“Piety is out of fashion. But we should rethink. Calvin saw piety as reverence joined with love of God given in our awareness of Christ’s benefits. Given that truth, we all should hunger for it. Dennis Ngien walks us through the highlights of Calvin’s classic, *The Institutes of the Christian Religion*, in such a way that we not only come to know the triune God better, but we are also increasingly led to revere him and trust in his goodness.”

—Mark Mattes, Chair of the Theology and Philosophy Department, Grand View University, Des Moines, Iowa

“This book is a profound gift. Demonstrating with great care that ‘Calvin’s theology is basically practical,’ Ngien illuminates Calvin’s trinitarian dynamic of salvation. I have waited for some time for a book like this, one that unfolds the soteriological heartbeat of Calvin’s trinitarianism. Students of Calvin and Christian doctrine more broadly are once again in Ngien’s debts. With masterful understanding on display, we see the unity of doctrine and life, the former as the principle and wellspring of the latter.”

—Christopher Holmes, Professor of Systematic Theology, University of Otago, New Zealand

“It was the Lutheran divine Philip Melanchthon who once described Calvin, his contemporary and a Reformed author, as ‘the theologian’ of his day. This fresh study of Calvin’s *Institutes* by Professor Ngien reaffirms Melanchthon’s epithet for the French pastor. With clarity, precision, and insight, Ngien leads the reader through the main contours of Calvin’s thought. All in all, a magisterial study.”

—Michael A. G. Azad Haykin, Professor of Church History, The Southern Baptist Theological Seminary

“Popular portraits, literal and metaphorical, of ‘dour’ Calvinism miss the mark. Calvin intends doctrine to direct the mind and delight the heart, for doctrine explains what God the Father has done through the Son by the Spirit for us, why, and to what end. True piety therefore leads to ‘worship in spirit and truth’ (John 4:23). In this timely book, Ngien ably guides readers through all four parts of Calvin’s *Institutes*, noting the doctrinal highlights (providence; union with Christ; Holy Spirit; ecclesiology) and demonstrating how each contributes to fostering true piety."

—Kevin J. Vanhoozer, Research Professor of Systematic Theology, Trinity Evangelical Divinity School

"Calvin understood that Christian doctrine has its term in the glorification of God, and that God is truly glorified as right teaching takes hold of the whole of the Christian life, transforming minds and hearts, and bearing good fruit in turn. Ngien's fine study of Calvin's *Institutes* seizes upon this fundamental horizon of the reformer's work, leading readers stepwise through this influential text to trace its trinitarian grammar and to discern and make manifest its practical ambition, namely, to serve the reshaping of life by the power of the gospel of God. Ngien thus invites us to contemplate the great theme of Calvin's lifework: namely, that true doctrine ministers to true piety to the glory of the one true God."

—Philip G. Ziegler, Professor of Christian Dogmatics, University of Aberdeen

"Calvin is all too easily misunderstood if part of his theology is analyzed in isolation from the whole, or if his doctrine is treated separately from his concern for practical piety and the life of the church. In *Calvin's Theology of Piety in the Institutes* Ngien provides an effective antidote to these ills, offering a wonderfully clear account of the overall shape of Calvin's theology in the *Institutes* while recognizing that for Calvin doctrine and life are one. The reformer's deep desire for our entire existence to be transformed by Christ leaps from the page. Rarely in scholarship has the passionately devotional nature of Calvin's theology been communicated so clearly."

—Stephen J. Chester, Lord and Lady Coggan Professor of New Testament, Wycliffe College, University of Toronto

"Dennis Ngien provides a clear systematic exposition of the trinitarian structure of Calvin's theology, piety, and ministry. By God's trinitarian movement, we are taken up in the Spirit through the Son to the Father and made to be 'not only partakers of all his benefits but also of himself.' Ngien illuminates just how holistically this theme permeates and integrates Calvin's thought. This is a book to enrich the mind, arouse the heart, encourage the affections, and motivate love-inspired devotion to the triune God, his mission, and his glory. A gift to the academy and the church!"

—Patrick S. Franklin, Alister E. McGrath Chair in Christian Thought and Spirituality, Tyndale University, Toronto

"Calvin famously begins his *Institutes* with a discussion of the knowledge of God that we attain to in relation to knowledge of ourselves; a two-fold knowledge that dialectically unfolds in the believer's soul. Dennis Ngien shows that, for Calvin, knowing God is therefore not merely speculative, it is also affective. True knowledge of God is loving knowledge. Given his long-standing academic interest in theology and piety, Ngien's book is at once serious theology and deep spiritual reflection. Calvin and Ngien help readers have head and heart filled with the knowledge of God for the glory of God."

—Ian Hugh Clary, Associate Professor of Historical Theology, Colorado Christian University

"Calvinism shaped—and still shapes—the lives of many across the world and through history. Yet Calvin's stereotype is of a cold, logical thinker, interested in doctrinal correctness, not emotion and the practicalities of the Christian life. Dennis Ngien punctures this image with this thorough, wide-ranging, and expert survey of Calvin's teaching on piety and spirituality. Whether writing about creation, the Holy Spirit, prayer, or the church, Ngien shows how Calvin displayed a God who engages affections and warms cold hearts."

—Graham Tomlin, Director, Centre for Cultural Witness, London

"In a time when spirituality is in and religion is out, this vital work calls us to ground Christian spirituality in robust Christian doctrine. Written in very accessible prose, the author explores five major spheres in Calvin's *Institutes*—epistemic foundations, union with Christ and the Holy Spirit, reaping fruits from the Law, Calvin's trinitarian ground of prayer, and the church as the ministerial vehicle of grace—and draws from a wealth of primary and secondary sources to illumine each topic. I most highly recommend it."

—Jimmy Tan, Lecturer in Pastoral and Practical Theology, Trinity Theological College, Singapore

"In this important work Dennis Ngien presents an engaging exposition of how Calvin's theology in the *Institutes* is shaped by a trinitarian theology that enables him to explicate the importance of union with Christ through the Holy Spirit for living the Christian life. Living by grace alone through faith in Christ means that we do not look to ourselves, but to God alone, for our salvation and thus for knowledge of the truth. This is a book that integrates dogmatic and practical theology in a way that deserves to be widely read."

—PAUL D. MOLNAR, Professor of Systematic Theology, St. John's University, New York

# Calvin's Theology of Piety in the *Institutes*

# Calvin's Theology of Piety in the *Institutes*

DENNIS NGIEN

Foreword by Alister E. McGrath

CASCADE *Books* · Eugene, Oregon

CALVIN'S THEOLOGY OF PIETY IN THE *INSTITUTES*



Cascade Books
An Imprint of Wipf and Stock Publishers
199 W. 8th Ave., Suite 3
Eugene, OR 97401

www.wipfandstock.com

PAPERBACK ISBN: 979-8-3852-5337-1
HARDCOVER ISBN: 979-8-3852-5338-8
EBOOK ISBN: 979-8-3852-5339-5

*Cataloguing-in-Publication data:*

Names: Ngien, Dennis, 1958– [author]. | Foreword by McGrath, Alister E. [author].

Title: Calvin's theology of piety in the *Institutes* / by Dennis Ngien ; with a foreword by Alister E. McGrath.

Description: Eugene, OR: Cascade Books, 2026 | Includes bibliographical references.

Identifiers: ISBN 979-8-3852-5337-1 (paperback) | ISBN 979-8-3852-5338-8 (hardcover) | ISBN 979-8-3852-5339-5 (ebook)

Subjects: LCSH: Calvin, Jean, 1509–1564. | Pastoral theology—Reformed church. | Theology—Early works to 1800. | Reformed Church—Doctrines. | Spiritual life—Reformed Church. | Calvinism. | Piety.

Classification: BX9420.A32 N45 2026 (print) | BX9420.A32 (ebook)

Dedicated to the benefactors and friends
of the Alister E. McGrath Chair
of Christian Thought and Spirituality,
Tyndale University, Toronto, Canada

# Contents

# Foreword

John Calvin remains a pivotal figure for church historians and historical theologians, as evidenced by the continually growing number of scholarly monographs addressing various aspects of his theology, historical significance, and foundational role in defining and sustaining a "Reformed" theological and ecclesiological identity. This intensive study of Calvin has revealed multiple dimensions of his importance, while calling into question the reliability of some earlier interpretations, which were often influenced by the concerns and agendas of previous generations.

Calvin is often portrayed, particularly by his critics, as a coldly logical and cerebral thinker who neglects the spiritual needs of his readers. In this important discussion of the significance of "piety" for Calvin, Dennis Ngien challenges this unhelpful and inadequate account of Calvin by highlighting the subjective and affective dimensions of Calvin's rich understanding of faith. At many points, Calvin distinguishes the objective and subjective aspects of salvation without separating them, envisioning them as informing the mind, nourishing the heart, and shaping the contours of Christian existence. In both his biblical commentaries and the *Institutes*, Calvin makes it clear that an encounter with Christ is both cognitively and existentially transformative.

Professor Ngien here offers a critical reexamination of Calvin's account of affectivity and commitment in the Christian faith, emphasizing the connections between Calvin's vision of Christian doctrine and its practical outworking in the Christian life. Christ does not merely change the way we think; he transforms our entire existence and experience. Knowing Christ, Calvin declares, "possesses the whole soul, and finds a seat and resting place in the inmost affection of the heart."

There has been growing interest in these questions in recent years. The Cambridge theologian Simeon Zahl, for example, has argued that Christian theology has always operated within a vibrant landscape of feeling and desire.[1] For Zahl, Martin Luther and Philip Melanchthon provide a responsible and engaging account of the experiential dynamics of faith, offering an important corrective to certain trends in contemporary theology, which has too often operated in problematic isolation from these dynamics. The same, it must be added, is true of Calvin. Ngien's work has the potential not only to inform historical reflection on Calvin's theology but also to enrich contemporary discussions on the nature and consequences of salvation in Christ, particularly by highlighting Calvin's strongly participatory understanding of salvation, which he maintains alongside an essentially forensic account of justification. Calvin clearly does not see a contradiction here, but an indication of the rich complexity of the biblical understanding of the believer's encounter and relationship with Christ.

Ngien's insightful analysis of Calvin's doctrine of salvation through Christ benefits readers in two key ways: first, by helping them grasp its conceptual depth, rooted in and enriched by the rich biblical testimony to God's work of salvation in Christ; and second, by enabling them to recognize Calvin's distinctive effort to integrate the multiple elements of the biblical account of core doctrines—such as salvation in Christ—without resorting to reductive simplification or distortion.

Finally, Ngien's important analysis will be valuable for reflections on spirituality, especially for those who recognize the significance of this concept and wish to remain firmly grounded in Reformational approaches to the subject. Some Reformed thinkers today have reservations about the notion of "spirituality," rightly noting that it is often used in broader cultural contexts to describe forms of self-focused and self-serving introspection rather than the outcome of God's transformative grace. Yet Ngien helps his readers understand how Calvin's rigorously objective account of salvation correlates with an appropriate and necessary inward response within the believer, expressed through obedience, contemplation, worship, and a fruitful Christian life. As Ngien puts it, "Calvin's theo-logic of piety" leads to "a profound sense of awe and devotion toward the majestic God, from whom we derive our identity, and receive an outpouring of benefactions for our well-being."

This work, I believe, will stimulate and inform discussions on how we might develop authentically Reformational approaches to spirituality, using Calvin as a guide. True piety is grounded in God's gracious

1. Zahl, *Holy Spirit.*

initiative toward us but results in the transformation of our hopes and fears, as well as the redirection and repurposing of our lives. As Professor Ngien makes clear, Calvin has much to say to us today!

Alister E. McGrath
Oxford University

# Acknowledgments

THIS WORK BEGAN DURING the COVID-19 pandemic when I was locked in my study room at home. Many mentors, colleagues, and students with whom I had had interactions encouraged me to produce a book on Calvin, specifically my reading of his *Institutes of the Christian Religion*. Immediately, I started reading, researching, and writing. Hugh Rendle, Leah Vetro, and the library team at Tyndale University were most helpful in securing relevant sources, and mailing books, including interlibrary-loaned materials, to my home for my purpose. Ceceilia, my wife, and Hansel, our boy, have been rooting for me. I am grateful to them both.

A team of Reformed friends to whom I presented the fruits of my work in the forms of public lectures, seminars, and table-talk over meals endured long hours of hearing about the book. They offered varied interpretative lenses to what Calvin's *Institutes* aimed to do. Their readings of Calvin's *Institutes* were instructive, and helped crystallize my own thinking. And I thank each of them immensely for playing the roles of shepherd, editor, and critic. Despite our differences, we all concur that Calvin is not an abstract theologian but a theologian who does theology with piety as the goal. Theology and piety are one; the former is the spring of the latter.

I am indebted to scholars who have read the book, commented on it, and suggested ways to improve it. These include a fine foreword from Alister E. McGrath, joined by a list of weighty endorsers, including Kevin J. Vanhoozer, Philip G. Ziegler, Christopher R. J. Holmes, Stephen J. Chester, Patrick S. Franklin, Jimmy Boon-Chai Tan, Mark C. Mattes, Graham Tomlin, Michael A. G. Haykin, Ian H. Clary, and Paul D. Molnar. I pray that *Calvin's Theology of Piety* will become a helpful resource for fostering true piety and care of the soul.

# Abbreviations

*CD* Karl Barth, *Church Dogmatics*. Translated by G. T. Thomson et al. Edinburgh: T&T Clark, 1936–77.

*CF* *Commentaries on the Four Last Books of Moses*. Translated by Charles William Bingham. 4 vols. Reprint, Grand Rapids: Eerdmans, 1950.

*CI* *Commentary on the Book of the Prophet Isaiah*. Translated by William Pringle. 4 vols. Reprint, Grand Rapids: Baker, 1979.

*CJL* *Commentaries on the Book of the Prophet Jeremiah and the Lamentations*. Translated and edited by John Owen. 5 vols. Reprint, Grand Rapids: Baker, 1979.

*CNTC* *Calvin's New Testament Commentaries*. Edited by David W. Torrance and Thomas F. Torrance. 12 vols. Grand Rapids: Eerdmans, 1959–72.

CO *Ioannis Calvini opera quae supersunt omnia*. Edited by Wilhelm Baum et al. 59 vols. *Corpus Reformatorum*, vols. 29–87. Braunschweig: Schwetschke, 1863–1900.

*Comm.* Commentary on

*CP* *Commentary on the Book of Psalms*. Translated by James Anderson. 5 vols. Reprint, Grand Rapids: Eerdmans, 1949.

*CR* *Corpus Reformatorum*. Edited by Karl Gottlieb Bretschneider et al. 101 vols. Halle and Braunschweig: Schwetschke, 1834–1909.

*CTMP* *Commentaries on the Twelve Minor Prophets*. Translated by John Owen. 5 vols. 1847. Reprint, Grand Rapids: Eerdmans, 1950.

| | |
|---|---|
| CTS | *Calvin's Commentaries.* 46 vols. 1844–55. Reprint, 22 vols. Grand Rapids: Baker, 1979. |
| *Inst.* | *Institutes of the Christian Religion.* Edited by John T. McNeill. Translated by Ford Lewis Battles. 2 vols. Library of Christian Classics, vols 20–21. Philadelphia: Westminster, 1960. |
| LW | *Luther's Works: American Edition.* Edited by Jaroslav Pelikan. Vols. 1–30. St. Louis: Concordia, 1955–73. |
| | *Luther's Works: American Edition.* Edited by Helmut T. Lehman. Vols. 31–55. Philadelphia: Fortress, 1957–86. |
| | *Luther's Works: American Edition*, new series. Edited by Christopher Boyd Brown et al. Vols. 56–82. St. Louis: Concordia, 2009–. |
| *SG* | John Calvin. *Sermons on Galatians.* Translated by Kathy Childress. Edinburgh: Banner of Truth Trust, 1997. |
| *STC* | *John Calvin's Sermons on the Ten Commandments.* Edited and translated by Benjamin W. Farley. Foreword by Ford Lewis Battles. Grand Rapids: Baker, 2002. |
| Vg. | Latin Vulgate |
| WA | *D. Martin Luthers Werke: Kritische Gesamtausgabe.* 65 vols. Weimar: Hermann Böhlau, 1883–1929. Abteilung 1: Schriften vols. 1–56. |

# Introduction

ALISTER MCGRATH RECOGNIZES THAT in his initial attempt to offer a summary of Christian beliefs, Calvin assumes as his model the order of topics Luther has for his *Small Catechism*: the Decalogue, the Apostles' Creed, the Lord's Prayer, the Sacraments, and Christian Duties.[1] Unsatisfied with this structure, Calvin makes changes with each new edition of his *Institutes* until he finally adopts the model that comprises the four books we now have. Book 1 deals with God the Father, including the doctrines of creation, the Trinity, providence, and Holy Scripture. Book 2 looks at God the Son, focusing on the foundations of the doctrine of redemption, including a discussion of human sin and an elaborated treatment of the redemptive activities of the incarnate Son. Book 3 applies Christ's redemption to the individual by discussing God the Holy Spirit, and includes analysis of the doctrines of faith, regeneration, justification, and predestination. And Book 4 explores the church, the life of the redeemed community, including the ministry of word and sacrament, and the church's relation to the state. The organization helps us to locate the appropriate materials within his work.

The four books of the final edition of Calvin's *Institutes* (1559) seem to bear the division after the Apostles' Creed.[2] "The major objection to this division," Charles Partee argues, "is that Calvin did not use the term 'Holy Spirit' in his title for Book III nor are all the topics treated there indirectly related to the Holy Spirit as would seem necessary if Calvin were using a Trinitarian outline."[3] The trinitarian structure is apparent in the 1559 *Institutes*, McGrath notes, although "it must not be regarded as

1. McGrath, *Reformation Thought*, 274. See also Elwood, *Brief Introduction*, 19.

2. Our discussion is based on the 1559 edition of Calvin's *Institutes*, edited by John T. McNeill, and translated by Ford Lewis Battles. I shall occasionally use Henry Beveridge's translation.

3. Partee, "Centra Dogma," 193.

having been in Calvin's mind as he organized the materials. For example, he fails to refer to the Holy Spirit in his own summary of the contents of Book III."[4] Union with Christ figures in Calvin's commentaries and sermons where Calvin discusses his doctrine of soteriology. Union with Christ is, for Calvin, the "central dogma" upon which all other doctrines are based, according to Charles Partee.[5] Contrary to Partee, Richard A. Muller insists that union with Christ is not to be understood as an independent reality, separated from the effective agency of the Spirit. He contends,

> To claim that the doctrine [union with Christ] is the central motif or "viewpoint" accounting for the structure of the entire 1559 *Institutes* and serving as a "comprehensive way of introducing and surveying Calvin's theology" would be, of course, absurd and a serious distortion of Calvin's patterns of exposition and argumentation—to place it, however, not in isolation, but together with the work of the Holy Spirit is foundational to Calvin's understanding of "the manner of receiving the grace of Christ," is crucial to a reading of Calvin's approach to the ordering of several aspects or elements of the work of salvation.[6]

While Calvin scholars have adopted various approaches to Calvin's theology,[7] this book assumes the trinitarian outline in Calvin's doctrines of soteriology and the Christian life. This outline can be gleaned from the way he divides the materials, although without elevating the Trinity as the "central dogma." In Book 1, Calvin states that due to the ruin of the fall, no one recognizes God's fatherly goodness in creation, until Christ the Mediator appeared as the remedy and reconciled him to us.[8] The same content occurs in his transition to the knowledge of God the Redeemer in Book 2: The whole knowledge of God the Creator does not profit us unless faith follows, setting forth for us the knowledge of God the Redeemer.[9] The Son's mediatory office is of no avail to us unless the Spirit leads us to appropriate it. This is evident in the transition from Book 2, which speaks of union with Christ, from whom we receive the

4. McGrath, *Life of John Calvin*, 152.

5. For a detailed discussion on the "central dogma," see Partee, "Central Dogma," 191–99.

6. Muller, *Calvin and the Reformed Tradition*, 206.

7. See Partee, *Theology*, 40–43; "Central Dogma," 192, 194, 196–99.

8. *Inst.* 1.2.1.

9. *Inst.* 2.6.1.

double grace, to Book 3, which speaks of the Holy Spirit, from whom "we receive those benefits which the Father bestows on his only-begotten Son—not for Christ's own private use, but that he might enrich the poor and needy."[10] The trinitarian dynamic of salvation, as this book aims to show, already appears at the outset of Book 3 of the 1559 *Institutes*, where Calvin teaches that the reception of Christ's benefits in Book 2 occurs through union with Christ effected by the Holy Spirit in Book 3:

> As long as Christ remains outside of us, and we are separated from him, all that he has suffered and done for the salvation of the human race remains useless and of no value to us. . . . Therefore, to share what he has received from the Father, he has to become ours and to dwell within us. . . . [Through] the secret energy of the Spirit . . . we come to enjoy Christ and all his benefits. . . . To sum up, the Holy Spirit is the bond by which Christ effectually unites us to himself.[11]

Calvin affirms the unity and distinction of the immanent and economic Trinity. Calvin's *Institutes* dwells on the economic Trinity, on what the triune God does in us and for us. The economic Trinity—God's way of being himself for us—stands as the foreground, through which we apprehend God as the immanent Trinity—that is, God as he is in himself, eternally triune. Our understanding of God, shaped by our encounter with the economic Trinity, must be grounded in the eternal nature of God (the immanent Trinity) to reflect his being truly. Our knowledge of God's external relationship with humanity corresponds to our understanding of his internal relationship with himself. Thomas Torrance argued unequivocally that authentic knowledge of God originates not from ourselves or from some external authority but solely from God. In his own words, "The truth of God is that he is who he is and that he reveals who he is as he is. . . . What God is towards men he is eternally in himself, and what he is in himself is faithfully towards men. He is truth and keeps truth for ever, and as such is the source and standard of all truth."[12] God is indivisibly one, so the actions of the triune God are inseparably one. Augustine writes, "Although just as Father, Son and Holy Spirit are inseparable, so do they work inseparably."[13] With Augustine,

10. *Inst.* 3.1.1.
11. *Inst.* 3.1.1.
12. Torrance, "Truth and Authority," 215.
13. Augustine, *Trinity* 1.2.7, 70.

Calvin accentuates that all three persons act in full unity with himself externally (*ad extra*) to reach us. The weight of Calvin's thinking falls on the soteriological significance of Christology and Trinity, rather than abstract theories of them. Timothy George summarizes the soteriological concerns in Calvin's trinitarian perspective:

> Why was the Trinity such an important issue for (Calvin)? [He] was not interested in the metaphysical niceties of abstract theology, nor was he slavishly attached to traditional terminology. *The Trinity was crucial because it was a witness to the deity of Jesus Christ and thus to the certainty of salvation procured by Him.* The purpose of Calvin's trinitarianism was, like that of Athanasius, soteriological. He wanted to safeguard the biblical message, "God is manifest in the flesh," against false interpretations, such as that of Servetus who "confounded the Son and the Holy Spirit with the creatures."[14]

Some might perceive Calvin's *Institutes* (1559) as a document of abstract doctrines, with no reference to piety and the shaping of it. But John T. McNeill identified the Reformation as an applied movement of the care of the soul: "In matters concerning the cure of souls the German Reformation had its inception."[15] Ronald Wallace rightly said, "The Reformation itself was a pastoral care movement growing directly out of care for the salvation of the soul."[16] The genius of Calvin lies in the usage of the word of God as the primary source of instruction and pastoral care. Calvin's *Institutes* is not to be equated with Scripture; they are the filters of God's word which acquaints us with a proper knowledge of God's majesty and how it nourishes the souls that are seized by it. His *Institutes* is, McGrath writes, "at its best, systematic theology . . . viewed as an extended engagement with and commentary on the Bible. It is intended to assist the believer in this encounter rather than excuse him from that encounter or deny him access to the identity-giving and faith-enhancing Word of God."[17] These observations reflect Calvin's intention in writing the *Institutes*, which, as stated in his preface addressed to King Francis I of France, was "solely to transmit certain rudiments by which those who

14. George, *Theology*, 208, italics original; cf. *Inst.* 1.13.22.

15. McNeill, *Cure*, 163.

16. Wallace, *Geneva*, 169.

17. McGrath, "Evangelical Theological Method," 20.

are touched with any zeal for religion might be shaped to true godliness [*pietas*]."[18] This he spells out in Book 2:

> True religion must come first, to direct our minds to the living God. Thus, steeped in the knowledge of him, they may aspire to contemplate, fear, and worship, his majesty; to participate in his blessings, to seek his help at all times, to recognize and by praises to celebrate, the greatness of his works—as the only goal of all the activities of this life. Then . . . we are to drive away all invented gods and not to rend asunder the worship that the one God claims for himself. For it is unlawful to take away even a particle from his glory; rather, all things proper to him must remain with him.[19]

Alister McGrath writes, "The word *spirituality* has gained virtually universal acceptance as the best means of designating the group of spiritual disciplines that focus on deepening the believer's relationship with God and enhancing the life of the Spirit."[20] The word "spirituality" permeates modern discussion on the topic. It has been used as the alternative word for "piety," "godliness," and "spiritual theology," focusing on the habitual life of spiritual practices. Calvin's term is not spirituality but "piety," translated as "godliness." John McNeill rightly describes Calvin's theology in the *Institutes* as "his piety described at length. His task is to expound (in the language of his original title) 'the whole sum of piety and whatever it is necessary to know in the doctrine of salvation.'"[21] Calvin's definition of piety in his 1559 *Institutes* resonates with what he writes in his 1537 *Instruction in Faith*, where he guides how a Christian thinks and lives: "The gist of true piety does not consist in a fear which would gladly flee the judgment of God, but . . . rather in a pure and true zeal which loves God altogether as Father and reveres him as Lord, embraces his justice and dreads to offend him more than to die."[22] Commenting on 1 Timothy 4:7–8, Calvin declares that the entire life of the Christian is bound up with an exercise in godliness, "the beginning, middle and end of Christian living. Where it is complete, there is nothing lacking."[23]

18. *Inst.*, Prefatory Address, §1, p. 9.

19. *Inst.* 2.8.16.

20. McGrath, "Evangelical Theological Method," 20.

21. McNeill, "Introduction," li, in *Inst.*; also cited in Hesselink, "Development," 214–15.

22. Calvin, *Instruction*, 18.

23. *Comm. 1 Tim.* 4:7–8, *CNTC* 10:243–44.

Calvin's *Institutes* is an exercise of theology within the confines of piety, therefore bringing together the mind and the heart.[24] Piety, for him, does not refer to an unreflective kind of religiosity, an inward turn to the self, and a private, subjective discipline, devoid of the substance of the gospel message. Calvin provides his own definition of piety:

> I call "piety" that reverence joined with love of God which the knowledge of his benefits induces. For until men recognize that they owe everything to God, that they are nourished by his fatherly care, that he is the Author of their every good, that they should seek nothing beyond him—they will never yield him willing service. Nay, unless they establish their complete happiness in him, they will never yield themselves truly and sincerely to him.[25]

For Calvin, Jimmy Boon-Chai Tan writes, "genuine piety is the fruit of knowing the immensity of God's grace and blessings on us and the expression of a life-long response of love and reverence to God."[26] Piety, Lucien Joseph Richard notes, comprises "the right attitude of man towards God, an attitude which implies true knowledge and true worship."[27] This right attitude, Joel Beeke says, includes also "saving faith, filial fear, prayerful submission, and reverential love."[28]

Doctrine, life, and vocation are governed by piety, a comprehensive term. Doctrine is not worthy of any "legitimate commendation" unless it instructs us in reverential fear of God; one cannot be called "the best disciple" of Christ unless one exemplifies "most progress in godliness," and one is "a real theologian" if one is able to establish people's "consciences in the fear of God."[29] For Calvin, doctrine and life are one: the former is the causal agent of the latter. The knowledge of Christ reaches the affective condition of the human heart and causes it to be fruitful; "its efficacy" ought to "affect the whole man a hundred times more deeply than the cold exhortation of the philosophers." The knowledge of Christ, Calvin says,

24. See Gerrish, "Theology," 67–87.

25. *Inst.* 1.2.1.

26. Tan, *How Then Shall We Guide?*, 156.

27. Richard, *Spirituality*, 100–101.

28. Beeke, "Calvin on Piety," 126.

29. *Comm. Titus* 1:1, *CNTC* 10:353.

> is a doctrine not of the tongue but of life. It is not apprehended by the understanding and memory alone, as other disciplines are, but it is received only when it possesses the whole soul, and finds a seat and resting place in the inmost affection of the heart. . . . We have given the first place to the doctrine in which our religion is contained, since our salvation begins with it. But it must enter our heart and pass into our daily living, and so transform us into itself that it may not be unfruitful for us.[30]

A "real theologian," which Calvin is, aims to build people's lives in the fear of God, the very thing that grips him and his vocation. As Hesselink observes, "*pietas* was [Calvin's] entire theological direction and goal, rather than merely one theme in his theology."[31] This book expands what Calvin means by "aspiring to contemplate, fear, and worship, his majesty" and reap from it the salutary fruits for our souls. It is not an attempt to offer a "how to" manual of spiritual exercises or habits; rather it presents Calvin's theo-logic of piety, centering on inculcating a profound sense of awe and devotion toward the majestic God, from whom we derive our identity and receive an outpouring of benefactions for our well-being, and to whom we owe everything so that whatever is rightly his—adoration, affection, thanksgiving, reverence, and submission—belongs to him and cannot be attached to others but to God alone, the primal reality of all that is external to himself.

Chapter 1 deals with the epistemic condition in which the pious can perceive knowledge of God and the fatherly goodness in creation with clarity and accuracy, enjoy the riches of God's providence, and recognize Holy Scripture as divinely inspired. Chapter 2 focuses on the soteriological connection between the second and third article of faith: The benefits of Christ's mediatorial office is made known to us by the Spirit, the participative power of the believer's reception of the benefits through union with Christ. Chapter 3 dwells on the end and uses of law, to reap from them fruits for godly living on earth in a way that is not incompatible with piety. Chapter 4 articulates Calvin's trinitarian ground of prayer, the "chief exercise of faith"[32] through which we dig up God's treasures hidden in Christ by the Spirit. And chapter 5 underscores the ministerial, not magisterial, role of the church, which the Spirit uses to regenerate us and keep us within the body of Christ.

30. *Inst.* 3.6.4.

31. Hesselink, *Catechism*, 45.

32. *Inst.* 3.20.1.

Calvin's primary occupation is not with how God is to himself but how he relates to us. How God is to himself is hidden in himself, and we have nothing to do with that; how God is to us has relevance to us. For Calvin, the knowledge of God as he exists in himself is hidden in himself and is beyond human speculation. Calvin begins with how God reveals himself to us and then proceeds to apprehend God as he is in his own nature. The truth of God's eternal existence is rooted in God alone and is not dependent on anything outside of himself. Discourse on God's essence, for Calvin, is forbidden; the God who hides in himself is beyond us.[33] The speculative question "What is God?" (*quid sit Deus*) must give way to the revelatory question "What is God like?" (*quails sit Deus*).[34] Calvin, like Luther, is not a "theologian of glory" who aspires "with a foolish and insane curiosity to inquire into his *Essence*," but a "theologian of the cross" who applies "the whole force of his mind to a consideration" of "the works of God."[35] The proper way to find God and live before the face of God is not through a consideration of his majestic greatness, which terrifies us, but through his accommodated mode in which he shows his immanence and familiarity to us in the way we could grasp. Paul Helm writes, "Divine accommodation, as Calvin treats it, is not primarily our theory about theological language, it is an account of some of the conditions under which God chooses to say and must say certain things about himself in order to achieve certain ends. It is an integral feature of his gracious self-revelation."[36] The way God reaches us radically differs from the way we reach him: "God accommodates himself to us: we do not accommodate God to ourselves."[37] The former is God's proper response to the weaknesses of the human condition; the latter is the impious forging of God in our images to reach God. As God's accommodation to us is set against human accommodation to God, so the true God is set against idols. The former relates to God's gracious coming to us in a way that we could come to him; the latter is idolatry, conceived as the human attempt to come to God via images of ill imagination, which is repugnant to reverence. God is robbed of his majesty through vain inventions of corrupt affections.

33. See Gerrish, "'Unknown,'" 131–59.

34. *Inst.* 1.2.2; 1.10.2; 3.2.6. See Helm, *Ideas*, 12.

35. *Comm. Gen*, *Argument*, CTS 1:60. The phrases "theologian of the cross" and "theologian of glory" are Luther's.

36. Helm, *Ideas*, 196.

37. Helm, *Ideas*, 196.

The knowledge of what God is like is known to us through his attributes or powers mentioned in Scripture. God imprints conspicuously the marks of his glory in creation, "so clear and so prominent that" none can "plead the excuse of ignorance."[38] Calvin's creational theology, to use William J. Bouwsma's phrase, "was based largely on seeing"[39] rather than idle speculation. God has put himself on public display, not so that we might speculate on him as he is in himself, but so that we might contemplate him as he manifests himself. Calvin asserts, "Hence the majesty of God is in itself incomprehensible to us, but he makes himself known by his works and by his word."[40] The universe as the "theater"[41] of God's glory underscores God's actions in creation, as in theatrical drama. God displays himself in creatures not only to instruct but to invite or draw us to a proper contemplation of him for our benefits. However, natural knowledge of God "profits nothing," as "most people, immersed in their own errors, are struck blind in such dazzling theater," and hence "scarcely one man in a hundred is a true spectator"[42] of the Creator's glory in nature. The appropriate epistemic condition suffers malfunction due to Adam's fall, and thus sinners cannot of themselves perceive the true and clear knowledge of God unless through the spectacles of Scripture, Christ's restoration of epistemic cognition, and the inner revelation of faith. The knowledge of God the Redeemer is temporally apprehended before the knowledge of God the Creator. The knowledge of God the Redeemer in the second article of faith sheds light on the knowledge of God the Creator in the first article. The cognitive condition of creatures lost through the dullness of mind is restored by faith in Christ, apart from which nothing of the divine mysteries in creation is transparent. Christ's regeneration restores the sense of divinity, and supplies an appropriate cognitive condition in which Christians are given, Alvin Plantinga writes, "a much clearer view of the beauty, splendor, loveliness, attractiveness, and glory of God."[43] Christ's redemption restores our epistemic condition so that we can read the book of nature clearly as God's revelation and truly perceive the world as the theater of God's glory. The renewal of human persons

38. *Inst.* 1.5.1.

39. Bouwsma, *Calvin*, 103. Bouwsma uses the phrase "natural theology" to speak of the universe as the place of sight and contemplation. I prefer "creational theology."

40. *Comm. Hab* 2:20, CTS 14:130.

41. *Inst.* 1.5.8.

42. *Inst.* 1.5.8.

43. Plantinga, *Warranted Christian Belief*, 291.

precedes and grounds the renewal of nature. Nature's revelatory function is restored to its original condition so that it can reflect God's glory and beauty, and participate in people's joy. Through Christ's redemption, which has begun now and will reach its consummation in the last day, all negativities—confusion, disorder, and corruption—are ended. The piety of reverence and love for God lost in sin are restored in Christ. Brian Gerrish sums up Calvin's piety grounded in faith:

> For Calvin, redemption is not only the restoration of piety, but also a deepening of it. Nevertheless, the Creator's love and the Redeemer's love are not two loves, any more than the Creator and the Redeemer are two Gods. Creation and redemption are works of the one true God who wants us to know him as father, and it would not be incorrect to say that, in Calvin's thinking, the significance of faith is that it makes piety a possibility once more. The first step to piety is to recognize God as father, but apart from faith in Christ this knowledge is no longer open to us. Only the recognition of faith can evoke the attitude of piety. This is why piety is instilled into the breasts of believers alone, and why faith can be called the "root of true piety" [*verae pietatis radix*]: because it is faith that "teaches us to expect and to desire all good things from God alone and disposes us to obey him."[44]

Calvin links the knowledge of the Creator to the first article of faith, with its emphasis on the economic action of the Father. The Almighty God creates us *ex nihilo*, and preserves us by his faithful and fatherly care. God's glorious powers or acts in creatures form the template of sight and contemplation by which we feel their causal effects on us. As soon as we recognize God as the Creator of the majestic and beauteous universe, and him as "the Lord and Father," our hearts must necessarily be enraptured by God's marvelous beauty and fear at his infinite powers.[45] Calvin's piety thus comprehends both strands, one that dwells on "a sense of awe at God's majesty" upholding the transcendence of God, the other inviting us onto the journey of "delight on God's beauty," ravished with wonderment over such an astounding display of glory.[46] Ecologically sensitive persons will find Calvin's creational piety appealing. The theater of God's glory calls forth a passionate delight from spectators seized by the beauty

44. Gerrish, *Grace and Gratitude*, 70. His analysis is based on *Inst.* 2.6.4; 1.2.1; 2.6.1; 3.6.3; *Comm. Ps.* 78:22, CO 31:729.

45. *Inst.* 1.14.22.

46. Lane, *Ravished by Beauty*, 27.

of God. Not only does God rule us by the power of his majesty, but he allures us by various creaturely images, as a father does to his beloved child, to taste of his goodness displayed in creation.

Calvin's creational theology shows no contempt for the natural world. Nicholas Wolterstorff highly esteems Calvin with this tribute: "If ever there was a theologian who saw the universe sacramentally it was Calvin. For him, reality was drenched with sacrality. . . . Calvin's reforms meant a radical turn towards the world."[47] What Calvin repudiates is not the world's substance but its abuse. Godliness is not measured by an ascetic withdrawal from the world but by constructive engagement with ordinary life on earth, enjoying God's abundant gifts in creation, and using them as helps and not as a basis of our identity, for we are pilgrims on a journey to the heavenly kingdom where our identity truly resides. We thus reap from Christ's redemption the restoration of our affections and desires so that the garden with all its pleasures can be heartily enjoyed, and God's gifts properly used, without being bound to them.

Providence belongs to Calvin's doctrine of creation. The God who creates is not the Epicureans' idle deity but is ceaselessly active in the governance of his own universe. All created beings owe their being to God, apart from whom they recede into nothingness. A few quotations prove Calvin's point: "Not one drop of rain falls without God's sure command";[48] "There is no erratic power, or action, or motion in creatures, but that they are governed by God's secret plan in such a way that nothing happens except what is knowingly and willingly decreed by him";[49] and "God so attends to the regulation of individual events, and they all so proceed from his set plan, that nothing takes place by chance."[50] Despite the atrocities and horrors that befall us, Calvin remains convinced that God governs all natures—human nature generally, and each individual's own nature particularly—in such a manner that God's glory does not suffer, and human beings receive the best care, despite the discrepancy we feel about the account of his governance.

> When that light of divine providence has once shone upon a godly man, he is then relieved and set free not only from the extreme anxiety and fear that were pressing him before, but

47. Wolterstorff, *Justice and Peace*, 160.

48. *Inst.* 1.16.5.

49. *Inst.* 1.16.3.

50. *Inst.* 1.16.4.

> from every care. For as he justly dreads fortune, so he fearlessly dares commit himself to God. His solace . . . is to know that his Heavenly Father so holds all things in his power, so rules by his authority and will, so governs by his wisdom, that nothing can befall except he determines it. Moreover, it comforts him to know that he has been received into God's safekeeping and entrusted to the care of his angels, and that neither water, nor fire, nor iron can harm him, except in so far as it pleases God as governor to give them occasion.[51]

The majesty of God's word reigns above all; it performs what it says. Religious fanaticism (without the word) or rigid orthodoxy (without the Spirit), the fall to either extreme, can be avoided by the unity of the word and the Spirit. Scripture mediates God's majesty; God's majesty inheres in Scripture. Self-witnessing is the ground of complete reliability. Paul Helm notes, "Only if God *directly* witnesses to himself is that witness thoroughly trustworthy."[52] Church tradition is subservient to Scripture and serves as a secondary aid to belief. Calvin does not deny that the writings of Demosthenes, Plato, and others of the same ilk may enrapture us in some measure. But Scripture itself enables its readers to "see" that it "breathe[s] something divine."[53] Through the inward testimony of the Spirit, readers feel the force of Scripture's truth and recognize its authority without needing to prove it. To see Scripture's authority thus is to be predicated upon being seized by the power of the majestic God that inheres within it, and that is stronger than all other proofs. The late James I. Packer summarizes Calvin's position:

> Rejecting both the Roman contention that the Scripture is to be received as authoritative on the church's authority, and the idea that Scripture could be proved divinely authoritative by rational argument alone, Calvin affirms Scripture to be self-authenticating through the inner witness of Holy Spirit. What is this "inner witness"? Not a special quality of experience, nor a new, private revelation, nor an existential "decision," but a work of enlightenment whereby, through the medium of verbal testimony, the blind eyes of the spirit are opened, and divine realities come to be recognized and embraced for what they are.[54]

51. *Inst.* 1.17.11.
52. Helm, *Calvin*, 31, italics original.
53. *Inst.* 1.8.1.
54. Packer, "Calvin the Theologian," 166.

Derek Thomas rightly observes, "Calvin's Christology is not a narrowly conceived Christocentrism, but part of a trinitarian understanding of the doctrine of God."[55] Calvin notes, "Whenever the name of God is mentioned without particularization, there are designated no less the Son and the Spirit than the Father; but where the Son is joined to the Father, then the relation of the two enters in; and we distinguish amongst the persons."[56] The majesty of God is hidden in his Son whom the Father sent to achieve redemption for the hopeless race. "The situation would surely have been hopeless had the very majesty of God not descended to us, since it was not in our power to ascend to him. Hence, it was necessary for the Son of God to become for us 'Immanuel, that is, God with us' [Isa. 7:14; Matt. 1:23], and in such a way that his divinity and our human nature might by mutual connection grow together."[57] Calvin's emphasis is not on the hypostatic union per se, but rather on the Son assuming our human nature to draw near to us and dwell with us, lest his majesty terrify us. Thus, Paul reminds us that this Mediator is "the man, Jesus Christ" (1 Tim 2:5). The Spirit presents before us the nearness of God in his Son, who became one of us so that troubled souls know where to seek the Mediator. Calvin writes,

> [Paul] could have said "God" or he could at least have omitted the word "man" just as he did the word "God." Because the Spirit speaking through his mouth knew our weakness, at the right moment he used a most appropriate remedy to meet it: he set the Son of God familiarly among us as one of ourselves. Therefore, lest anyone be troubled about where to seek the Mediator . . . the Spirit called him "man," thus teaching us that he is near us, indeed touches us, since he is our flesh.[58]

By the Spirit, believers through faith reap from union with Christ the two gifts of justification and sanctification, gifts he received from the Father. Following Calvin, Karl Barth formulates, "Justification and sanctification are one in divine origin and one in human experience, but two for the purpose of analysis. . . . This distinction is a matter of strong

55. Thomas, "Mediator," 206.

56. *Inst.* 1.13.20.

57. *Inst.* 2.12.1.

58. *Inst.* 2.12.1, as quoted in Edmondson, *Christology*, 202.

emphasis but not of exclusive definition."[59] Todd Billings articulates Calvin's trinitarian dynamic of divine–human intimacy thus:

> The inseparability of justification and sanctification is found in the person of Christ. By participation in Christ through faith, believers enter into a trinitarian drama of encountering a gracious Father who pardons our sin because of Christ's blamelessness (justification), and a powerful Spirit who sanctifies believers for new life (sanctification). Both of these aspects are accessed through participation in Christ—but both aspects would be dramatically altered if the two sides of the double grace were mixed, or collapsed into one another.[60]

Christology and Pneumatology are one; thus, what Christ does for us is followed up by what the Spirit does in us. In Christ, we are fully endowed, and thus need not seek outside him for the formation of our identity and security. Outside Christ, God is hostile and wrathful to us; in Christ, God is friendly and merciful to us. The greatest antithesis is not between law and sin, but between God's mercy and his wrath, which Christ has banished. God can only fully love sinners once Christ appeases the wrath of God by his death. The acquisition of benefits from the Father via the efficacious activities of Christ's vicarious obedience forms the content of the gospel. The incarnate Christ truly assumed sin, guilt, wrath, condemnation, and death as his own; or else these frightful contraries remain with us, and we are lost eternally. The Son mediates between God and us, effecting for us the blessing of God's reconciliation with us against the curse of God's hostility toward us. What Christ achieves for us is of no use to us unless the Spirit mediates between Christ and us, applying to us the fruit of Christ's victory over all contraries of justification—sin, wrath, death, and devil—so that they no longer bar our access to the heavenly sanctuary. The benefits Christ acquires from his Father are transferred to us through the Holy Spirit; conversely, the Spirit unites us to Christ, to receive from him God's fatherly goodness. The Spirit cements in our hearts the epistemic certainty that the opposition between the terror of God's wrath and the consolation of God's mercy is conquered through union with Christ. The economic action of the Spirit receives so much attention in Calvin that Benjamin B. Warfield labels him "the theologian

59. Barth, *CD* 4/2:502.

60. Billings, "Soteriology," 435.

of the Spirit"[61] as much as he is one of grace, justification, and sanctification. Calvin's trinitarian dynamic of grace encompasses both directions, descent and ascent. The effectual ascent to God, which is by the Holy Spirit through the Son to the Father, parallels the gracious descent to us, which is from the Father through the Son in the Spirit.

Through union with Christ, we are made "not only partakers of all his benefits but also of himself."[62] These benefits include his nearness with God, his worship of God, and his proximate communion and dominion with the Father. The worship that is lost due to sin is now restored by God the Son: Christ's efficacious act as the Mediator alone sanctions our worship as the true sacrifice. The mediatorial activity of Christ has abolished the inaccessibility of God and elevated us to royal honor, a fitting status that grants us a share in God's glory. God commands worship from us that we in ourselves could not give. Yet God in Christ supplies what he commands. In John Thompson's words, "Christ is the One who as the God-man comes as God reveals himself, but also as the representative man, being and doing in our place what we cannot be and do for ourselves."[63] Our priesthood, defiled in itself, cannot reach God unless it is sanctified in Christ. Our priesthood has no other basis than Christ's own person, who brings God's blessings to us and brings us ("his companion"),[64] together with our praise or adoration to God. Because Christ enters the holy of holies "in our name," our worship "in the name of Jesus" also culminates in the same place. We worship through Christ the Mediator alone, who stands before God for us in our name, and who is our altar (Heb 13:10) where we place our sacrifices. As our leader, Christ proclaims the praises of God amid his people (Heb 2:12). The only basis we have for coming to God is the one-time efficacious response the Son made to the Father, accessible to those who are united to Christ by the Spirit. Stephen Chester writes, "Human reciprocity participates in the responsiveness of the Son to the Father through the power of the Spirit."[65] The Spirit is the dynamic of human response that allows us to share in the Son's faithful response and thus in his Sonship. The human response to God's grace that the Father offers us through Christ's restoration of divine image is passive, empowered by the Holy Spirit, who applies to us

61. Warfield, *Calvin and Augustine*, 21.

62. *Inst.* 3.2.24.

63. Thompson, *Modern Trinitarian Perspectives*, 99.

64. *Inst.* 2.15.6.

65. Chester, *Reading Paul*, 291.

the power of Christ's mediatorial work. In Calvin's terms, "*The 'works' are ours by God's gift, but God's by his prompting*."[66]

Just as God uses the gospel to create faith in us, so too he uses the law to engender piety in us. For Calvin, the use of the law is threefold, which David Clyde Jones sums up in three convenient words: "preparative, preservative, and restorative."[67] The law is perfect not only in itself but also in the work it performs. It never fails to be an agent of exposure: It reveals the righteousness God requires of us, and unmasks its opposite, our unrighteousness before a holy God. Negatively, the law performs its punitive function—that is, the "accidental" function when it collides with sin.[68] The law is the occasion of life but becomes the occasion of death because of Adam's fall. Sin results in a movement from life to death; Christ's redemption reverses the movement, from death to life. The abolition of the law Paul taught in Romans 7:6 does not pertain to its content, the righteousness God approves in the law; rather it applies to its effect, the curse God imposes on the ones who disobey it. What is suspended is not the law's contents but its "accidental" function. The teaching of the law remains, but its power to bind the conscience with a threat of a curse is abolished.[69] This is because Christ has redeemed us from the curse of the law (Gal 4:4–5). Under the "bare law,"[70] consciences agonize with fear and trembling; under the gospel, they are emancipated, filled with freedom and joy. In Christ, our conscience no longer has to reckon with what the law requires to render God favorable; rather it finds relief from the law's requirement in Christ alone, the sole righteousness.

Calvin retains the two kinds of freedom from the law. First, we are set free from worrying about the law and its power to condemn. Second, we are set free to obey the law joyfully, since we, by faith, have obtained our deliverance from the law's condemnation. The contradiction between law and gospel is resolved for those whose sole trust is in Christ. The law, which no longer frightens our conscience, is not abrogated, but continues and is deemed the best method of conformity to the commands of God. Obedience is characteristic of those in whom Christ's Spirit dwells and reigns. The law, stripped of its accusing function, causes us to obey God. Edward Dowey writes, "Once the legal curse is removed and so long as

66. *Inst.* 2.5.15, italics original.

67. Jones, "Law and the Spirit," 302.

68. *Comm. Gal.* 3:10, *CNTC* 11:53.

69. *Inst.* 2.7.14.

70. *Inst.* 2.7.2.

all justification by works of any kind is banished, the law can return to its original and proper role of being an articulation of the love of God and thus is helpful in the Christian life."[71] The law is the expression of God's will. As Hesselink affirms, "Calvin's view [of the law as a guide] could be Deuteronomic, for to him law and love are not antithetical, but are correlates."[72]

Through the law, the Holy Spirit remakes us according to the image of God. Because sin resides, the old Adam continues to need purification from the law. When the spur of the law fails to arouse in us a piety of joyous obedience but a despair of God's mercies, Calvin advises us to set it aside and make the most of God's sweet promises by which God gently woos us to obey. God's gracious invitation is by far a much stronger impetus to obedience than the law or by compulsion from terror. "Not that it is any more improper for God to punish than it is for him to be gracious, but he wishes to show us that his goodness is much greater, and in brief, that he is not harsh. Rather he only wants to open his heart to us if we will permit him. In fact, he wills to be known as good and merciful; and it is in that that his glory principally shines."[73] God commends to those who worship him aright the magnitude of his mercy, which he extends to a thousand generations, while he has imposed his vengeance upon the idolaters only for four generations. This sharp contrast between the largeness of God's mercy and brevity of God's wrath shows that God's nature is sheer mercy. Even in punishing evils, God wills to be revealed as merciful, in which God's glory "principally shines." Wrath is not an ontological attribute; it is a proper reaction to sin, something he does that is contrary to his nature.

Calvin stresses the Holy Spirit as the dynamic of a threefold transformation of the attitude toward the law in the faithful: epistemic perception (that believers come to a new realization that the law is sweet), affective reception (that they delight in it and long for it), and conative apprehension (that they desire to live in conformity to it). By the Spirit, the transition is made from "being in Christ," where our identity as God's beloved is founded, to "acting like Christ," where we express that new identity in conformity to the law.[74] The law of God is "one everlasting and unchange-

71. Dowey, "Law in Luther and Calvin," 151.

72. Hesselink, "Law," 215–16.

73. *STC*, 78.

74. Kolb and Trueman, *Between Wittenberg and Geneva*, 58, where the unity and distinction of "being in Christ" and "acting like Christ" appear.

able rule to live by,"[75] and that rule that reigns over us is Jesus Christ, who is apprehended in the law, and whose character is reproduced in us by the Spirit. The Christian expresses her adoption in two ways: first, passively by the gift of righteousness through the gospel, which faith appropriates by the Holy Spirit; and second, actively by performing what the Father has imposed on us in the law for a productive human life, involving us in self-giving acts in the sociopolitical realm. The activity of God in justification does not exclude human responsibility in sanctification. Holiness flows out of union with Christ, as does justification. "By treating these two elements, which had hitherto been regarded as independent entities requiring correlation, as subordinate to the believer's union with Christ," McGrath writes, "Calvin is able to uphold both total gratuitousness of our acceptance before God and the subsequent demands of obedience placed upon us."[76]

Was there a time in which civil order was not? For Calvin, civil order is not necessitated by the fall; it belongs to God's created order. Its function is "like trees, on whose fruits mortals feed and under whose shadow they rest."[77] The dignity of civil government is not derived from its postlapsarian remedy to any waywardness but from its being a created dispensation, appointed by God to produce peace and order of society, just as the earth is appointed to produce food for our physical well-being. In the prelapsarian state, law and gospel do not exist as an antithesis. The law before sin works good until the subject to whom it is applied changes from a righteous person to a sinner. The latter incurs the negative imposition of political power hurled against his wicked deeds. Likewise, civil government is ordained by God to protect human life, unless the subject to which it is administered is the wicked, who necessarily falls under the sword of the political order. In his commentary on Isaiah 24:12, Calvin avows, "How much God is pleased with government and the well constituted order of all things; and also how great a privilege it is to have it preserved among us. . . . When these fall, civilization itself falls along with them."[78]

The transitional statement "The Way We Receive the Grace of Christ" appears after Calvin's discussion of union with Christ and his benefits. The significance of this statement, T. H. L. Parker observes, lies

75. *Inst.* 2.7.13.

76. McGrath, *Life of John Calvin*, 166.

77. *Comm. Dan.* 4:10–16, CO 40, 657, as cited in Milner, *Church*, 30.

78. *Comm. Isa* 24:12, CO 36, 400, as cited in Milner, *Church*, 30n1.

in that it leads to the subject at hand, where Calvin regards prayer as a vehicle through which believers receive the treasures of his grace.[79] Calvin begins his chapter on prayer with a trinitarian presupposition, bringing together union with Christ, the acquisition of his benefits for us, and the Spirit—all of which we receive through prayer, "the chief exercise of faith."[80] The Father initiates salvation; the Son implements it; the Holy Spirit completes it. All three persons work together externally as one God in the economy of salvation. The same procedure applies to effectual prayer, which commences with the Father's invitation in Christ through whom it culminates in the Father by the Spirit. The abundance of treasures the Father prepares for us in his Son remains outside us and thus does not profit us unless the Holy Spirit seals it in our hearts, causing us to grasp these treasures by prayer. Purely out of nothing, God saves us by bestowing on us his heavenly goods in Christ; so too out of nothing we pray to God through the Son to receive his gifts. Prayer alone invokes the abundance of God's preexistent goods stored up in heaven.

In Calvin's discussion on prayer, the role of the Spirit looms large. Calvin shows himself more than a theologian who instructs people in the faith, but also a pastor who leads his people to "pray in the Spirit" for the weaknesses of their faith. Calvin does not deny darkness as part of the life of faith. Self-confidence is given up in favor of filial confidence in "the double grace"—justification and sanctification—obtained through union with Christ by the Holy Spirit. Believers take refuge in "the fruit of reconciliation,"[81] the antinomy between God's mercy and his wrath having been resolved, and are assured by the Spirit that their adoption is not vitiated by imperfect prayers. Paul, in speaking of the Spirit's intercession, wanted to, in Calvin's words, "more significantly ascribe the whole to the grace of the Spirit. We are indeed bidden to knock; but no one can of himself premeditate even one syllable, except God by the secret impulse of his Spirit knocks at our door, and thus opens for himself our hearts."[82] God not only instructs us to pray according to his word, especially the Lord's Prayer; he also "gives us the Spirit as our teacher in prayer, to tell us what is right and temper our emotions."[83] Elsewhere Calvin writes, "[The Spirit] stirs up in our hearts the prayers which it is proper for us

79. Parker, *Biography*, 41.

80. *Inst.* 3.20.1.

81. *Inst.* 3.20.9.

82. *Comm. Rom.* 8:26, CNTC 8:178.

83. *Inst.* 3.20.5.

to address to God."[84] As instructed in the Geneva Catechism, we are not to await passively for the Spirit to move us to pray; we are to "flee to God and demand" that we be "inflamed with the fiery darts of his Spirit, so as to be rendered fit for prayer."[85] While believers count on the Spirit's help, they are not exempted from the fervency and anguish of true prayer. This is already implied in the metaphor of "groans,"[86] which believers give forth under the secret prompting of the Spirit. "[The Spirit] affects our hearts in such a way that these prayers penetrate into heaven itself by their fervency."[87] True prayer presupposes the outwardness, a going outside of oneself, and the abandonment of all self-reliance or self-assurance.

Calvin relates the concept of divine accommodation to his theology of church and her ministries. In Calvin's words, "Shut up as we are in the prison house of our flesh, we have not yet attained angelic rank. God, therefore, in his wonderful providence accommodating himself to our capacity, has prescribed a way for us, though still far off, to draw near to him."[88] As God hides his majesty in the frail, weak humanity of Jesus to meet us, so God hides his majesty in the weak, tangible forms of God's word to come to us. Pedagogically, God accommodates himself to us as a mother does to her child. In order to mature us, God who is our Father constitutes the church as our Mother "into whose bosom God is pleased to gather his sons, not only that they be nourished by her help and ministry as long as they are infants and children, but also that they be guided by her motherly care until they mature and at least reach the goal of faith."[89] While the word of God is the "foundation," the sacraments are "pillars" through which believers contemplate the riches of God's grace.[90] The audible word and the visible word are God's instituted means through which God's grace comes to nurture, strengthen, and support the weak faith of believers. Public worship is a saving event in which the church hears and receives his word of promise conveyed through preaching and celebration of the sacraments. Preachers are the instruments of God's power. This is borne out in his commentary on 2 Corinthians 3:6: "And so

84. *Comm. Rom.* 8:26, *CNTC* 8:178.

85. Calvin, *Theological Treatises*, 121; also quoted in Calhoun, "Prayer," 358. The quotation comes from the Geneva Catechism, question 245.

86. *Inst.* 3.20.5.

87. *Comm. Rom.* 8:26, *CNTC* 8:178.

88. *Inst.* 4.1.1.

89. *Inst.* 4.1.1.

90. *Inst.* 4.14.6.

we are the Ministers of the Spirit not because we hold Him bound or captive and not because at our own whim we can confer His grace upon all or upon whom we please, but because through us Christ enlightens men's minds, renews their hearts and wholly regenerates them. It is because of this bond and conjunction between Christ's grace and man's work that a minister is often given credit for what belongs to God alone."[91] The efficacy of preaching rests entirely on the work of the Spirit, and the sermon is the means which the Spirit employs to do the work of justification and regeneration. The majesty of God shines in preaching through which God himself, not just ideas or memories about him, is fully disclosed through the Spirit to the heart of the worshipers. The word preached in the power of the Spirit ensures that God's presence is truly felt in present times, as certain as in the past. The Spirit-fired sermon is itself a divine encounter, not a preparation for it. For preaching, says Heiko Oberman, "forces for itself a way to the heart and mind of the congregation,"[92] forging an intimate communion between God and the hearers. To borrow from John L. Austin's speech act theory, the word proclaimed, for Calvin, is not a "constative utterance," that which merely describes a situation, but a "performative utterance," that which actually delivers what it says.[93] As Lane sums up, "To issue the utterance is to perform the act. The language participates in (and creates) the reality."[94] To speak is to perform, bringing about that which has not occurred before.

Calvin is at odds with the view that the Spirit achieves everything by "his intrinsic power" apart from external means. He also dismisses the position that God "resigns his office to the outward symbols"[95] so that the material signs themselves are efficacious, inherently possessing the power to justify. For him, the outward symbols are the instruments God uses to work grace in us, without detracting anything from his "original activity."[96] Sacraments accomplish their office only when accompanied by the Spirit, the inward teacher, who causes the minds and hearts to be opened to receive the sacramental gifts. Christ together with all his benefits are bestowed on us through sacramental signs; to transfer efficacy to the sacraments themselves is to rob God of his majesty and glory. The

91. *Comm. 2 Cor.* 3:6, *CNTC* 10:43.

92. Oberman, "Preaching," 18.

93. See Austin, "Performative-Constative," 13–22.

94. Lane, *Ravished by Beauty*, 80.

95. *Inst.* 4.14.17.

96. *Inst.* 4.14.17.

promise of God benefits those who receive it with sure faith; it is vitiated by unbelief, yet the promise remains firm and valid.

Calvin differs from the Lutherans regarding the presence and location of Christ's body. While Lutherans affirm a real, physical presence of Christ's body and blood in the elements, Calvin affirms a real spiritual presence, because Christ's body is circumscribed in heaven. Lutherans place the emphasis on the downward movement of Christ's body from heaven, thereby locating it in the eucharistic elements. However, Calvin puts the emphasis on the upward movement of the faithful participants by the Spirit to Christ's ascended throne, to partake of Christ's body there. In Butin's apt estimation, "Calvin's approach at this point thus complements and completes the 'downward' Lutheran emphasis on incarnation with an equal 'upward' emphasis on resurrection and ascension."[97] To this, Horton adds Pentecost, since "it is the Spirit's work especially that Calvin highlights in discussing how we are united to Christ as coheirs with him of the Father's estate."[98] Calvin's emphasis is not on what happens to the eucharistic elements but on what happens to those who partake of them in faith. In eucharistic worship, Christ is not relocated to earth to feed us from below; instead, the Spirit lifts the faithful communicants up to heaven, where Christ nourishes them with his body. What enters us is not Christ's body but the fullness of life from his body. The dynamic between the Spirit's descent and Christ's ascent is where Calvin's doctrine of the Supper is framed and receives its central meaning. Milner summarizes Calvin's view aptly: "The Spirit join us to Christ, and makes possible a true participation in his flesh and blood, not by bringing Christ down to us; rather, the Spirit raises us up to him, brings us into the presence of Christ. The most profound action of the sacrament, therefore, takes place in heaven, not on earth."[99] The sacramental signs are God's gracious invitation extended to his faithful communicants to "enjoy Christ," that is, the "whole Christ."[100]

True piety consists in receiving the Spirit's gift of union with God in Christ through faith alone. Fallen sinners are stripped of all residual moral powers that orient them toward God, and of all natural capacities that allow them to achieve communion with God. Introspection is of no use; of ourselves, we do not have the necessary resources to meet

97. Butin, *Revelation*, 118.

98. Horton, *Christian Life*, 93.

99. Milner, *Church*, 129.

100. *Inst.* 4.17.18; 4.17.30.

God. But by extrospection, by looking outside of ourselves, we seek the resources that do meet our need. Calvin's piety has grace as its origin and end, and it is trinitarian in shape. Calvin's trinitarian piety of grace assumes the posterior, backward movement of the Trinity, moving from the third article (the Holy Spirit) through the second (the Son) to the first (the Father), a movement that presupposes the prior, forward movement of the Trinity—namely, from the Father through the Son in the Spirit. Calvin's piety spells the death of ascent either by way of good works we do for the neighbor, or by inward solitude or meditation on God apart from the external word and sacrament. To live by grace is to "forget ourselves and all that is ours, . . . to be wise in nothing and to will nothing through ourselves but to follow the leading of the Lord alone."[101] Karl Barth's formulation of grace reflects Calvin's: "Grace points them away from self, frightens them out of themselves, deprives them of any root or soil or country in themselves, summons them to hold to the promise, to trust in Him, to boast in Him, to take guidance and counsel of Him and Him alone."[102] By God's gentle invitation, we enter into the trinitarian drama of God's glorious actions in creation, redemption, and sanctification, and reap from each the benefits for our souls. The sweetness of communion with the triune God is a privilege given to God's beloved, which in turn marks our life as receptive. We live a beggarly life, characterized not by active, self-propelled progress toward God in faith, but by receiving God's unconditional promises passively by faith. The extrinsic nature of faith in Calvin's theology engenders in us a piety not of turning inward to the self for fulfillment, but of turning outward to God in an affective act of loving God as Father as much as fearing him as Lord. To live before the majestic God is to leave ourselves behind by cleaving to the triune God in whom true happiness resides. Calvin would accept William Ames's definition of theology as "the doctrine of living to God."[103] We live, not by anything we inherit or acquire, but by the gratuitous gift of God in creating and preserving us, restoring us to divine favor from the fall, and adopting us as his children along with all the heavenly inheritances. The crucial thing, as this book demonstrates, is that Calvin's theology is basically practical, showing us how the gospel leads the way to the triune God, whose majesty governs all aspects of a life lived under him.

101. *Inst.* 3.7.1.

102. Barth, *CD* 1/2:393.

103. Ames, *Marrow*, 77.

# 1

# Epistemic Condition and Revelation

## *Creation, Providence, and Holy Scripture*

Book 1 of Calvin's *Institutes* is not occupied with the knowledge of God the Redeemer, but "with only of the primal and simple knowledge to which the very order of nature would have led us if Adam had remained upright."[1] Natural knowledge of God is open to all eyes to see. All of us are given the appropriate epistemic condition in which the capacity for the natural awareness of God is innately operative. But it does not profit much, for the contemplation of such knowledge, due to the fall, does not direct us to the true God. Apart from "the spectacles"[2] of Holy Scripture, we cannot see clearly that the God revealed in creation is indeed the God revealed in Scripture. Just as Scripture's authority is temporally apprehended by the inward testimony of the Spirit, so too the knowledge of God the Redeemer is temporally apprehended by the inner revelation of faith before the knowledge of God the Creator is recognized, though the logical order is from creation to redemption. Word and Spirit imply each other; they do not collapse into each other. The knowledge of the Creator God is incomplete unless accompanied by the scriptural witness to the providential care of his universe. Scripture yields salutary insights into how God governs his people and the universe with his power, justice, and wisdom so that they turn to God for all good. Only faith grasps divine providence from which proceeds nothing but good, even when the outworking of it is hidden from us.

1. *Inst.* 1.2.1.
2. *Inst.* 1.6.1.

The search for God is not by a consideration of God's essence, which terrifies us, but by gazing upon God's individual works in creation, which allure us. Fruitful contemplation moves from his works to his nature, not the reverse. Calvin teaches us to regard the universe as the school of contemplation—focusing on God's glorious powers, which we see in creatures—and be caught up in awe and wonder of his glory hidden therein. Our cognitive and affective condition must undergo regeneration so that we might see clearly the splendorous glory of God in creation and feel its causal effect on us, that we are rapt outside of ourselves in wonder and awe before the majestic God. True knowledge of God is born not out of idle speculation but from a revelatory encounter with God, whose nature is not located in some transcendent sphere, separated from his glorious acts upon us that faith grasps. Calvin affirms a correspondence between God's nature and God's act, but with an emphasis on the latter as the starting point of his contemplation. Paul Helm writes,

> God's nature, then, is expressed and summed up in what he is towards us. What God does, including what God reveals of himself, is what God has chosen to do. So we know God's nature through those activities that God has chosen to undertake. These activities express God's nature directly—for example, in the wisdom and righteousness that they display—but they express his essence only obliquely.[3]

The first book of the *Institutes* opens with a foundational assertion: "Nearly all the wisdom, true and sound wisdom, comprises two parts: the knowledge of God and knowledge of ourselves."[4] The knowledge of God is essential to knowing ourselves; conversely, the knowledge of ourselves is crucial to knowing God. The two forms of knowledge are distinct but inseparably one. It is not easy to discern which one is prior and issues forth the other.[5] Both occur concurrently so that we cannot have either in isolation. At every point of our life, we must confront a delicately balanced interaction between God and the world, the Creator and his creation. Rather than choosing one or the other as the starting point, Calvin insists on looking at both, moving back and forth between reflection on who God is and who we are within the context of the relation between

3. Helm, *Ideas*, 14.
4. *Inst.* 1.1.1.
5. *Inst.* 1.1.3.

them. Yet, "the order of right teaching"[6] requires that we discuss the knowledge of God first, then, following that, the knowledge of ourselves.

Natural knowledge of God is discernible in creation. Inherent in this assertion, McGrath notes, are two grounds, one subjective and the other objective.[7]

## THE SUBJECTIVE GROUND: A SENSE OF DIVINITY

The subjective ground is "a sense of divinity" (*sensus divinitatis*), or "the seed of religion," or "the worm of conscience," which constitutes our creaturely status.[8] The sense of divinity is inscribed in, and never effaced from, the hearts of all. All humans are given the epistemic condition whereby the knowledge of God in nature is universally known. No matter how far people deviate from God, even to the point of denying God's existence, still that seed remains and can never be uprooted.[9] "This is not a doctrine which is first learned at school"; rather, it is one "which nature itself permits no one to forget, though many strive with every nerve to this end."[10] Although the structure of the sense of divinity remains intact after the fall, its integrity is compromised. Three disastrous consequences flow out of the noetic effects of sin upon this structure.

First, the seed of divinity is so corrupted by sin that it gives rise necessarily to bitter fruit. In the created order, sin corrupts this luminous knowledge of God, and sinners become idolaters rather than those who worship God "in spirit and in truth" (John 4:25). The natural awareness or knowledge of God is distorted by the curvature of the soul, unless healed by grace.[11] The sense of divinity may be used as a point of contact for Christian proclamation, but not with God, as it bears no saving power to move from unbelief to faith. It is no agent of exposing sin, preparing us for a reception of grace. In fact, it works just the opposite, leading us away from God. Calvin says it bears no godliness. He writes, "As experience shows, God has sown a seed of religion in all men. But scarcely one man in a hundred is met with who fosters it, once received, in his heart,

6. *Inst.* 1.1.3.

7. McGrath, *Life of John Calvin*, 152–53.

8. *Inst.* 1.3.1; 1.4.4; 1.5.1.

9. See Jones, *Rhetoric*, 168–70.

10. *Inst.* 1.3.3.

11. Warfield, *Calvin and Augustine*, 32.

and none in whom it ripens—much less shows fruit in season [cf. 1:3]."[12] Alvin Plantinga notes, "The knowledge of God provided by the *sensus divinitatis*, prior to faith and regeneration, is both narrowed and partially suppressed."[13] The human mind, for Calvin, is "a perpetual factory of idols";[14] it tends to imagine or construct a god according to its own image. Engrossed in ignorance, it invents "an empty appearance as God," devoid of reality. The implication of this sense of divinity is that idolatry is inevitable, but atheism impossible. By the word "imagine," Calvin is against "the ravings or evil imaginings of our flesh,"[15] a vain invention of perverted affections; it is not to be confused with true imagining, an intellectual reflection of that which seizes our minds.

The second disastrous consequence is a troubled conscience, which arises from the vengeance of God's majesty against those who are despisers of God.[16] They try to hide from the Lord's presence, as though it can be effaced from their minds. Occasionally it may disappear, but it always abides and returns "with new force."[17] There is no respite from anxiety of conscience, as "they are continually troubled with dire and frightful dreams."[18] The impious activities in which they hide is sure proof that some ideas of God remain ever alive in people's minds.[19]

The third consequence is a servile fear of God exacerbated by the threat of God's inescapable judgment. Because sinful humans can neither eradicate the innate sense of divinity nor flee from it, they hide away in trepidation.[20] They then become hypocrites, resorting to twisting paths to approach the God from whom they flee. Instead of placing their trust in God, they seek to placate God's wrath through some impious acts of expiation. Eventually they lapse into numerous errors through blind wickedness. Those sparks of God's glory they once perceived in creation gradually diminish until they finally are extinguished through "the fault of dullness" in us.[21]

12. *Inst.* 1.4.1.
13. Plantinga, *Warranted Christian Belief*, 184.
14. *Inst.* 1.11.8.
15. *Inst.* 1.5.11.
16. *Inst.* 1.3.2.
17. *Inst.* 1.3.2.
18. *Inst.* 1.3.2.
19. Dowey, *Knowledge of God*, 54.
20. *Inst.* 1.4.4.
21. *Inst.* 1.5.15.

## THE OBJECTIVE GROUND: THE WORLD AS THE SCHOOL OF CONTEMPLATION

The second ground lies in rational reflection upon and experience of the created order. The invisible God hides under the form of creaturely and visible things. God's self-disclosure is so perspicuous that all could perceive him. God repeatedly renews the innate knowledge of divinity by his richest manifestations in nature and providence.[22] The inscrutable vastness of the universe and conspicuous sparks of divine glory in it escapes our surveying; quoting Calvin, "You cannot in one glance survey this most vast and beautiful system of the universe, in its wide expanse, without being completely overwhelmed by the boundless force of its brightness."[23] The "skillful ordering of the universe is for us a sort of mirror in which we can contemplate God, who is otherwise invisible."[24] The pious person is given the eyes of faith, through which he is bound to contemplate God's self-revelation in creation. Calvin writes, "Therefore, as soon as the name of God sounds in our ears, or the thought of God occurs to our minds, let us also clothe God with this most beautiful ornament, the universe."[25] "The contemplation of heaven and earth," for Calvin, "is the very school of God's children."[26] If we truly "desire to know God," he adds, we should regard "the world" as "our school,"[27] which teaches us to contemplate the knowledge of God the Creator aright, beginning from the heavens and ending in ourselves. Because, as Taylor argues, "the experience of the creation is an intensively sensory one,"[28] sight and contemplation of the visible world should not be done, in Calvin's words, "cursorily, and, so to speak, with a fleeting glance, but we should ponder them at length, turn them over in our minds seriously, and faithfully, and recollect them repeatedly."[29] All could see God's powers portrayed in his works. But the learned, Calvin argues, penetrate more deeply into God's wisdom displayed for all eyes to see.

22. *Inst.* 1.3.1. See Jones, *Rhetoric*, 163–64.

23. *Inst.* 1.5.1.

24. *Inst.* 1.5.1.

25. *Comm. Gen, Argument*, CTS 1:60.

26. *Inst.* 1.6.4.

27. *Comm. Gen, Argument*, CTS 1:60.

28. Taylor, *Theater*, 40.

29. *Inst.* 1.14.21.

> There are innumerable evidences both in heaven and on earth that declare his wonderful wisdom; not only those more recondite matters for the closer observation of which astronomy, medicine, and all natural sciences are intended, but also those which thrust themselves upon the sight of even the most untutored and ignorant persons, so that they cannot open their eyes without being compelled to witness them. Indeed, men who have either qualified or even tasted the liberal arts penetrate with their aid far more deeply into the secrets of all the divine wisdom.[30]

Natural reason bears no power to attain to the certainty of knowing God. This in no way means that there is no knowledge to be gained from liberal arts and science. Creaturely knowledge is God's natural gift, freely bestowed for our benefit. Quoting Calvin, "These men whom Scripture [1 Cor. 2:4] calls 'natural men' were, indeed, sharp and penetrating in their investigation of inferior things";[31] and "if we regard the Spirit of God as the sole fountain of truth, we shall neither reject the truth itself, nor despise it wherever it shall appear, unless we wish to dishonor the Spirit. For by holding the gifts of the Spirit in slight esteem, we condemn and reproach the Spirit."[32] Creaturely gifts which we gain from these sciences—"physics, dialectic, mathematics, and other like disciplines, by the work and ministry of the ungodly"—are of the Holy Spirit, and can be of help to us.[33] "Since God is the source of all knowledge," Susan E. Schreiner writes, "pagan wisdom can be legitimately appropriated as an aid in investigations of nature and for governing society."[34] Any disdain of these gifts dishonors the Creator and thus incurs just punishments for it.

On Genesis 4:20, Calvin highly esteems the invention of arts that work good for the common life and are "a gift of God." Such arts show that "the rays of divine light have shone on unbelieving nations, for the benefit of the present life; and we see, at the present time, that the excellent gifts of the Spirit are diffused through the whole human race."[35] The pious in particular are given fresh eyes to see and enjoy these gifts, not to be shared with the impious. They have the duty to study them for

30. *Inst.* 1.5.2.
31. *Inst.* 2.2.15.
32. *Inst.* 2.2.15.
33. *Inst.* 2.2.15.
34. Schreiner, *Theater*, 120.
35. *Comm. Gen.* 4:20, CTS 1:217.

themselves, and consequently are caught up in wonderment over such natural wisdom or insights. Contemplating God in all creatures leads to a thoughtful recognition of the majesty of God and the allurement of his astounding beauty. Calvin writes, "As soon as we acknowledge God to be the supreme architect, who has erected the beauteous fabric of the universe, our minds must necessarily be ravished [*rapi necesse est*] with wonder at his infinite goodness, wisdom, and power."[36]

## The Proper Starting Point: God's Essence or God's Works?

Calvin affirms, "Indeed, his essence is incomprehensible."[37] God's essence is not to be confused with God's glory that permeates the natural world. Lane clarifies, "Though God's 'unveiled presence' is never discerned in the external world, nature is shot through with evidences of God's 'glory.' This distinction between 'essence' and 'glory' . . . allows people to speak of God's vivid presence in the physical universe without confusing the two. Calvin knew that direct experience of divine glory would wholly obliterate us, hence we glimpse God only obliquely (though beautifully) through the mirror of God's works in the world."[38] The transcendence of God's otherness is maintained alongside the knowability of God. Contemplation thus is to be done not by an investigation of God's essence, whose majestic greatness may frighten us, but a pondering of God's actions in creation through which our hearts are aroused to trust, praise, and love him.[39] Calvin writes,

> Consequently, we know the most perfect way of seeking God, and the most suitable order, is not for us to attempt with bold curiosity to penetrate to the investigation of his essence, which we ought more to adore than meticulously to search out, but for us to contemplate him in his works whereby he renders himself near and familiar to us, and in some manner communicates himself. The apostle was referring to us, when he said that we need not seek him far away, seeing that he dwells by his present power in each of us [Acts 17:27–28].[40]

36. *Comm. Ps.* 19:1, CO:195, CTS 4:309.
37. *Inst.* 1.5.1.
38. Lane, *Ravished by Beauty*, 68.
39. *Inst.* 1.14.22.
40. *Inst.* 1.5.9.

Calvin regards David as a good example of how to rightly seek God. David, who "having first confessed his [God's] unspeakable greatness [Ps. 145:3], afterwards proceeds to mention his works and professes that he will declare his greatness [Ps. 145:5–6; cf. Ps. 40:5]." Such an approach "may so hold our mental powers suspended in wonderment as at the same time to stir us deeply."[41] Calvin draws from Augustine, for whom the search for God proceeds from a consideration of God's creative goodness (act) to his majestic greatness (being), not the reverse. He sums up Augustine's thought: "And as Augustine teaches elsewhere, because, disheartened by his greatness, we cannot grasp him, we ought to gaze upon his works, that we may be restored by his goodness."[42] It bears no saving significance to simply know of God's essence. Such knowledge could remain an abstract kind, totally detached from the affective dimension of faith. It does not penetrate "the inmost affection of the heart,"[43] and create a faith that nourishes obedience to God and trust in his goodness. God's majesty assumes his essential greatness as the content, and the accommodated form in which the majesty appears, not as he really is in himself but as he manifests himself to us. We hold on to God, "not as he is in himself, but as he is toward us; so that this recognition of him consists more in living experience than in vain and high-flown speculation."[44] The contrast between "not as he is in himself, but as he is toward us" reflects two opposite ways of seeking God. The former refers to God's majesty, which drives us away; the latter is God's gracious coming to us in an accommodated mode that draws us to him. God hides his majesty from us, and reveals himself in a familiar way so that we can bear him. As John Chrysostom writes, "God appears not as He is, but that he shows Himself in a way that the one who beholds Him can bear, because he proportions what He reveals to the weakness (ἀσθενεία) of the beholder."[45] Calvin's theological task is not to engage in idle speculation on God's essence ("What is God?") but in contemplation of God's revelation ("What is God like?"). Horton sums up aptly: "The goal for Calvin, then, is not to find

41. *Inst.* 1.5.9.

42. *Inst.* 1.5.9. See Augustine, *Psalms*, Ps 144:6 (MPL 37. 1872; tr. LF *Psalms* 6. 319), as cited in *Inst.* 1.5.9, 62n30.

43. *Inst.* 3.6.4.

44. *Inst.* 1.10.2.

45. See Chrysostom, *Sur l'incompréhensibilité de Dieu* (*Homélies* 1–4), ed. Jean Daniélou and Anne-Marie Malingrey, trans. Robert Flacelière. SC 28bis. Cerf: Paris, 2000, as quoted in Huijgen, *Divine Accommodation*, 76.

a 'what' but a 'who', not an essence, but an active agent in history. That requires a story, not a speculation."[46] That story is about God's gracious activity toward us in which God's true nature is known. "What help is it, in short, to know a God with whom we have nothing to do?"[47] The God with whom we have to do does not dwell in his transcendent solitariness and rigid aloofness; instead, he dwells in us by his ever-present power (Acts 17:27–28), bestowing on us his manifold gifts. God's nature is not located in some remote sphere, but in his operations in and upon the world. God communicates himself in his works in which he is most godly. Thus, we seek God where he has made himself near and accessible to us, that we may "grasp what befits us and is proper to his glory, in fine, what is to our advantage to know of him."[48]

For Calvin, the word "know" carries a richer meaning than the merely cognitive; as Helm argues, "To know in the full sense is to be not only in the appropriate epistemic condition, but also in a positive affective and conative condition towards the one whom one knows."[49] Helm's analysis finds support in Calvin, who writes, "Indeed, we shall not say that, properly speaking, God is known where there is no religion or piety."[50] True knowledge of God stems not from philosophical speculation but a living encounter with God. In this regard, Calvin contends that the Athenians or Aratus have only an intimation of God, not the knowledge of the true God. An intimate relationship with God is the fruit of true piety, marked by reverence and love of God. Calvin reverts to Paul's basic principle, "that God cannot be worshipped in a proper and devout manner until He has been made known."[51] To know that there is a god, as Athenians know, is not the same as to know what God is like. Unless God discloses what he is like, we really do not know what God is. Calvin argues that Paul, in his debate with Athenians in Mars Hill, did not begin from "the first point," that "there is some deity to whom worship is due from men," something the Athenians already accepted; rather, "Paul passes on to the second point," to show that "the true God ought to be distinguished from all fabrications."[52] God belongs to an ontologically

46. Horton, *Christian Life*, 47.

47. *Inst.* 1.2.2.

48. *Inst.* 1.2.1.

49. Helm, *Ideas*, 222.

50. *Inst.* 1.2.1.

51. *Comm. Acts* 17, *CNTC* 7:111.

52. *Comm. Acts* 17, *CNTC* 7:112.

different category, not to be reduced to, or confused with, the category of creatures, lest his transcendence be compromised. On the first point, Calvin seems to concede that Athenians and Christians overlap in cognitive content (there is a God), but this overlap does not mean the pagans worship the true God, unless they are given appropriate moral and affective orientation toward God. Speculative knowledge "flits in the brain" and does not take "root in the heart."[53] Revelatory knowledge of the second point acquaints us with what God's will is toward us through which God is truly worshiped. Hence, Calvin concludes, "Paul certainly does not deal in a subtle way with the secret essence of God, but shows from His works what profitable knowledge of Him is."[54]

## Created Images and Fatherly Allurements

The language of desire, Belden C. Lane rightly observes, inheres in Calvin's references to the beauty of creation and the abundant benefits therein.[55] Calvin, in sensuous language, depicts joyous participation in God's benefits in nature. In his *Genesis Argumentum*, Calvin encourages his readers to humbly meditate on God's works to taste of his goodness: "We see, indeed, the world with our eyes, we tread the earth with our feet, we touch innumerable kinds of God's works with our hands, we inhale a sweet and pleasant fragrance from herbs and flowers, we enjoy boundless benefits; but in those things of which we attain some knowledge, there dwells such as an immensity of divine power, goodness, and wisdom, as absorbs all our senses. Therefore, let men be satisfied if they obtain only a moderate taste of them, suited to their capacity."[56] Calvin repeatedly stresses that human beings are not "mere witnesses" of creation but are "to enjoy all the riches" hidden in there.[57] Elsewhere, Calvin says, "It is no small honor that God for our sake has so magnificently adorned the world, in order that we may not only be spectators of this beauteous theater, but also enjoy the multiplied abundance of good things which are presented to us in it."[58] Calvin pictures the universe as a spacious house,

53. *Inst.* 1.5.9.

54. *Comm. Acts* 17, *CNTC* 7:112–13.

55. See Lane, *Ravished by Beauty*, 68–74. I am indebted to Lane's perspective.

56. *Comm. Gen, Argument*, CTS 1:57.

57. *Comm. Gen, Argument*, CTS 1:62.

58. *Comm. Ps.* 104.31, CTS 6:169.

in which God invites us to dwell and avail ourselves of its riches: "God has so wonderfully adorned heaven and earth with as unlimited abundance, variety, and beauty of all things as could possibly be, quite like a spacious and splendid house, provided and filled with the most exquisite and at the same time most abundant furnishings."[59] This created sphere is where Christians dwell, act, study, enjoy the riches, and make proper use of gifts. Our delight in creation does not originate with us but with God. As Calvin writes, "Here God is introduced by Moses as surveying his work, that he might take pleasure in it."[60] Human desire is grounded in God's own desire. "For God cannot either more gently allure, or more efficiently incite us to obedience, than by inviting and exhorting us to the imitation of himself."[61] Just as God enjoys his own creation, so we too enjoy the sensory riches of creation such as drinking wine with friends, wearing elegant clothes, living in a beautiful home, being playful in the garden, enjoying the beauty of garden, delighting in the smell of flowers and food, and enjoying fine music. "We have never been forbidden to laugh, or to be filled, or to join new possessions to old or ancestral ones, or to delight in musical harmony, or to drink wine."[62] He further underscores that creaturely gifts serve us with "necessity" and "delight."

> If we ponder to what end God created food, we shall find that he meant not only to provide for necessity but also for delight and good cheer. Thus the purpose of clothing, apart from necessity, was comeliness and decency. In grasses, trees, and fruits apart from their various uses, there is beauty of appearance and pleasantness of odor [cf. Gen. 2:9]. For if this were not true, the prophet would not have reckoned them among the benefits of God, "that wine gladdens the heart of man, that oil makes his face shine" [Ps. 104:15 p]. Scripture would not have reminded us repeatedly, in commending his kindness, that he gave all such things to us. And the natural qualities themselves of things demonstrate sufficiently to what end and extent we may enjoy them. Has the Lord clothed the flowers with the great beauty that greets our eyes, the sweetness of smell that is wafted upon our nostrils, and yet will it be unlawful for our eyes to be affected by that beauty, or our sense of smell by the sweetness of

59. *Inst.* 1.14.20.

60. *Comm. Gen.* 1:4, CTS 1:77.

61. *Comm. Gen.* 2:3, CTS 1:106.

62. *Inst.* 3.19.9.

> that odor? . . . Did he not, in short, render many things attractive to us, apart from their necessary use?[63]

The world as the theater of God—"this dazzling theater," "this most beautiful theater," and "this magnificent theater of heaven and earth, crammed with innumerable wonders"—invites us to contemplate what Paul calls the "wisdom of God." The image of "theater" denotes a place where something happens; the universe is where God's action is played out, as though a theatrical stage, and we are invited to participate in the drama. "Calvin," Belden C. Lane writes, "conceived of the world as a theatre for the contemplation of divine beauty, with *God* assuming the central role at the heart of the action on stage."[64] God's astounding beauty on display on the great stage of this world not only instructs us about God as the mystery of the world, but also evokes a corresponding desire in those who have been drawn into this dramatic presentation. All the images of the universe—"spectacle," "mirror," and "painting"[65]—Lane opines, "serve to underscore the two principal roles that the world as 'God's glorious theatre' plays": "both to delight and to instruct, ever pointing the spectators to the wonder of God's sustaining presence."[66] Calvin's creational theology elicits a balanced piety; Lane describes, "Calvin was as smitten by God's beauty as he was overwhelmed by his power."[67]

The powers of God in the theater—"the infinite goodness, justice, power, and wisdom of God"[68]—draw us to contemplate him. Zachman clarifies what Calvin means by powers:

> Powers are forces which we experience so that they are not just attributes that could be ascribed to God in an abstract manner, but are actually things that are revealed in what God does, that convey God's nature to us. God's nature, then, actually acts upon us. It is not very remote at all. It is quite intimate.[69]

63. *Inst.* 3.10.2.

64. Lane, "Spirituality," 2. He notes, "The word '*theatrum*' itself appears at least seven times in the *Institutes* and dozens of times in Calvin's sermons and biblical commentaries, especially in his commentaries on Genesis, Isaiah, and the Psalms" (4).

65. *Inst.* 1.5.1; 1.5.6; 1.5.10.

66. Lane, "Spirituality," 3.

67. Lane, *Ravished by Beauty*, 27, 57.

68. *Comm. Gen.* 2:3, CTS 1:105–6.

69. Zachman, *Reconsidering John Calvin*, 9–10.

God is intimate in his acts—creative and providential—on us. Contemplating God's glorious powers in creation leads to a recognition that all of his creation is for our good and salvation while concurrently causing us to feel the effect of his power and grace in us.[70] Calvin says, "For the Lord manifests himself by his powers, the force of which we feel within ourselves and the benefits of which we enjoy. We must therefore be much more profoundly affected by this knowledge than if we were to imagine a God of whom no perception came through to us."[71] Whatever we contemplate will have causal effects on us, that we feel his powers and enjoy his benefits. Meditation lifts us out of ourselves and introduces us to the domain of his providence, through which he governs the affairs of his people; of his omnipotence, through which he sustains the feeble hearts; of his goodness, through which he receives the miserable sinners into grace; of his justice, through which he executes his righteous judgment on evil; and of his wisdom, through which he guides and protects us against all forms of vices. These attributes of God—providence, omnipotence, goodness, justice, and wisdom—to which we appeal in meditation create in us the assurance that none of our ills escapes the Lord; our safety lies in him alone, who has both the power and motivation to ensure that we are provided with the best care. Believers know by the outworking of faith that meditation on these attributes supplies new fuel to the ardor that burns low.

We keep "God's individual works" before our gazes, Calvin notes, "especially as in a painting" by which "the whole of mankind is invited and attracted to recognition of him, and from this to true and complete happiness."[72] God's invitation extended to us bestirs in us a desire to turn to God for all good. W. David O. Taylor writes, "More than simple obedience, the invitation of the Creator to the creature is heartfelt trust in a benevolent Father."[73] He quotes Calvin: "Invited by the great sweetness of his beneficence and goodness, let us study to love and serve him with all our heart."[74] The more we are allured by God's glorious acts vividly portrayed in creation as in a painting, the more we feel their affective power on us, that not only are we stirred to repose in him but also we are rapt outside of ourselves with wonder. To the extent that we are seized by the

70. *Inst.* 1.14.22.

71. *Inst.* 1.5.9.

72. *Inst.* 1.5.10.

73. Taylor, *Theater*, 43.

74. *Inst.* 1.14.22.

glorious powers we see in God's creatures, to that extent we are enthralled with profound awe of his majesty, and wonder over the splendor of his glory displayed therein. We are reduced to silence. "It is not a silence before language," Zachman notes, but "a silence beyond language."[75]

Unless God introduces us into the orbit of his self-knowledge, we can never know God. Likewise, unless God informs us of our self, no one can know him- or herself. Calvin opines, "It is certain that man never achieves a clear knowledge of himself unless he has first looked upon God's face and then descends from contemplating him to scrutinize himself."[76] The thought of God as a creative agent leads to an immediate awareness of ourselves as a completely dependent agent. As Calvin writes, "For, how can the thought of God penetrate your mind without your realizing immediately that, since you are his handiwork, you have been made over and bound to his command by right of creation, that you owe your life to him?—that whatever you undertake, whatever you do, ought to be ascribed to him?"[77] The knowledge of God reveals our inaccurate self-perception; Calvin writes, "What in us seems perfection itself corresponds ill to the purity of God."[78] When God manifests his glory, no mortal souls can stand without being terrified and struck dumb, and, in Calvin's words, "are in fact overwhelmed by it and almost annihilated. As a consequence, we must infer that man is never sufficiently touched and affected by the awareness of his lowly state until he has compared himself with God's majesty."[79] God is high and exalted, filled with splendor, the opposite of humans, who are small and lowly, filled with uncomeliness. Calvin writes, "God's majesty is too lofty to be attained by mortal men, who are like grubs crawling upon the earth."[80] To know oneself as a lowly creature before God's majesty is to be overcome with "dread and wonder."[81]

The knowledge of the Creator is peculiar to the first article of the Creed. There it affirms the economic action of the Father as the origin and goal of all that is external to himself. To call God the Creator of this universe is to acknowledge his lordship over all things he has made, and

75. Zachman, *Reconsidering John Calvin*, 11.

76. *Inst.* 1.1.2.

77. *Inst.* 1.2.2.

78. *Inst.* 1.1.3.

79. *Inst.* 1.1.3.

80. *Inst.* 2.6.4.

81. *Inst.* 1.2.3.

receive them as gifts from a benevolent Father. We come face-to-face with God, who is both an awesome Creator, the Lord of all, and a loving Father who employs gentle and loving means to attract us to him. Impious minds wander off, and rashly go beyond God's will. The godly mind forgets itself, and is raised upward, attributing reverence, glory, and honor to God, the one and only true God. Knowing God has a causal effect on us; it creates in us a desire to trust in him, directing all activities to the worship of the living God so that not even "a particle [be detracted] from his glory; rather, all things proper to him must remain with him."[82] Calvin expands:

> Because it acknowledges him as Lord and Father, the pious mind also deems it meet and right to observe his authority in all things, reverence his majesty, take care to advance his glory, and obey his commandments. . . . Because it loves and reveres God as Father, it worships and adores him as Lord. . . . Here, indeed is pure and real religion: faith so joined with an earnest fear of God that this fear also embraces willing reverence, and carries with it such legitimate worship as is prescribed in the law.[83]

## CONTEMPT FOR THE PRESENT LIFE: USE AND MISUSE

The Christian life is governed by an eschatological hope for the future life. Thus meditation on the future should be part of spiritual discipline. The new creature draws "encouragement for the future, from the experience of past favor."[84] God continues to supply proof of miseries in this life to curb the affections of the mind so that we will not become so fixated on earthly allurements that we have no "desire" for the heavenly life.[85] By the manifold tribulations, "God weans us from excessive love" or "brutish" love of this world, causing us to meditate on the life to come. "The mind is never seriously aroused to desire and ponder the life to come unless it be previously imbued with contempt for the present life."[86] Such a phrase ("contempt for the present life") needs to be understood in its proper context—namely, in light of the eschatological glory toward which we

82. *Inst.* 2.8.16.

83. *Inst.* 1.2.2.

84. *Comm. Gen.* 19:20, CTS 1:510.

85. *Inst.* 3.9.4.

86. *Inst.* 3.9.1.

aspire, lest it be conceived as a contradiction of Calvin's celebrated piety of delight for the natural world. Van Vlastuin is helpful in saying, "Nevertheless, in his evaluation of this world, Calvin expresses that relative to the enjoyment of God, this world is to be held in contempt. This view flows from the believer's union with Christ and his participation in the new creation which implies that he is a stranger and pilgrim in this world."[87] The cultivation of a contempt for this world stems from a contemplation of the future. Calvin writes,

> For, if heaven is our homeland, what else is the earth but our place of exile? If departure from the world is entry into life, what else is the world but a sepulcher? And what else is it for us to remain in life but to be immersed in death? If to be freed from the body is to be released into perfect freedom, what else is the body but a prison? If to enjoy the presence of God is the summit of happiness, is not to be without this, misery? . . . Therefore, if the earthly life be compared with the heavenly, it is doubtless to be at once despised and trampled underfoot. Of course, it is never to be hated except in so far as it holds us subject to sin; although not even hatred of that condition may ever properly be turned against life itself.[88]

The contrast between present and future life is no indication of Calvin's disparagement of the created order; as he asserts, "It is never to be hated" unless it subjects us to sin. Rather, it highlights that the complete restoration of this present life occurs in the future life, a better life for those who are united to Christ, in comparison to this life dominated by the miseries of suffering and vices. In light of the tribulation and struggle that feature in the Christian life, Calvin speaks of the need to cultivate a contempt for this present life and to be aroused, thereby, to contemplate the future life. Contempt for this world, Cornelis P. Venema notes, does not "amount to a kind of monastic and otherworldly asceticism."[89] The theme of hope does not entail the disengagement of the Christian from worldly affairs or life in the body, but the renewal of life, which begins now and extends into the future. What Calvin rejects is not the perversity of this present life, but the "perverse love" of it that persuades the heart to seek its happiness there, not in God.[90] As pilgrims, "we ought to use

87. Van Vlastuin, "Kuyper's Spirituality," 533.

88. *Inst.* 3.9.4.

89. Venema, "Last Things," 458.

90. *Inst.* 3.9.4.

its good things in so far as they help rather than hinder" our pilgrimage to heaven.[91] The perfecting of the new creature presupposes the annihilation of the old creature and its vices, a lifelong battle of a regenerated life. "For many so enslave all their senses to delights that the mind lies overwhelmed," and thus sensitivity toward spiritual things is deadened. Calvin illustrates: "The smell of the kitchen or the sweetness of its odor so stupefies others that they are unable to smell anything spiritual."[92] Thus we must adopt a proper approach to this present life, as Paul taught in 1 Corinthians 7:30–31. We are to "use this world as if not using it"—that is, use it without attaching to or depending on it.[93] The phrase "use it as if not using it" guards against the negative—that is, the misuse of it in the way that hinders the future life. We are to use this world, as does a sojourner, as that which is lent to us for temporary use, or as if it belongs to others, not to ourselves.[94] "Those who use this world should be so affected as if they did not use it"[95]—that is, without being bound to creaturely existence. We are to use God's gifts in such a manner that neither "diverts [nor] hinders . . . from thought of the heavenly life and zeal to cultivate the soul."[96] In an attempt to excite believers to make progress in their pilgrimage to the heavenly kingdom, where real happiness lies, Calvin urges them to "burn with zeal for death and be constant in meditation"[97] on the life to come. This is, Venema explains, "an implication of what it means to live in conformity to Christ."[98] Thus, Calvin argues, Paul presents us with Christ to whom we live and die, whichever befits us, and in whose presence alone is "the summit of happiness." Paul, held at length in the prison of the body, lamented his condition and yearned with fervency for deliverance (Rom 7:24). Likewise, we sigh for the last day and the day of the resurrection of the body when all bondages of life—sin, death, devil, and hell—are annihilated, and we enter the perfect freedom which we enjoy, now in part but there in full. "But in comparison with the immortality to

91. *Inst.* 3.10.1.

92. *Inst.* 3.10.3.

93. *Inst.* 3.10.1.

94. *Comm. 1 Cor* 7:30, *CNTC* 9:160.

95. *Inst.* 3.10.4.

96. *Inst.* 3.10.4.

97. *Inst.* 3.9.4.

98. Venema, "Last Things," 458. For further discussion of meditation on future life, see Quistorp, *Last Things*, 40–51.

come," Calvin avows, "let us despise this life and long to renounce it, on account of bondage of sin, whenever it shall please the Lord."[99]

Faith grants us a new vision of God, that he is the Giver; all creaturely goods proceed from God's hands, not as merits of human agency, but as gratuitous gifts of divine agency. These gifts include a new attitude toward his created things, recognizing their goodness, and using them for necessity and delight; and a renewed affection toward God, that our hearts are aroused to thank and praise God. All creaturely things God provides for the enriching of this present life are sacred gifts of God; but they may be perverted, for "man's depravity seduces his mind from rightly seeking him."[100] As travelers on the way to heaven, we are to avoid the two extremes in the usage of God's gifts, which are, in Partee's formulation, "mistaken rigor" and "mistaken indulgence."[101] The severely strict "abstain from all things they could do without; thus, according to them, it would scarcely be permitted to add any food at all to plain bread and water." They permit only the exercise of the most necessary gifts; others cast all their gifts away, for fear that they would be destroyed by them if they do not first destroy them. The severely lax, under the pretext of freedom, give in to "licentious indulgence," making provision for the flesh without restraint.[102] In faith, all are equal in status; in gifts, all are different. Calvin warns against the gluttonous acquisition of goods and the indulgent use of them. The phrase in 1 Corinthians 7:13—"not using it to the full"—imports a sense of self-restraint or discipline in the usage of gifts. In abundance, we bear in moderation; in scarcity, we bear with patience.

"The singular consolation" belongs to those who operate on the "Lord's calling [as] a basis of our way of life."[103] All worldly ambition is curbed, knowing that all callings are equal before God. No task done in obedience to God is base, but is reckoned holy in God's sight. Calvin asserts, "The Lord's calling is in everything the beginning and foundation of well-doing."[104] Calvin expands on the salutary doctrine of vocation:

99. *Inst.* 3.9.4.

100. *Inst.* 1.2.2.

101. Partee, *Theology*, 220.

102. *Inst.* 3.10.1.

103. *Inst.* 3.10.6.

104. *Inst.* 3.10.6.

> Lest through our stupidity and rashness everything has turned topsy-turvy, he has appointed duties for every man in his particular way of life. And that no one may thoughtlessly transgress his limits, he has named these various kinds of living "callings." Therefore, each individual has his own kind of living assigned to him by the Lord as a sort of sentry post so that he may not heedlessly wander about throughout life.[105]

The idea of calling prevents us from being a wanderer, traveling throughout life hither and thither; it helps curb the restlessness and fickleness of human nature, which naturally leads to various self-governed pursuits and deviation from the straight path in duties, thus exceeding their due bounds. We are not aimless wanderers but guided pilgrims, whose life is to be ordered by God, our sole guide in everything.[106] God hides in various positions or vocations (such as the magistrate, the head of the household, or clergy) to mediate his rule. Michael Horton explains, "Here we are taken up in God's loving action toward his creation—not that we now become co-redeemers, but we do become instruments through whom he delivers his gifts of common and saving grace to others. We are not Santa, but his elves."[107] A life of faith is marked by God's mercy, not merits; God's gifts, not self-achievement; stewardship, not competition.

The correct use of earthly benefits in this life is directed toward God, the end for which God creates. God blesses us by means of earthly things not so that we may be held bondage by them, but so that we may rise above them to taste of the spiritual life. We are blessed with earthly things, though not as an end in itself. Through tasting in advance God's kindness manifested in them, we are aroused by that taste to long for the heavenly things, the desired outcome. Calvin writes, "For in this world God blesses us in such a way as to give us a mere foretaste of his kindness, and by that taste to entice us to desire heavenly blessing with which we may be satisfied."[108] Calvin cautions against the idolatry of misplaced trust, reposing in his gifts rather than the Giver. Those who worship idols will become idols themselves. One becomes precisely that in which the heart delights. Calvin illustrates, "Many are so delighted with marble, gold, and pictures that they become marble, they turn, as it were, into

105. *Inst.* 3.10.6.

106. *Inst.* 3.10.6.

107. Horton, *Christian life*, 233.

108. *Comm. 1 Tim.* 4:8, *CNTC* 10:244.

metals and are like painted figures."[109] Those who substitute the one true God for "prodigious trifles" become prodigious trifles themselves.[110] The vanity of this life, for Calvin, is not a reference to the creatures which in themselves are not evil, but to the condition of the heart, designated by the word "use." The fault lies not in the created things of God but in the misdirection of the affective and desiderative condition of the heart. Simeon Zahl's rendering is helpful: "An idol is not an idol inherently; rather, it becomes one through how it is 'used.'"[111] Creation is subject to vanity through no fault of its own but through unbelief or sinful abuse of it. Material things become idols when we attach divinity to them, setting our affection and desire on them. Calvin warns, "To be so occupied in the investigation of the secrets of nature, as never to turn the eyes to its Author, is a most perverted study; to enjoy everything in nature without acknowledging the Author of the benefit, is the basest ingratitude."[112] God creates and destines all things for our good, not so that we might idolize them, but so that we recognize him as Author and give thanks for his kindness toward us.

> Let us therefore remember, whenever each of us contemplates his own nature, that there is one God who so governs all natures that he would have us look unto him, direct our faith to him, and worship and call upon him. For nothing is more preposterous than to enjoy the very remarkable gifts that attest the divine nature within us, yet to overlook the Author who gives them to us at our asking.[113]

## SCRIPTURE AS SPECTACLES: EYES AND EARS

Based on Romans 1:19, Calvin argues that human beings are more than spectators of this world but are "endowed with eyes for the purpose of his being led to God himself, the Author of the world, by contemplating so magnificent an image."[114] Calvin's approach to creational theology is rooted in the idea of "seeing" God's presence and action in creation; it

109. *Inst.* 3.10.3.

110. See *Inst.* 1.5.11, where the phrase "prodigious trifles" occurs.

111. Zahl, "Tradition," 331.

112. *Comm. Gen, Argument*, CTS 1:60.

113. *Inst.* 1.5.6.

114. *Comm. Rom.* 1:19, *CNTC* 8:31.

is not a literal vision but a way of understanding creation through direct observation rather than through abstract speculation. All creatures are given the capacity to see God and glorify God. But such endowment no longer is open due to the fall. "But although the Lord represents both himself and his everlasting Kingdom in the mirror of his works with very great clarity, such is our stupidity that we grow increasingly dull toward so manifest testimonies, and they flow away without profiting us."[115] Corrupted minds are so inclined toward "vanity and error," profaning God's truth and indulging in "the imaginings of our flesh," that "we forsake the one true God for prodigious trifles."[116] Alvin Plantinga sums up well: "This natural knowledge of God has been compromised, weakened, reduced, smothered, overlaid, or impeded by sin and its consequences."[117] Humans are so blinded by sin that they cannot "see" God in creation. They do not "apprehend God as he offers himself, but imagine him as they have fashioned him in their own presumption."[118] They deviate from the right path to attain the certainty of truth. For this reason, God enlightens us with the knowledge of himself by giving us Scripture, which Calvin calls "spectacles."[119]

> Just as old or bleary-eyed men and those with weak vision, if you thrust before them a most beautiful volume, even if they recognize it to be some sort of writing, yet can scarcely construe two words, but with the aid of spectacles will begin to read distinctly; so Scripture, gathering up the otherwise confused knowledge of God in our minds, having dispersed dullness, clearly shows us the true God. This, therefore, is a special gift where God, to instruct the church, not merely uses mute teachers but also opens his own most hallowed lips. . . . His Word . . . is a more direct and more certain mark whereby he is to be recognized.[120]

The fall has so weakened sight that it requires the spectacles of Scripture to see more clearly. Scripture yields a true knowledge of God, something the revelation in creation cannot do due to the fall. It interprets us and the world around us. To lead us properly to God the Creator of the universe,

115. *Inst.* 1.5.11.

116. *Inst.* 1.5.11.

117. Plantinga, *Warranted Christian Belief*, 184.

118. *Inst.* 1.4.1.

119. *Inst.* 1.6.1.

120. *Inst.* 1.6.1.

God supplies the light of his word, "another and better help,"[121] which ultimately leads us to salvation. Calvin advises that we should "willingly leave to God the knowledge of himself. For, as Hilary says, he is the one fit witness to himself, and is not known except through himself."[122] Calvin cautions us against seeking God beyond what he has revealed himself, or speaking or thinking of him beyond what the word explicitly teaches.[123] "We must come," Calvin writes, "to the Word, where God is truly and vividly described to us from his works, while these very works are appraised not by our depraved judgment but by the rule of eternal truth."[124] Scripture corrects our misguided conception of the works of God, so that we might rightly see the powers of God displayed therein; and through the awareness of these powers, we arrive at the knowledge of the true God. In Zachman's assessment, "All right knowledge of God is born out of obedience to the Word of God in Scripture, for this alone reveals the Creator to us from the works God does in the universe."[125]

False imagining, that of the flesh, leads to a distortion of the likeness of things. As William A. Dyrness puts it, "The solution itself involves a reorientation of our sight, involving both a vision of God and a corrected apprehension of the visible world—which is a recognition of its true likeness."[126] Our vision of God (eyes) in creation lost in sin is restored to its original function by the hearing of the word (ears). Dyrness clarifies, "Notice how again sight and contemplation—directed outward toward heaven and earth—are given a special place, though, again, their limits are soon apparent. And Calvin will come to highlight the journey to God through the hearing of the word. But hearing for Calvin will complement, not undermine, the visual spectacle of creation. This dialectic between seeing and hearing, central to Calvin, is evident at the very beginning of the *Institutes*,"[127] where Calvin teaches,

> Therefore, however fitting it may be for man seriously to turn his eyes to contemplate God's works, since he has been placed in this most glorious theatre to be a spectator of them, it is fitting

121. *Inst.* 1.6.1.

122. *Inst.* 1.13.21. See Hilary of Poitiers, *On the Trinity* 1.18 (MPL 10. 38; tr. NPNF 2 ser. 9. 45), as cited in 146n46.

123. *Inst.* 1.13.21.

124. *Inst.* 1.6.3.

125. Zachman, "Scientific Inquiry," 72.

126. Dyrness, "Creation, Drama, and Time," 72.

127. Dyrness, "Creation, Drama, and Time," 69.

> that he prick up his ears to the Word, the better to profit. And it is therefore no wonder that those who were born in darkness become more and more hardened in their insensibility.[128]

Calvin accentuates the "ear" as an antidote to the "eyes" so that nature's eyes return to their revelatory function. "Unbelievers are deaf to all the voices of God" resounding in creation.[129] Hearing itself has no power to create obedience to God unless it hears the word, which the Spirit makes effective, restoring our sight and contemplation of the visible world. Calvin avers, "There is no other way of raising up the Church of God than by the light of the word, in which God himself, by his own voice, points out the way to salvation."[130] Just as God shouts in his incarnate Son to call us back, so too he hides in the preacher's voice to reinstate a right perception of nature, that we might see as did the innocent Adam. In Stephen H. Webb's assessment,

> Adam could "read" nature in ways that we no longer can—which leaves us with hearing as the primary means by which God works the most powerful divine rhetoric. Scripture expresses God's voice more directly than nature, but what enables us to listen to the Bible is the clearest divine speech of all—God's willingness to condescend to us in the incarnation. God will go to the greatest extreme in making the divine word effective. . . . God is forced by our deafness to shout the good news; hyperbole is the usual tenor of the divine voice.[131]

## FAITH IN CHRIST AND NATURAL KNOWLEDGE

The God we see in creation, for Calvin, is identical to the God that we have in Christ. These two revelations mutually reinforce each other. The knowledge of God, which is perceptible through nature, is nonetheless more truly and vividly explained in the word.[132] The knowledge of God after the fall and apart from the Mediator profits us "so little," as it possesses no power unto salvation (cf. Rom 1:16; 1 Cor 1:24). "The epistemic distance between God and humanity, already of enormous magnitude,"

128. *Inst.* 1.6.2, as cited in Dyrness, "Creation, Drama, and Time," 69.

129. *Inst.* 1.6.4.

130. *Comm. Mic* 4:1–2, *CTMP* 3:257.

131. Webb, *Divine Voice*, 154.

132. *Inst.* 1.10.1.

McGrath writes, "is increased still further on account of human sin."[133] Not only is the natural knowledge non-salvific, it is also inadequate as the basis of an accurate portrayal of the nature, character, and purpose of God. As stated in Book 1, the lost and accursed themselves do not apprehend God the Creator. "The primal and simple knowledge" in nature would have led us to the Creator, had Adam not fallen from grace. Piety that begins by acknowledging God as Father is no longer possible unless remedied by Christ's redemption. Calvin notes, "In this ruin of mankind no one now experiences God either as Father or as Author of salvation or favorable in any way, until Christ the Mediator comes forward to reconcile him to us."[134] The same sentiment recurs in Book 2:

> Therefore, since we have fallen from life into death, the whole knowledge of God the Creator [discussed in Book 1] would be useless unless faith also followed, setting forth for us God our Father in Christ. The natural order was that the frame of the universe should be the school in which we were to learn piety, and from it pass over to eternal life and perfect felicity. But after man's rebellion, our eyes—wherever they turn—encounter curse.[135]

Humans are created in God's image, and in their pristine stage, they are "the reflection of God's glory."[136] Nevertheless, fallen human nature still reflects God's glory, albeit imperfectly; only by Christ's restoration do we see that glory fully revealed. The created gifts of understanding and will become totally depraved and no longer function as they did before the fall. Partee rightly discerns the sequence where Calvin proceeds from corruption in Adam to restoration in Christ: "Corruption of the gifts of creation is treated more fully in II.1–5 as a preface to redemption, the subject that occupies the remainder of the *Institutes*."[137] Human reason "is gravely wounded by sin, and . . . the will has been very much enslaved by evil desires."[138] Therefore it does not know "who the true God is or what sort of God he wishes to be toward us."[139] Humanity's epistemic condition is corrupted by sin; no one can by contemplating the universe

133. McGrath, *Life of John Calvin*, 154.

134. *Inst.* 1.2.1.

135. *Inst.* 2.6.1.

136. *Inst.* 1.15.4.

137. Partee, *Theology*, 85.

138. *Inst.* 2.2.4.

139. *Inst.* 2.2.18.

deduce that God is a gracious Father. Rather, conscience presses us within and exposes our systemic defilement, the just cause of God's curse upon his children. Perversion of our senses and ingratitude of heart follow, for our minds, having been blinded by sin, do not perceive what is true. "For it is true, that this world is like a theater, in which the Lord shows to us a striking spectacle of His glory. However such a sight lies open before our eyes, we are quite blind, not because the revelation is obscure, but because we are 'alienated in mind' (*mente alienati*, Col. I.21), meaning that not only the will but also the power for this activity fails us."[140] Sparks of divine glory are smothered through "the fault of dullness." Even when surrounded by multitude of "burning lamps" in creation that radiate the glory of the Creator, we lack the natural ability to arrive at the pure and clear knowledge of God. Nature's eyes fail to grasp displays of God's glory unless faith is added.

> Although they [burning lamps] bathe us wholly in their radiance, yet they can of themselves in no way lead us into the right path. . . . For this reason, the apostle, in that very passage where he calls the worlds the images of things invisible, adds that through faith we understand that they have been fashioned by God's word [Heb. 11:3]. He means by this that the invisible divinity is made manifest in such spectacles, but that we have not the eyes to see this unless they be illumined by the inner revelation of God through faith.[141]

The integrity of this epistemic condition is lost through Adam's fall unless restored by faith in Christ. Commenting on 1 Corinthians 1, Calvin says, "This magnificent theater of heaven and earth, crammed with innumerable miracles, Paul calls 'the wisdom of God.' Contemplating it, we ought in wisdom to have known God. But because we have profited so little by it, he calls us to the faith of Christ, which, because it appears foolish, the unbelievers despise."[142] "This," Zachman comments, "is the rhythm of Calvin's thought, that he passes from the knowledge of God the Creator to the knowledge of the Redeemer, and uses this text in the *Institutes* as his transitional text, 1 Corinthians 1."[143] Thus Paul proclaims the necessity of preaching the cross as a remedy for the fall: "Since in the wisdom of God the world did not know God through wisdom, it pleased

140. *Comm. 1 Cor* 1:21, *CNTC* 9:40.

141. *Inst.* 1.5.14.

142. *Inst.* 2.6.1.

143. Zachman, *Reconsidering John Calvin*, 7.

God through the folly of preaching to save those who believe" (1 Cor 1:21). Faith in Christ effects our return to God our Author and Maker from whom sin has estranged us. Our epistemic perception of God's glory is restored whereby we recognize God as the Almighty Creator; through faith in the knowledge of God our Redeemer, we see clearly and truly God's glory displayed in creatures. "For notwithstanding that God shows Himself openly, yet it is only by the eye of faith that we can look at Him."[144]

God's works in creation point to Jesus Christ, that image in which God presents to our sight. Calvin uses these metaphors drawn from the natural world—"heart" and "hands and feet"—to highlight faith in Christ as the lens through which the book of nature is read rightly. The *heart* refers to "that secret love with which he embraces us" (cross), and his *hands* and *feet* refer to "[his works] displayed before our eyes" (creation).[145] The procedure is from faith in Christ to his works in creation; in Lane's assessment, "If we know the *heart* of the risen Lord through the witness of the Holy Spirit in Scripture, we know his *hands and feet*."[146] So faith in Christ, says Calvin, "does not prevent us from applying our senses to the consideration of heaven and earth, that we may thence seek confirmation in the true knowledge of God."[147]

In the theatrical drama of divine agency, God's creative act is followed by Christ's redemptive act. The created order on account of sin's bondage requires redemption.

> For in the cross of Christ, as in a splendid theater, the incomparable goodness of God is set before the whole world. The glory of God shines, indeed, in all creatures on high and below, but never more brightly than in the cross, in which there was a wonderful change of things (*admirabilis rerum conversio*)—the condemnation of all men was manifested, sin blotted, salvation restored to men; in short, the whole world was renewed and all things restored to order.[148]

In his commentary on Romans 8:19–23, Calvin deduces that "the creatures, which are subject to corruption, cannot be renewed until the

144. *Comm. 1 Cor* 1:21, *CNTC* 9:40.

145. *Comm. Gen, Argument*, CTS 1:64.

146. Lane, *Ravished by Beauty*, 29, italics original.

147. *Comm. Gen, Argument*, CTS 1:64.

148. *Comm. John* 13:31, *CNTC* 5:68.

sons of God are wholly renewed." The renewal of nature follows the renewal of *human* nature. Every part of creation is subject to ecological ruin by the noetic effects of sin and is eagerly longing for liberation. "There is no element and no part of the world which, touched with the knowledge of its present misery, is not intent on the hope of resurrection." The whole creation "groans," which means "the creatures are not content with their present condition [of corruption], and yet they are not so distressed as to pine away irremediably. They are . . . in labor" but "sustained by [the] hope" of being reconstituted to a better state awaiting them. All creatures (including "irrational creatures" such as the sun, the moon, stars, and planets) are "bound by great anxiety and held in suspense by a great longing, [and] look for that day which will openly exhibit the glory of the sons of God."[149] The earth and its creatures are included in Christ's eventual restoration of the world. Hence, Calvin writes, "the brute animals, and even inanimate creatures—even trees and stones—conscious of the emptiness of their present existence, long for the final day of resurrection, to be released from emptiness with the children of God."[150] God "promises under the reign of Christ the complete restoration of a sound and well-constituted nature."[151] The restoration of order initiated by Christ awaits its perfection at the last judgment.

> Christ, by his death, has already restored all things as far as the power to achieve this and the cause of it are concerned; but the effect of it is still not fully visible because this restoration is still in the process of completion and so, too, our redemption, insofar as we still groan under the burden of servitude. Therefore, if, at the present time, we see much confusion in the world, let that faith encourage us and revive us, the faith that Christ shall one day come and restore all things to their former condition [*in integrum*].[152]

Christ's redemption reestablishes the relational image of God lost in Adam's fall. Calvin writes, "For how is the whole man entire, except when his thoughts are pure and holy, his affections all honorable and well-ordered, and when his body also devotes its energies and services to good works along? . . . For man is pure and whole if he thinks nothing

149. *Comm. Rom.* 8:19–20, *CNTC* 8:172.73; CO 49:151-52; *Comm. Rom.* 8:22, CTS 19:306; *Comm. Ps.* 96:11, CTS 6:58.

150. *Inst.* 3.9.5.

151. *Comm. Gen.* 3:14, CTS 1:167.

152. *Comm. Acts* 3:21, CO 48:72–73.

with the mind, desires nothing with the heart, nor does anything with the body except that which is approved by God."[153] In the restored condition, where we stand in a right relationship with God, the mind participates in a renewed contemplation of nature, the will can conform to God's law, and hearts may refer their gifts back to God, and find happiness in God. Schreiner writes, "With the soul's restoration, nature once again serves God's original purpose: to manifest the divine majesty to the human creation in praise of their common Creator."[154] On Psalm 96:11, "Let the earth rejoice and let the earth be glad," Calvin teaches that the heavens and earth cannot "experience the slightest measure of true joy, as long as we have not seen the face of God." In the restored order, nature's revelatory function returns to its original condition so that it participates in the people's joy, the blessedness that stems from faith.

> The Psalmist calls upon the irrational things themselves, the trees, the earth, the seas, and the heavens, to join in the general joy. Nor are we to understand that by the heavens he means the angels, and by the earth men; for he calls even upon the dumb fishes of the deep to shout for joy. The language must therefore be hyperbolical, designed to express the desirableness and the blessedness of being brought unto the faith of God. . . . As all the elements in the creation groan and travail together with us, according to Paul's declaration (Rom 8:22), they may reasonably rejoice in the restoration of all things to their earnest desire.[155]

Praise as the peculiar nature of creatures is borne out in Calvin's commentary on Isaiah 43:20, "The beasts of the field shall honor me," where he asserts, "The meaning is, that the power of God will be so visible and manifest [when God does a 'new thing'], that the very beasts, impressed with the feeling of it, shall acknowledge and worship God. . . . [And] they will stand still, as if in astonishment, when they see the miracles."[156]

All creatures benefit from Christ's gradual restoration now in part but then in full, when the restoration reaches its perfection. Just as Christ's restoration of the created order is progressive, so too is the joyous

153. *Comm. 1 Thess* 5:23, CO 52:179.

154. Schreiner, *Theater*, 113.

155. *Comm. Ps.* 96:11, CTS 6:58.

156. *Comm. Isa* 43:20, CTS 8:343–44, as quoted in Taylor, *Theater*, 44, parentheses original.

participation in the benefits that come from it. Susan E. Schreiner sums up the matter well:

> As the human soul is gradually restored to (and even surpasses) the original order characteristic of the image of God, so too the believer returns to that originally intended activity: namely, the contemplating of God's revelation written in the book of nature and revealed in the visible splendor of the world. As the perpetual breakdown caused by sin is healed by the Spirit and Scriptures, nature regains its revelatory function as a mirror, a painting, and a theater of the divine glory.[157]

The redeemed people reap from Christ's redemption the restoration of the epistemic condition that enables them to see God's revelation in the book of nature and perceive God's glory displayed in the universe. The benefit of Christ's redemption applies also to the restoration of the affective condition. The misuse of created things through the fall is set against their proper use through Christ's redemption. The depraved affections must be healed by Christ's redemption, so that the house or garden will be heartily enjoyed, and God's gifts properly used, without people basing their identity in them.

For Calvin, we are to read backward from the second article of faith (Son as the redeemer) to shed light on the first article (Father as the Creator). In the logical order of *being*, creation precedes redemption; in the temporal order of *knowing*, redemption is prior to creation. Without the second article of faith, the book of nature will not be rightly read. "The relation of the knowledge of God the Creator to the knowledge of God the Redeemer," Edward Dowey writes, "remains a dialectical one or . . . a double presupposition. Each presupposes the other, but in a different way."

> (1) The redemptive knowledge must be seen to have come from God, the Creator of heaven and earth, the same God to whom Scripture points in the natural order and the moral law, whom Scripture describes as the Triune Creator and Sustainer of the world. This is a logical or conceptual presupposition. . . . We know the Creator only in the gratuitous promise of mercy in Christ—which is the other presupposition: (2) The knowledge of God the Creator comes only to those illuminated by the Spirit in faith, although the knowledge of faith, properly speaking, is not God as seen in his general creative activity, but as seen in

157. Schreiner, *Theater*, 121.

> the special work in redemption in Christ. Thus, the knowledge of the Redeemer is an epistemological presupposition of the knowledge of the Creator.[158]

To sum up, piety is rooted in Scripture, "the spectacles" through which the knowledge of God the Creator is confirmed; it is enhanced by the eyes of faith that "discern the sparks of his glory as it were shining out in every individual creature."[159] Believers also have "faith in Christ," which establishes the knowledge of God the Creator from the knowledge of God the Redeemer. Not until we are grasped by God the Redeemer do we grasp with certainty and clarity God the Creator. The self-revelation of God in Jesus Christ does not eclipse the self-disclosure of God in creation; it confirms it. The knowledge of God the Creator necessarily leads to the knowledge of God the Redeemer, and vice versa.

## SCRIPTURE AND TRADITION: GOD AS A FITTING WITNESS

Calvin's elaborated efforts at showing the self-authenticating nature of Scripture was inevitably spirited by the state of controversy with Rome, which held that only the church can assure us that Scripture is God's word. In which case, Calvin argues, Rome set the church above Scripture. This immediate context was the impetus for Calvin's preoccupation in Book 1 of the *Institutes* with establishing the credibility of the doctrine of Holy Scripture.[160] Contrary to Rome, Calvin avers that Scripture is logically prior to the church. The church does not confer authority to the Scripture; rather she recognizes the authority that is inherent in it. Calvin does not deny that the church witnesses to Scripture, and that we indeed receive the canonical writings from the Catholic Church. Concerning the question of authority, Calvin raises two questions: How can we be certain of the divine authorship of Scripture, and how can we know which books are in the canon? The answer to the former question remains the inner witness of the Spirit. Concerning the latter, Calvin does not suggest that individual believers look for the inner witness of the Spirit. Such an approach to the canon was too subjective and was alien to Calvin. Sebastian Castellio, for example, was refused admission into the pastorate because

158. Dowey, *Knowledge of God*, 238–39.

159. *Comm. Heb.* 11:3, *CNTC* 19:184.

160. *Inst.* 1.7.4.

he denied the canonicity of the Song of Solomon.[161] It was the Spirit, not private judgment, who opened the eyes of the church over the ages to determine the limits of the canon. Calvin could side with Luther who said, "The Scripture is the womb from which are born the divine truth and the church."[162] The church does not make Scripture God's word, any more than the apostles made Jesus the Son of God. The Bible is above the church; it also constitutes her, not vice versa.

To expand the relation between Scripture and church, Calvin introduces a statement of Augustine: "For my part, I should not believe the gospel, except as moved by the authority of the catholic church."[163] This statement aroused much debate in the Reformation period. It is, for Calvin, a description of the ungodly; those who have yet to be inwardly moved by the Spirit of God "are rendered teachable by reverence for the church, so that they may persevere in learning faith in Christ from the gospel."[164] This does not mean that the faith of the godly rests on the authority of the church; nor does it imply that the certainty of the gospel is derived from it. Rather, Augustine argues that "there would be no certainty of the gospel for unbelievers to win them to Christ if the consensus of the church did not impel them."[165] The majesty of God makes it necessary that the church plays an instrumental or ministerial role of preparing the ungodly for a consideration of faith in the gospel. To relegate Scripture's authority to human judgment as foundational is to deprive God of his majesty. Scripture's authority, for Augustine, rests upon "a far different foundation" than human judgment.[166] Calvin writes, "Therefore, Scripture will ultimately suffice for a saving knowledge of God only when its certainty is founded upon the inward persuasion of the Holy Spirit."[167] What Calvin opposes is not the witness of the church, but the claim that the certainty regarding Scripture is predicated upon the consent of the church, and thus Scripture bears only so much weight

161. Van 't Spijker, *Calvin*, 80.

162. See Luther's *Lectures on the Psalms*, WA 3:454, as quoted in *Inst.* 1.7.2, 76n4.

163. Augustine, *Contra epistolam Manichaei quam vovant fundamenti* v (MPL 42. 176; tr. NPNF 4. 131), as quoted in *Inst.* 1.7.3, 76n6; cf. Luther's *That the Doctrines of Men Are to Be Rejected* (1522), WA 10:2.89. Luther here anticipates Calvin's understanding of Augustine's statement.

164. *Inst.* 1.7.3.

165. *Inst.* 1.7.3.

166. *Inst.* 1.7.3.

167. *Inst.* 1.8.13.

as is granted by the church. Rational, apologetic arguments aid not in fortifying the credibility of Scripture, which is a domain of the Holy Spirit, but in vindicating the truth of Scripture against the wiles of its slanderers. Prophecies in the Old Testament, miracles, the consent of the church, and human testimonies might buttress already-existing faith, but they do not bring faith into existence. They are secondary aids to our weakness; they follow the inward testimony of the Holy Spirit, "that chief and highest testimony."[168]

The conviction that Scripture is God's word flows from the self-authenticating character of Scripture.[169] Hilary writes, "For He whom we can know only through his own utterances is a fitting witness concerning himself."[170] With Hilary, Calvin asserts, "For God alone is a fit witness of himself in his Word."[171] In other words: "Scripture exhibits fully as clear evidence of its own truth as white and black things do of their color, or sweet and bitter things do of their taste."[172] The recognition of color or taste for oneself is immediate and beyond analysis; it is, to borrow Helm's phrase, "a one-step procedure not involving inference, or only involving it in a minimal fashion." Likewise, the epistemic perception of Scripture's authority is "a direct, one-step endorsement" by the inner testimony of the Spirit.[173] The category of Scripture is not human endorsement or reasoning but witness or testimony. How does the Spirit witness? Not by a leap of faith into the vacuum but by providing an appropriate epistemic condition in which we are inwardly persuaded of Scripture as divinely commanded.[174] By nature, we do not look at Scripture with a pure eye and sense.[175] We need the Holy Spirit to open our blind eyes to see; to use Calvin's analogy, we need spectacles in order to achieve an accurate perception of the beauty of a landscape. These glasses do not constitute Scripture as God's word, nor do they prove it to be such; they merely enable us to recognize it. With conviction, Calvin writes, "Yes, if we turn pure eyes and upright senses toward it, the majesty of God will

168. *Inst.* 1.8.13.

169. *Inst.* 1.7.5.

170. Hilary of Poitiers, *On the Trinity* 1.18 (MPL 10. 38; tr. NPNF 2 ser. 9. 45), as cited in *Inst.* 1.7.4., 79n15.

171. *Inst.* 1.7.4.

172. *Inst.*1.7.2.

173. Helm, *Ideas*, 147–48.

174. *Inst.* 1.7.3.

175. *Inst.* 1.7.4.

immediately come to view, subdue our bold rejection, and compel us to obey."[176]

The dignity and majesty of Scripture is a predicate of divine revelation, not human judgment. No human reasoning or proof can provide a firm faith, Calvin avows, "until our heavenly Father, revealing his majesty, lifts reverence for Scripture beyond the realm of controversy."[177] Elsewhere, Calvin states, "For even if it wins reverence for itself by its own majesty, it seriously affects us only when it is sealed upon our hearts through the Holy Spirit."[178] In Piper's assessment, "There is the key for Calvin: the witness of God to Scripture is the immediate, unassailable, life-giving revelation to our minds of the majesty of God that is manifest in the Scriptures themselves. The majesty of God is the ground of our confidence in his Word."[179] Divine majesty appears in a creaturely form, as in Abraham's vision in Genesis 15:2. Calvin writes, "Not that God appeared as he really is, but only so far as he might be comprehended by the human mind."[180] On this verse, Rebekah Earnshaw comments, "Divine majesty guarantees that it is genuinely God who is met in his Word. Therefore, that Word can be fully trusted because its authentic authority is grounded in God himself. Divine majesty ratifies the truth of the divine Word so it can be trusted."[181] Readers are seized by the majesty of God himself, whose illuminating power flows into them, causing them to consciously and willingly reverence and obey him.

> Therefore, illumined by his power, we believe neither by our own nor anyone else's judgment that Scripture is from God; but above human judgment we affirm with utter certainty (just as if we were gazing upon the majesty of God himself) that it has flowed to us from the very mouth of God by the ministry of men. . . . We feel that the undoubted power of his divine majesty lives and breathes there. By this power we are drawn and inflamed, knowingly and willingly, to obey him, yet also more vitally and more effectively than by mere human willing or knowing.[182]

176. *Inst.* 1.7.4.

177. *Inst.* 1.8.13.

178. *Inst.* 1.7.5.

179. Piper, *Calvin*, 26–27.

180. *Comm. Gen.* 15:2, CTS 1:400.

181. Earnshaw, "Usefulness," 197.

182. *Inst.* 1.7.5.

"The highest proof of Scripture" is intrinsically linked to the assertion that the majesty of God "lives and breathes there"; Calvin stresses, "God in person speaks in it"[183] so that the word finds acceptance in human hearts, without any human agency. The word should receive the same reverence as God himself because it originates solely from God, without human influence. Calvin does not set the words of God against the person of God, as they are one. Nor does he collapse the two into one. The majesty of God and the word of God mutually co-inhere; Piper sums up aptly: "The Word mediated the majesty, and the majesty vindicated the Word."[184] The message God delivers is objectively clear and true; it is not vague nor ambiguous, because the Holy Spirit illuminates our minds and creates faith in what was spoken through the prophets and apostles, whom God constituted as servants of the living word. They "do not boast either of their keenness or of anything that obtains credit for them as they speak; nor do they dwell upon rational proofs. Rather, they bring forward God's holy name, that by it the whole world may be brought into obedience to him."[185] Thereafter, their testimony to God becomes the context whereby we are apprehended by the word of the living God. Just as the patriarchs in the era of the law and prophets apprehended God in his word, the self-utterances of God, so now we apprehend God in his written word. Not just a privileged few, but every believer, past and present, can experience within herself a heartfelt conviction of Scripture as God's truth, a "feeling" that arises from heavenly disclosure.[186] For when God speaks, it is God himself who speaks; it is not just a message abstracted from God's person. We do not bypass the person of God while searching Scripture. The majesty of God inheres in Scripture, and thus it is so glorious and wonderful that no amount of our theological edifice and articulation could do justice to it. Acquisition of information from theological study, which may leave our hearts unaffected, is categorically different from a living encounter with God, by whose voice our hearts are effectively inflamed to obey God. And the latter requires the Holy Spirit, by whose testimony we are drawn into the affective knowledge of God. The truth that illuminates our minds cognitively now reaches the hearts affectively. "Then, in spite of yourself, so deeply will [Scripture] affect you, so penetrate your heart, so fix itself in your very marrow,

183. *Inst.* 1.7.4.

184. Piper, *Calvin*, 27.

185. *Inst.* 1.7.4.

186. *Inst.* 1.7.5.

that compared with its deep impression, such rigor as the orators and philosophers have will nearly vanish."[187] Ultimately, it is God himself, not humans, who must testify to his own word, its origin and its authority. Scripture is written in a "rude and undefined style," but its contents are divinely conceived, convincing us of its truth by the Spirit.[188] Of the biblical writers, Calvin notes that "the truth cries out openly that these men who, previously contemptible among common folk, suddenly began to discourse so gloriously of the heavenly mysteries must have been instructed by the Holy Spirit."[189]

Scripture's authority requires no human reason or keenness to prove it. It is not contra reason but concurs with the "best reason," causing the mind to repose in it more confidently than in any other way.[190] Rationalistic proofs do not inflame our hearts as does the Holy Spirit. Spirit-actuated certainty is "far more excellent"[191] than human reasons, judgments, or opinions. Those who attempt to establish their faith in Scripture through rational disputation, for Calvin, "are doing things backwards," robbing God of his majesty and glory.[192] With Augustine, Calvin warns, any attempt to "prove to unbelievers that Scripture is the Word of God [is] acting foolishly, for only by faith can this be known."[193]

## BEDROCK: WORD AND SPIRIT IN UNITY

Word and Spirit in unity is the bedrock of Calvin's doctrine of Scripture. Calvin quotes Isaiah 59:21: "My Spirit which is in you, and the words that I have put in your mouth, and the mouths of your offspring, shall never fail." This is Calvin's interpretation: "Under the reign of Christ the new church will have this true and complete happiness: to be ruled no less by the voice [word] of God than by the Spirit."[194] Word and Spirit always imply each other. They are distinguished but not separated from each other. The word is the instrument by which the Lord works in believers the

187. *Inst.* 1.8.2.

188. *Inst.* 1.8.2.

189. *Inst.* 1.8.11.

190. *Inst.* 1.7.5.

191. *Inst.* 1.7.4.

192. *Inst.* 1.7.4.

193. *Inst.* 1.8.13. See 92n15, which cites Augustine, *The Usefulness of Belief*, 18.36 (MPL 42. 92; tr. LCC 6. 322).

194. *Inst.* 1.9.1.

illumination of his Spirit. It is by the same Spirit who dwelled and spoke in the apostles through whose writings we are continually ushered into his presence.[195] The Holy Spirit is given not to impart new doctrine but to instill in our minds the doctrine that we have received. In Calvin's own words, "Therefore the Spirit, promised to us, has not the task of inventing new and unheard-of revelations, or of forging a new doctrine, to lead us away from the received doctrine of the gospel, but of sealing our minds with that very doctrine which is commended by the gospel."[196]

Without the word, religious experience breeds fanaticism or frenzy. The Anabaptists, who try to reach God directly, despising Scripture, are carried away with "frenzy."[197] Does the Holy Spirit bring new revelations today? This age-old question plagued Calvin in his time as it plagues us in ours. Calvin was at odd with the radicals of the Reformation who subordinated Scripture to fresh experience, elevating the Spirit above the word. The Anabaptists tore apart the inviolable bond between word and the Spirit. Experience is real and is part of the Christian life in Christ, which Paul did not deny. Paul's ecstatic experience of being "caught up in the third heaven" (2 Cor 12:2), though vivid and valid, does not reign above Scripture; nor does it render superfluous the doctrine of the Law and the Prophets. Not experience but "Christ and him crucified" (1 Cor 2:2) is the content of the gospel. Whoever desires a richer experience of the Holy Spirit must apply himself "both to read and to hearken to Scripture."[198] Calvin thus warns that those who are zealous about the Spirit-filled life might unconsciously fall under the grip of the spirit of Satan, "the angel of light" (2 Cor 11:14). To avoid such danger, he advises us to "recognize the Holy Spirit in his own image, namely, in his Word."[199] When the Holy Spirit shines in his word, he causes us to behold God's face—namely, Jesus Christ. We then in turn may endorse the work of the Spirit without fear of being deceived. Spirit and word work together in unity, disclosing the face of God in Jesus Christ. The one Spirit who authors Scripture binds us to Christ, the "express"[200] content of both Old and New Testaments. It is the Holy Spirit's office to enlighten us with no

195. *Inst.* 1.9.3.
196. *Inst.* 1.9.1.
197. *Inst.* 1.9.1.
198. *Inst.* 1.9.2.
199. *Inst.* 1.9.2–3.
200. *Inst.* 1.6.1.

other glory than the glory of the cross. When that glory shines in our hearts, we are led to embrace the Holy Spirit wholeheartedly.

In keeping with his pastoral instinct, Calvin allows experience a legitimate place in his theology. The affective language of faith—"feeling," "feel," "taste," "hear," "enjoy," "embrace," "inflame," "sweetness," "contemplate," and "glory in" God—appears frequently in Calvin's writings.[201] But the linkage of the word to the creation of human experience is essential to proper piety. "Indeed, with experience as our teacher we find God just as he declares himself in his Word."[202] We cannot hear God apart from Scripture; in Scripture, we hear God in person speaking, clearly and without ambiguity. For God cannot violate himself by revealing in his image (word) a God contradicting the one whom we experience. Our experience of God, if it were truly Spirit-induced, finds confirmation in the word, or else God is not trustworthy. No contradiction between Scripture and the work of the Spirit occurs in post-apostolic times; and for that reason, Calvin frequently speaks of Scripture as the image of the Holy Spirit.[203] He affirms,

> For by a kind of mutual bond the Lord has joined together the certainty of his Word and of his Spirit so that the perfect region of the Word may abide in our minds when the Spirit, who causes us to contemplate God's face, shines; and that we in turn may embrace the Spirit with no fear of being deceived when we recognize him in his own image, namely, in the Word.[204]

Without the Spirit, it breeds rigid rationalism or dead orthodoxy. "The letter, therefore, is dead . . . and, leaving the heart untouched, sounds in the ears alone."[205] Scripture itself is spiritually inert, but when charged with the Holy Spirit, it moves our hearts. The Holy Spirit inheres in the truth expressed in Scripture and emits his efficacious power so that "reverence and dignity are given to the Word."[206] The apostle thus calls his preaching "the ministration of the Spirit" (2 Cor 3:8). Through the Spirit, the letter highlights Christ.[207] Without the Spirit, preaching to the

201. *Inst.* 1.5.9; 1.7.4–5; 1.8.2; 1.9.3; 1.14.22; 1.16.1; 1.17.1.

202. *Inst.* 1.11.2.

203. Lopes and da Conceicao, "Calvin, Theologian of the Holy Spirit," 46.

204. *Inst.* 1:9:3.

205. *Inst.* 1.9.3.

206. *Inst.* 1.9.3.

207. *Inst.* 1.9.3.

ungodly has no effect; it is like the brightness of the sun shining on the blind, who cannot see the divine reality of God in Scripture.[208] Calvin asserts, "Now, all of us are blind by nature. . . . Accordingly it [the word of God] cannot penetrate our minds unless the Spirit, as the inner teacher, through his illumination makes entry for it."[209] The word the Lord sent forth is not temporary, to be abolished at the descent of the Spirit; rather he poured forth the same Spirit by whose power he had delivered the word, which he makes effective to complete his work in us.[210] The Spirit enables the human mind to gain a deeper understanding of the Bible's truth: "For the soul, illumined by him, takes on a new keenness, as it were, to contemplate the heavenly mysteries, whose splendor had previously blinded it. And man's understanding, thus beamed by the light of the Holy Spirit, then at last truly begins to taste those things which belong to the Kingdom of God, having formerly been quite foolish and dull in tasting them."[211] True piety does not relinquish the word, nor does it renounce the Spirit, for both are one, working together in the production of true piety. Anthony Lane summarizes Calvin's position on the unity of the word and the Spirit for godly living:

> "The Spirit without the word: dangerous; the word without the Spirit: deadly; the word with the Spirit: dynamite." Or again, more succinctly, "too much word—dry up; too much Spirit—blow up; word and Spirit: grow up."[212]

## THE OUTWORKING OF PROVIDENTIAL CARE: OMNIPOTENCE AND GOD'S WILL

The knowledge of God the Creator, for Calvin, is incomplete unless it includes the scriptural witness to God's providential care for the universe. Alister McGrath writes, "Calvin's discussion of God the creator [in the 1559 *Institutes*] ends with an exposition of the notion of divine providence. . . . It seems that Calvin wishes to affirm that God's providence is an extension of his creation."[213] In general, philosophers and human minds

208. *Inst.* 3.2.34.

209. *Inst.* 3.2.34.

210. *Inst.* 1.9.3.

211. *Inst.* 3.2.34.

212. Lane, "Witness," 6.

213. McGrath, *Life of John Calvin*, 156.

attribute the created universe to God's secret inspiration.[214] However, Christians must go beyond the general conception of God to perceive God's special and fatherly care.[215] Whenever we call God the Creator of the universe, we must at the same time acknowledge God as our Father, whose children we are, and who has received us into "the great sweetness of his beneficence."[216] Terry J. Wright rightly points out that, for Calvin, "creation has a fundamentally anthropological orientation: 'God himself has shown by the order of Creation that he created all things for man's sake.'"[217] God's providential care of human creatures occurs "before we were born"—that is, "before he fashioned man, he prepared everything he foresaw would be useful and salutary for him."[218] However, this does not mean Calvin shows no concern for the non-human creation. For God is not a distant onlooker, idly observing from heaven what occurs on earth, but rather an ever-present deity, actively involved in the dispensation and governance of all events. Calvin enumerates three aspects under which providence may be understood. First, God's providence covers future as well as past events; second, it works either through or without an intermediary, or even contrary to every intermediary; finally, it has as its end God's ultimate concern for the whole human race, but especially his vigilance in watching the church more closely.[219]

The word "omnipotence," Calvin avers, is "not the empty, idle, and almost unconscious sort" of the Sophists, "but a watchful, effective, active sort, engaged in ceaseless activity."[220] The majesty of God is enacted in his ceaseless activity toward his created world, holding every piece together without confusion. By way of the metaphor of a "machine," Calvin writes, "The whole machinery of the world would fall out of gear [*diffluerct tota mundi machina*: the whole frame would collapse] at almost every moment and all its parts fail in the sorrowful confusion which followed the fall of Adam, were they not borne up from elsewhere by some hidden support."[221] Unlike the Epicureans' deity, who is idle and indolent, the

214. *Inst.* 1.16.1.

215. *Inst.* 1.16.1; Niesel, *Theology*, 63.

216. *Inst.* 1.14.22.

217. Wright, *Providence*, 29, citing *Inst.* 1.14.22.

218. *Inst.* 1.14.22.

219. *Inst.* 1.17.6. I shall discuss God's special care for the church when dealing with Book 4 of the *Institutes*.

220. *Inst.* 1.16.3.

221. *Comm. Rom.* 8:20, CO 49:152–53, *CNTC* 8:173.

Christian God is never deistically aloof and uninvolved. He is the Lord of all, regulating all things so that nothing occurs by chance and without his deliberation (cf. Ps 115:3). "Providence means not that by which God idly observes from heaven what takes place on earth, but that by which, as keeper of the keys, he governs all events. Thus it pertains no less to his hands than to his eyes."[222] God's providence extends to all and is not narrowly confined to the realm of nature. "Indeed, those as much defraud God of his glory as themselves of a most profitable doctrine who confine God's providence to such narrow limits as though he allowed all things by a free course to be borne along according to a universal law of nature."[223] God's ceaseless activity rules and governs all things; this he carries out by his might and wisdom, in accordance with what he has decreed from eternity. God governs the created order, and the plans and intentions of humans, teleologically, straight to their proper end.[224] All actions, good or evil, are decreed by God, and ultimately serve God's will, "the highest and first cause of all things because nothing happens except from his command or permission."[225] Believers cling to "God's singular providence," knowing that God does not suffer anything to perish but works its good and salvation.[226] Through "pious and holy meditation on providence," Calvin avows, they "receive the best and sweetest fruit": solace.[227] The Christian is persuaded to "ever look to God as the principal cause of things, yet will give attention to the secondary causes in their proper place."[228] Secondary causes are "instruments in [God's] hand," through which God acts in a manner that does not destroy creaturely action but is appropriate to it.[229]

Sinners, if left without any light but their own, cannot understand how God's providence works. Carnal reason attributes all occurrences—prosperous or perverse—to fortune;[230] it can perceive only the effects of chance or natural forces. With realism, Calvin contends, "God's providence does not always meet us in its naked form, but God in a sense

222. *Inst.* 1.16.4.

223. *Inst.* 1.16.3.

224. *Inst.* 1.16.8.

225. *Inst.* 1.16.8.

226. *Inst.* 1.17.6.

227. *Inst.* 1.17.6.

228. *Inst.* 1.17.6.

229. Calvin, *Libertines*, 243.

230. *Inst.* 1.16.2.

clothes it with the means employed."[231] Providence appears disguised, and we do not always recognize God's fatherly care in the turbulences and trials of life. Calvin shuns speculative incursion into the hidden God with respect to God's governance. The atrocious adversity that visits us does not disclose its own meaning, and the full significance of the event as it occurs can never be grasped on earth until we enter the heavenly glory. Here Calvin speaks of a hidden will, which is not a reference to two wills in God.[232] Instead it indicates that the outworking of his will is compared to a "deep abyss" (Ps 36:6). Even when the true causes of events or the significance of horrific occurrences are hidden from us, faith believes that God's providence works greatest benefit for us. Despite its hiddenness, believers can lay hold of divine providence, for they, unlike the Athenians (Acts 17:28), can experience "that earnest feeling of grace" and "taste God's special care by which alone his fatherly favor is known."[233] We should not flee from God but to God, hiding in God's fatherly goodness and his beneficent will, which is an expression of his providence.[234] The world has no access to such intimacy with God, nor does it confer such benefit, for the experiential aspect of faith (feeling and tasting) is given to the faithful, assuring them that God has not abandoned them, even when God's providence does not appear distinct. Though the disturbances in the world defy rational justification, we trust that God's power works alongside with his justice and his wisdom, tempering and directing all things to their appointed end.[235] Zachman writes, "For Calvin, the thought of God's power alone is terrifying, but when seen in the service of God's justice, it is alluringly beautiful."[236] Faith clings to God, who showers upon us his bountiful goods so that we might in turn look to him for all good; or else the present experience of God's absence will leave us bewildered and without hope. Suffering was not something alien to Calvin, and the pilgrims in Geneva also bore innumerable evils. Calvin describes, "We need not go beyond ourselves, since our body is the receptacle of a thousand diseases—in fact holds within itself and fosters the causes of diseases—a man cannot go about unburdened by many forms of his own destruction, and without drawing out of a life enveloped, as it

231. *Inst.* 1.17.4.

232. *Inst.* 1.17.2, 212–13n4.

233. *Inst.* 1.16.1.

234. *Inst.* 1.10.1.

235. *Inst.* 1.17.1.

236. Zachman, *Image and Word*, 94.

were, with death."[237] Yet a heart that is grasped by certainty about God's providence is filled with a "joyous trust toward God."[238]

Calvin's pastoral sensitivity shines when he asserts that God always has "the best reason for his plan."[239] Calvin counsels that if life caves in, it is because God wants to instruct his own people in patience; if frustrations surround us, it is because God wants to correct the wicked affections and tame the lust within us; if the present life is filled with hardship, it is because God wants to arouse us from sluggishness and crucify vices within us. However, if the present life is filled with ease and comfort, it is because God aims to reward faithfulness. "The quiet and composed minds" cling to divine providence, "that determinative principle of all things, from which flows nothing but right,"[240] even when the final outcome of his plan is hidden from them. Apart from it, we cannot reduce the force of "these uncontrolled and superstitious fears,"[241] which repeatedly hassle our minds when facing dangers. Our fears are real; they are untamed unless God allays them. "In short," says Calvin, "there is nothing that God does not temper in the best way."[242]

## THE PRINCIPLE OF CONCURRENCE: DIVINE AND HUMAN AGENCY

Every creature is a secondary cause through which God accomplishes the judgments he has determined with himself. God operates by the principle of concurrence: God acts through secondary causes, says Calvin, "to serve His goodness, righteousness, and judgment according to His present will to help His servants, to punish the wicked, and to test the patience of His faithful or to chastise them in His fatherly kindness."[243] Nothing occurs by fortune or chance, but everything by God's "special ordinance by which He governs all things." Calvin elaborates on the purposive usage of God's secondary causation:

237. *Inst.* 1.17.10.
238. *Inst.* 1.17.11.
239. *Inst.* 1.17.1.
240. *Inst.* 1.17.1–2.
241. *Inst.* 1.16.3.
242. *Inst.* 1.5.8.
243. Calvin, *Libertines*, 243–44.

> Therefore, let us adopt this resolution: that prosperity and adversity alike, rain, wind, sleet, hail, good weather, abundance, famine, war, and peace are all works of God's hand; and that creatures who constitute secondary causes are only means by which He fulfils His will; and consequently He commands and uses them as it pleases Him in order to bring them to that end which He has ordained should come to pass.[244]

Calvin illustrates this principle of concurrence by means of the stories of Joseph and Job. Joseph recognized his brothers' treachery as the Lord's work; he forgot the injustice, and inclined to show gentleness, comforting them with this: "It is not you who sold me into Egypt, but I was sent before you by God's will, that I might save your life" (Gen 45:5, 7–8). "Indeed you intended evil against me, but the Lord turned it into good" (Gen 50:20). God does not need evil to work good. God does not will evil, though he wills the acts of the wicked. Apart from God's willing and power, Joseph's brothers could not even do evil; nor could Satan have the power to act until he receives God's command (Job 1:5; 2:1).[245] As Augustine writes, "For through the bad wills of evil men God fulfills what he righteously wills."[246] Calvin further expands,

> By their defection the apostate angels and all the wicked, from their point of view, had done what God did not will, but from the point of view of God's omnipotence they could in no way have done this, because while they act against God's will, his will is done upon them. Whence he exclaims: "Great are God's works, sought out in all his wills" [Ps. 111:2; cf. Ps. 110:2, Vg.]; so that in a wonderful and ineffable manner nothing is done without God's will, not even that which is against his will. For it would not be done if he did not permit it; yet he does not unwillingly permit it, but willingly; nor would he, being good, allow evil to be done, unless being also almighty he could make good even out of evil.[247]

244. Calvin, *Libertines*, 244–45.

245. *Inst.* 1.18.1.

246. Augustine, *Enchiridion* 26. 100f., as cited in *Inst.* 1.18.3.

247. *Inst.* 1.18.3. See also Augustine, *Psalms*, Ps 111.2 (Latin, Ps 110.2), as cited in *Inst.* 1:18.3, 235n7. The paragraph quoted here is unclear in where the quotation begins. English translations have only a closing quotation (after "make good even out of evil") without an opening quotation. So I insert an opening quotation beginning with "By their defection . . ."

Omnipotence is understood not as the power to achieve anything but God's power to achieve his purpose. God's almighty power is teleologically conceived as "a watchful, effective, active sort," ceaselessly active in directing all things to the appointed end. God is most renowned or majestic when his purpose remains sturdy and established, despite apparent contradictions. God's action and human action coincide in such a manner that the Lord's purpose is not thwarted, and human choices, which are truly their own, are not exempted from judgment. The distinction between the two parties does not collapse, so that the Lord and his plan remain righteous, and humans, whose evil deeds serve God's purpose, remain wicked. "And in this way we serve his just ordinance by doing evil, for so great and boundless is his wisdom that he knows right well how to use evil instruments to do good."[248]

Commenting on Job 1:17, Calvin attributes the same work to God, to Satan, and to humans as authors, without either excusing Satan or the wicked of their evil deed, or making God the origin of evil. All three parties are involved in the same event to produce a certain outcome, although without sharing the same purpose. Job's life is an example of such principle.[249] First, the Lord's end is to exercise Job's patience in suffering; second, Satan aims to cause Job to despair; third, the Chaldeans endeavor to acquire profit from another by illegal means. Considering the manner of acting, the Lord permits Satan to assault Job and subjugates the Chaldeans to Satan's affliction, having constituted them as his instruments for Job's assault. Satan provoked the wicked minds of the Chaldeans to implement that evil deed. Each deed bears its own purpose. Calvin expands, "The distinction in purpose and manner causes God's righteousness to shine forth blameless there, while the wickedness of Satan and of man betrays itself by its own disgrace."[250] God's justice is not at stake, even when he fulfills his purpose through the deeds of the godless. The wicked remain wholly inexcusable, for their deeds emerge out of their evil covetousness. They are bent toward evil, not because God has created it in them, but because they themselves are by nature wicked and thus utterly intent on rebellion against God.[251] Though God makes use of the deeds of the wicked for his purpose, he is free from every stain or defilement. God's character is holy, and he never does evil himself. He accomplishes

248. *Inst.* 1.17.5.

249. *Inst.* 2.4.2. See Wendel, *Calvin*, 182–83.

250. *Inst.* 2.4.2.

251. *Inst.* 1.14.17.

his righteous purpose through the wicked intention of people, which he constitutes as a means to a good end. The diabolic intervention as a means of his providence might cast doubt on God's goodness, but not so for the pious, as they find abundant comfort in the knowledge that the powers of evil do not have free rein but "are completely restrained by God's hand as by a bridle."[252]

Calvin is indebted to Augustine,[253] according to whom the wicked are condemned on account of their own evil intention. In Judas's betrayal, it is improper to ascribe the guilt of the crime to God, who willed the death of his Son, and to transfer the credit for salvation to Judas, whom God used as his tool to fulfill his appointed end. Here paradox inheres in the mystery of the cross of Christ, that same event in which God surrendered his own Son, and Judas betrayed his Lord; the cause of their acting is not identical. Judas's betrayal is included in God's design as an instrument to fulfill his saving purpose. In this way, God's righteousness is exalted. Yet, evil that he was, Judas was not exonerated from culpability. "In the same act," Calvin notes, "as man's evil deed shows itself, so God's justice shines forth."[254] God acts through secondary causes, but in such a way that "does not prevent each creature . . . from having and retaining its own quality and nature and from following its own inclination."[255]

Knowing that God's providence works blessings is no cause for passivity. As proof, Calvin cites Proverb 19:9, "Man's heart plans his way, but the Lord will direct his steps."[256] Providence does not relieve us of our responsibility, for we are not hindered by God's eternal decrees. God has set the limits to our life and has at the same time provided means and helps to preserve it. It would be folly not to seek counsel from people, whom God uses as means in the fulfillment of his intended goal. We must attend to what our duty is, so that if the Lord has offered helps to protect life, our duty is to use them to preserve life. By neglecting God's ordained means and suspension of human judgment, we may bring ills upon ourselves, but not in a way that conditions or supersedes God's will. Gratitude fills the Christian heart that has felt God's beneficence through the ministry of people and inanimate creatures.[257]

252. *Inst.* 1.17.11.

253. *Inst.* 1.18.4, 237n8, citing Augustine, *Letters* 93 .2 (MPL 33. 324).

254. *Inst.* 1.18.4.

255. Calvin, *Libertines*, 243.

256. *Inst.* 1.16.6.

257. This reflects the third part of the Heidelberg Catechism, which prescribes God's mercy as an antidote to misery, culminating in thanks as a response.

The aforementioned biblical instances and discussions are clear scriptural proofs of God's providential care, especially of fatherly goodness, even when human reason fails to grasp them. Calvin closes the section on providence with an exhortation: "For our wisdom ought to be nothing else than to embrace with humble teachableness, and at least without finding fault, whatever is taught in Sacred Scripture."[258]

## CONCLUSION

Foundationally, Calvin's piety is drawn from Scripture, the "spectacles" through which we come to know God and his dealing with creation. His piety rests on word and Spirit, bound inseparably together as "a kind of mutual bond," by which we are preserved from slipping into the extremes of cold rationalism and erratic frenzy. The Spirit's witness to his own word constitutes an essential aspect of the entire life of faith. Scripture possesses its own authority, which is not to be borrowed from extraneous factors such as rational apologetic or human judgments. The significance of Scripture lies not so much in an impartation of some information about God as it does in an encounter with the God himself. In this regard, the Bible, theology, and Christian experience interpenetrate, and are of one piece, strengthening each other.

Creation is the realm of God's activities upon which we are to contemplate, not speculate, so as to draw benefits from God's fatherly goodness displayed therein. Alluring images of God as the awesome Creator and a benevolent Father, through which God gently attracts us to contemplate him and enjoy all his riches, permeate Calvin's creational piety. Creation itself is good but is subject to vanity through misuse. The corruption of the created order through Adam's fall is restored through Christ's redemption. Faith lays hold of God who "promises under the reign of Christ the complete restoration of a sound and well-constituted nature."[259] The aim of this restoration is so that all of creation, humans and other creatures, might return to a blissful communion with the life of the Trinity. Calvin does not deny the natural knowledge of God in creation; but, due to the fall, the image of God is so corrupted that we cannot know God naturally unless aided by the Holy Spirit.[260] The knowledge of

258. *Inst.* 1.18.4.

259. *Comm. Gen.* 3:14, CTS 1:67.

260. Parker, *Knowledge*, 53.

creation flows from the knowledge of redemption. When our epistemic condition is restored to its original state, our eyes are opened to see clearly God's splendorous glory in creation; thus, nature's revelatory power is returned to its proper function of reflecting the awesome beauty of God in creation. Faith in Christ leads us to the knowledge of God the Creator, from whom we reap bountiful benefits through a proper contemplation of the powers or works of God in the natural order. Creation is where God acts and dwells, and where we enjoy the riches of God's provision. Zachman notes, "More importantly, by our feeling and enjoyment of the powers of God—which we behold in the theater of the world—we are invited, allured, and attracted to seek the God who is the source of all these powers, in whom alone is found human happiness and blessedness."[261]

Forgoing speculation on the theodicy question, "If God, why evil?," it suffices us to know from Scripture that nothing flows from God except his boundless might with which he creates and sustains the universe, his infinite wisdom with which he regulates the created order, his perfect righteousness with which he rules us, and his everlasting mercy with which he provides for us and covers us.[262] While "ignorance of providence" is the root of "all miseries," knowledge of it is the basis of "the highest blessedness."[263] Faith, not reason, grasps with certainty that nothing can handcuff God's purpose, even when the means by which God implements his providence and the meaning of a given occurrence are hidden from us. Life is miserable when we are consumed with excessive worry about the many dangers we face, and so we are to trust God and find solace in the "singular proofs," despite appearances to the contrary, of God's fatherly care for his own.[264]

261. Zachman, "Universe," 303.

262. *Inst.* 1.2.1.

263. *Inst.* 1.17.11.

264. *Inst.* 1.17.6.

# 2

# Union with Christ and the Holy Spirit

## *Efficacy and Participation*

THE CATEGORY OF MEDIATOR occupies the center of Calvin's Christology.[1] With Chalcedon, Calvin accentuates the unity of two natures in Christ. With Paul, Calvin urges us to attend to two distinct powers of the Son of God:

> First, in so far as he is God's eternal Word, he is the "first-born of all creation" [Col. 1:15]. . . . Secondly in so far as he was made man, he was the "first-born from the dead" [Col. 1:18]. The apostle in one short passage sets forth two things to be considered: (1) "through the Son all things have been created," that he may rule over the angels [Col. 1:16 p]; (2) he was made man that he might begin to be our Redeemer [cf. Col. 1:14].[2]

Calvin's emphasis is not on how God and man are one in Christ, although they are, but on the economic actions of God in Christ for us. The significance of the person of Christ lies not in who he is in essence but in the redemptive acts he came to accomplish for the hopeless human race. Thus Calvin asserts, "For it would be of little advantage to know who Christ is, if this second point were not added, what he wishes to be toward us, and for what purpose the Father sent him."[3] In Book 1 of the *Institutes*, Calvin instructs his readers not to dwell on knowing that God is

1. Wendel, *Calvin*, 208–31.
2. *Inst.* 2.12.7.
3. *Comm. John* 9:37, CTS 1.389, CO 47:232, as cited in Edmondson, *Christology*, 87.

or what God is, but to know how God is for us so that we look to God for all good.[4] Likewise, in Book 2 of the *Institutes*, Calvin counsels that our faith must not be fixed on Christ's essence, simply knowing him as God's Son, but that we must attend to his power and office as our Mediator. Hence Calvin begins his section on Christology proper in the *Institutes* with an affirmation of Christ's identity as the God-man, bringing him into the foreground as the Mediator who atones for sin by submitting the weakness of his human nature to death, and who, through combating death by the power of his divine nature, gains victory for us. To despoil Christ of either his divinity or his humanity is, for Calvin, "to diminish his majesty and glory, or obscure his goodness."[5] On the one hand, Calvin is at odds with Osiander, who argues that Christ was mediator between God and humanity only according to his divinity, not his humanity; on the other hand, Calvin opposes Francesco Stancaro, who contends that Christ's mediation between God and humanity occurs only through his humanity, not his divinity. To refute both views, Calvin contends that Christ's dual nature is essential to the role he, the God-man, plays as the Mediator between God and humanity.[6] Richard Muller augments: "The function of mediation becomes determinative, and the person of Christ must be considered in and through his office."[7] The indivisible person of Christ, who bears the properties of both natures, effects for us reconciliation with God. In Calvin's words,

> In short, since neither as God alone could he feel death, nor as man alone could he overcome it, he coupled human nature with divine that to atone for sin he might submit the weakness of the one to death; and that, wrestling with death by the power of the other nature, he might win victory for us.[8]

"As important as Christ's prophetic and royal ministry are for his service to us," Michael Horton intimates, "Calvin believes that Scripture places the spotlight especially on his priestly ministry." He quotes Calvin: "Let us therefore bear in mind that the entire gospel consists mainly in the death and resurrection of Christ."[9] The import of Christ's mediato-

4. *Inst.* 1.2.1.
5. *Inst.* 2.12.3.
6. Tylenda, "Christ the Mediator," 161–72.
7. Muller, *Christ and the Decree*, 28.
8. *Inst.* 2.12.3.
9. Horton, *Christian Life*, 85; cf. *Comm. 1 Cor* 15:14, CTS 20:19.

rial office is that Christ "has nothing that is not to be put to our benefit, because He was given to us by the Father [so that] everything that is His should be ours."[10] Christ's vicarious obedience to the Father acquires for us the benefits; our faith acquires the benefits Christ has obtained for us. Hence, Calvin affirms, "We enjoy Christ only as we embrace Christ clad in his own promises."[11] All that Christ has acquired for us—justification and sanctification, which Calvin calls "double grace"—is of no use to us unless the Spirit makes it real in us through faith.[12] Believers enter the adoption in which what is Christ's by nature—his natural Sonship—is imparted to us by grace, making us the children of God, equally loved as is the Son by the Father.

Christology and pneumatology are one. Both Christ and the Spirit are mediators: Christ mediates between the Father and us by effecting restoration to his favor through his death, and the Spirit mediates between Christ and us by applying to us the power of Christ's victory over all enemies of life. In the economy of salvation, Christ himself must first be grasped before his properties. The person of Christ and his benefits are one, and they become ours through the receptive character of faith which the Spirit works in us. The Spirit makes us sharers in the efficacy of Christ's mediation whereby all contradiction, antithesis, and discord between opposites—righteousness and unrighteousness, mercy and wrath—are resolved for those who believe. The noetic contradiction between God loving us and hating us is resolved through union with the Son effected by the Spirit through the instrument of faith. Calvin's trinitarian dynamic of grace assumes both directions: descent and ascent. The gracious descent to us from the Father through the Son in the Spirit is the abiding presupposition to the Spirit's effective ascent to God through the Son to the Father.

## UNION WITH CHRIST: JUSTIFICATION AND SANCTIFICATION

Christ first must make himself ours and dwell within us as "our head" (Eph 4:15); second, by faith we are "engrafted into him," and as his

10. *Comm. Heb.* 7:25, *CNTC* 12:101, as cited in Clark, "Principal Point," 141.

11. *Inst.* 2.9.3.

12. See Billings, "John Calvin's Soteriology," 428.

members receive what Christ has acquired (Rom 11:7).[13] As McGrath writes, "Thus Calvin speaks of the believer's being 'grafted into Christ', so that the concept of incorporation becomes central to his understanding of justification."[14] The two consequences of the believer's incorporation into Christ are what Calvin calls "a double grace"—the twin benefits of union with Christ—"namely, that being reconciled to God through Christ's blamelessness, we may have in heaven instead of a Judge a gracious Father; and secondly, that sanctified by Christ's Spirit we may cultivate blamelessness and purity of life."[15]

Justification and sanctification are distinguished but not separated. Calvin teaches this by way of analogy. "The sun, by its heat, quickens and fructifies the earth, by its beams brightens and illumines it. Here is a mutual and indivisible connection. Yet reason forbids us to transfer the peculiar qualities of the one to the other."[16] For Calvin, Billings notes, "there is no temporal gap between the [two] gifts."[17] Justification and sanctification are one subject, though Calvin deals with them in separate sections. Justification by free imputation of righteousness or faith alone does not exclude actual holiness of life; they are one in Christ. In Partee's formulation,

> justification and sanctification are one in divine origin and one in human experience, but two for the purpose of analysis. Since justification is accomplished once-for-all by the work of Jesus Christ, and sanctification is being accomplished day-by-day through the work of the Holy Spirit, the doctrines are single in confession but dual in explanation. . . . This distinction is a matter of strong emphasis but not of exclusive definition.[18]

Engrafted in Christ, we grasp his righteousness while at the same time grasp his holiness. This is summed up in Calvin's exposition of 1 Corinthians 1:30: "Therefore Christ justifies no one whom he does not at the same time sanctify. These benefits are joined together by an everlasting and indissoluble bond, so that those whom he illumines by his wisdom, he redeems; those whom he redeems, he justifies; those whom

13. *Inst.* 3.1.1.

14. McGrath, *Iustitia Dei*, 222.

15. *Inst.* 3.11.1.

16. *Inst.* 3.11.6.

17. Billings, "John Calvin's Soteriology," 428.

18. Partee, *Theology*, 211.

he justifies, he sanctifies."[19] To separate sanctification from justification is to tear asunder the unity of the one Christ. As Stephen Chester writes, "Since Christ is a living person, his saving benefits cannot be detached from his person and can only be received in union with him. For the same reason, these saving benefits cannot be separated from each other. They are received together in him or not at all."[20] The soteriological priority of union with Christ, for Calvin, evinces this order: from person to property, that Christ the person must first be grasped, followed by his properties (such as righteousness and holiness). Such a rationale is opposite to "later popular Protestant concepts of imputation where forensic justification is the gateway to union with Christ."[21] We receive the whole Christ, not part of him, so any separation of the two interconnected soteriological elements is inconceivable for a life of union with Christ. Both justification and sanctification are conceived christologically, under the rubric of union with Christ, so that the discussion of which is prior is meaningless, and any conception of justification as existing apart from sanctification is denied. They together constitute, McGrath notes,

> the chief *beneficia Christi*, bestowed simultaneously and inseparably upon believers as a consequence of their *insitio in Christum*. Sanctification is not the effect of justification; both justification and sanctification are effects of union with Christ. Notice also how sanctification is now conceived Christologically, in terms of "becoming what we are"—that is to say, actualising our new status in Christ in our lives through the process of being conformed to Christ.[22]

Through "mystical union" with Christ, he is made ours and we are made his, resembling the connection between body and head. "Christ, having been made ours, makes us sharers with him in the gifts with which he has been endowed."[23] His benefits—redemption, righteousness, sanctification, and eternal life—would be useless to us unless Christ first makes himself ours.[24] By engrafting us into his body, Christ makes us participants in himself and all that he achieves for us. His righteousness absolves our sin, his salvation cancels our condemnation, his worthiness

19. *Inst*. 3.16.1.

20. Chester, *Reading Paul*, 282.

21. Chester, *Reading Paul*, 282.

22. McGrath, *Iustitia Dei*, 224.

23. *Inst*. 4.11.10.

24. *Inst*. 4.17.11.

covers our unworthiness. In so far as Christ remains outside us, and we are estranged from him, all that he has acquired for us remains outside us and does not benefit us. In this connection, we are not to contemplate ourselves, which is sure despair and damnation; we contemplate Christ, not "standing afar off" but rather "dwelling in us,"[25] which is sure joy and salvation. Christ is so united to us that his person and all his benefits are ours by faith; hence we must not sever Christ from ourselves or vice versa.[26] "Rather," Calvin stresses, "we ought to hold fast bravely with both arms to that fellowship by which he has bound himself to us."[27]

Justification occurs outside us, in Christ. That Christ must become ours entails this: The spotless righteousness of Christ becomes ours by faith. "Our righteousness is not in us but in Christ," which we possess "because we are partakers of Christ."[28] Thomas Schreiner writes, "Our justification is perfect from the beginning. Believers don't become more justified as they progress in holiness, for justification does not denote inner renewal, but the declaration from God that one is acquitted and not guilty before him."[29] Justification involves a change in God's judgment toward us, that we appear before the face of God not as a sinner but as a righteous person; as Calvin writes, "Therefore, we explain justification simply as the acceptance with which God receives us into his favor as righteous men." And it comprises "the remission of sins and the imputation of Christ's righteousness."[30] Because our iniquities are covered by Christ's sinlessness, so our deeds are righteous and are regarded holy on account of Christ's purity.[31] The fruit of sanctification follows justifying faith, just as heat follows the sun. "The importance of this point," McGrath notes, "is perhaps best seen from one of Calvin's responses to Jacopo Sadoleto, who considered evangelical approaches to justification to be incoherent, lacking any place for human moral agency." He quotes Calvin:

> While we deny that good works have any role in justification, we recognise their proper place in the lives of the righteous. For someone who is justified possesses Christ . . . who as the Apostle teaches, (1 Corinthians 1:30), has been given to us for

25. *Inst.* 3.2.24.
26. *Inst.* 3.2.24.
27. *Inst.* 3.2.24.
28. *Inst.* 3.11.23.
29. Schreiner, *Faith Alone*, 59.
30. *Inst.* 3.11.2.
31. *Inst.* 3.11.23.

> our justification and for sanctification. And where there is this righteousness of faith, which we maintain to be freely given, Christ is there as well. And wherever Christ is, there also is the Spirit of holiness, who gives new life to the soul.[32]

Justification is solely by faith alone, yet that justifying faith is not without works. Commenting on Galatians 5:6, Calvin avers,

> It is not our doctrine that the faith which justifies is alone. We maintain that it is always joined with good works. But we contend that faith avails by itself for justification. The Papists . . . tear faith to pieces, sometimes making it *informis* [unformed] and empty of love, and sometimes *formata* [formed]. But we deny that true faith can be separated from the Spirit of regeneration. When we debate justification, however, we exclude all works.[33]

The same sentiment appears in his *Institutes* (1559), where Calvin stresses, "We are justified not without works, but not through works, since in our sharing in Christ, which justifies us, sanctification is just as much included as righteousness."[34]

In his *Institutes*, Calvin employs several words to describe union with Christ: "engrafting," "communion," "fellowship," "participation," and "adoption."[35] All of these images are relational, not substantive. For Osiander, the union of believers with Christ is a mingling of Christ's essence with ours, from which he deduces that "we are substantially righteous in God by the infusion of both of his essence and of his quality."[36] Christ's essence is so mixed with ours, and so transfused into us, that he makes us part of his being. Justification occurs "when we are made partakers in God's righteousness when God is united to us in essence."[37] For Calvin, justification occurs solely by Christ's imputed righteousness outside us, not by any righteousness inherent in us; it is extrinsic, not intrinsic. Canlis argues that Osiander's ontology is "introspective," focusing on the human being as a substance, and analyzing how an individual subject was essentially righteous; on the contrary, Calvin's ontology is "extrospective,"

32. Calvin, *Reply to Sadoleto*, 43; OS 1:470, as cited in McGrath, *Iustitia Dei*, 223.
33. *Comm. Gal.* 5:6, *CNTC* 11:96.
34. *Inst.* 3.16.1.
35. Tamburello, *Union with Christ*, 90.
36. *Inst.* 3.11.5.
37. *Inst.* 3.11.5.

outside ourselves but in Christ.[38] The true identity of the human person is not derived from a rational exploration of our human nature but from the revelation of God in Christ, in whom the perfect image of God consists. Thus human identity, says Thomas Torrance, "has no independent status."[39] Calvin combines forensic and familial terms to describe union with Christ. He teaches that as soon as we are engrafted into Christ through the receptivity of faith, we become "a son of God, an heir of heaven, a partaker in righteousness, a possessor of life; . . . you obtain not the opportunity to gain merit but all the merits of Christ, for they are communicated to you."[40] The union of believers with Christ by the Spirit, for Calvin, is not one of substance but one of status and relationship in which the Son's uniqueness as God's child by nature and our uniqueness as God's children by adoption is maintained. Calvin's "rejection of Osiander's view," Partee discerns, "precludes a simple ontological identification between the believer and the redeemer."[41] Osiander and Calvin share a different participative motif: infusion versus fellowship.[42] Calvin rejects the infusionist language of substance in favor of the language of participation in the Spirit, the bond of unity between the two "unlikes"—that is, God and humans.[43] As Calvin asserts, "For we hold ourselves to be united with Christ by the secret power of his Spirit."[44] The Spirit, the agent of union, deigns to join us with Christ, not by the physical mingling of substance, but by "the fellowship of righteousness with him" through the grace of the Mediator.[45] "Not only does he cleave to us by an indivisible bond of fellowship, but with a wonderful communion, day by day, he grows more and more into one body with us, until he becomes completely one with us."[46] The union Calvin has in view is not an ontological

38. Canlis, *Calvin's Ladder*, 146.

39. Torrance, *Doctrine of Man*, 13.

40. *Inst.* 3.15.6.

41. Partee, "Central Dogma," 198. He further notes, "The union with Christ for Calvin is not mystical (in the sense of imitation) nor substantial (in an ontological sense) but real (in a genuine but unspecified and unspecifiable sense)."

42. See Canlis, *Calvin's Ladder*, 143. She contrasts two kinds of participation: "participation-as-infusion" and "participation-as-*koinonia*." The former she calls "Platonic participation," the latter "Trinitarian participation."

43. *Inst.* 3.11.5. Canlis coins the word "unlikes" to speak of dissimilar essences; see *Calvin's Ladder*, 142.

44. *Inst.* 3.11.5.

45. *Inst.* 3.11.10.

46. *Inst.* 3.2.24.

union but a "spiritual bond,"[47] which has "the sense of being effected and maintained by the Holy Spirit."[48] Osiander repudiates the "spiritual bond," thereby forcing "a gross mingling of Christ with believers."[49] Osiander's mode of participation has oneness of essence as its aim; Calvin's mode of participation aims at an intimate relationship in a differentiated union of both parties.[50] Canlis argues that Osiander's flaw lies in thinking that the Spirit cannot effect the union of two "unlikes" or dissimilar essences.[51] In the same vein, Chester writes, "The believer and Christ are one, but this does not mean sameness. Instead, their unity is the 'bringing together of two 'unlikes' in a relationship of mutual dwelling.'"[52] Righteousness that flows from union with Christ is a gift, not a natural possession. For Calvin, Willem van Vlasuin notes, "we do not merely believe in Christ or are saved by Christ, but that Christ forms a spiritual union with us through the Holy Spirit."[53] Therefore, the Spirit-produced bond does not obliterate created humanity but rather restores it.[54] Nor does the bond replace our humanity; rather it renews it.[55] There is no diminution of our humanity; rather it is sanctified.

## THE SOLE PRIESTHOOD OF CHRIST: THE VICARIOUS HUMANITY OF CHRIST

As Stephen Edmondson writes, "The human predicament of broken relationship with God and the divine intention to heal this brokenness" form the condition of possibility for the descent of God in human flesh.[56] Incarnation occurs not by absolute necessity, or by factors outside of God's own character and will.[57] The motive of the incarnation is God's

47. *Inst.* 3.11.10.

48. Gaffin, "Justification and Union," 262.

49. *Inst.* 3.11.10.

50. See Canlis, *Calvin's Ladder*, 13, where she states, "These relationships are qualitatively different from Platonic schemes of 'participation' in that they are characterized by intimacy and differentiation, not consubstantiality."

51. Canlis, *Calvin's Ladder*, 142.

52. Chester, *Reading Paul*, 289. See also Canlis, *Calvin's Ladder*, 142.

53. Van Vlastuin, "Kuyper's Spirituality," 530.

54. Billings, "John Calvin's Soteriology," 436.

55. Canlis, "Human Identity," 19.

56. Edmondson, *Christology*, 202.

57. *Inst.* 2.12.1.

loving and free determination to fulfill his saving purpose for humanity. This free and unmerited act of love begins in eternity but is manifested in history as a remedy to the plight of human sin. Calvin says, "In short, from the time when he took on the form of a servant, he began to pay the price of liberation in order to redeem us."[58] While Osiander claimed that the incarnation would have occurred even without sin, Calvin insists that the sole reason for the incarnation was to appease the wrath of God by accepting the chastisement that brings us peace.[59]

Justification is "the main hinge on which religion turns."[60] Christ is "the material cause" and "the Author and Minister of this great benefit"—righteousness.[61] How have we been justified? Calvin writes, "For even though God alone is the source of righteousness, and we are righteous only by participation in him, yet, because we have been estranged from his righteousness by unhappy disagreement, we must have recourse to this lower remedy that Christ may justify us by the power of his death and resurrection."[62] Before defection, the image of God we bear includes "true piety, righteousness, purity, and intelligence";[63] but it is lost subsequently in Adam's fall. The structure of the image of God survives the fall but not its integrity. Calvin avers, "Nothing remains after the ruin except what is confused, mutilated, and disease-ridden."[64] The knowledge of our fallenness from God's image, "the perfect excellency of the human nature,"[65] is set against the knowledge of Christ as the cure for it. The truth of who we are, the image of God in the pristine state, "can be nowhere better recognized than" through its opposite—that is, "from the restoration of his corrupted nature" in Christ.

> Therefore, even though we grant that God's image was not totally annihilated and destroyed by him, yet it was so corrupted that whatever remains is frightful deformity. Consequently, the beginning of our recovery of salvation is in that restoration which

58. *Inst.* 2.16.5.
59. *Inst.* 2.12.4.
60. *Inst.* 3.11.1.
61. *Inst.* 3.11.7.
62. *Inst.* 3.11.8.
63. *Inst.* 1.15.4.
64. *Inst.* 1.15.4.
65. *Inst.* 1.15.4.

> we obtain through Christ, who is called the Second Adam for the reason that he restores us to true and complete integrity.[66]

Because the work of righteousness lies beyond human nature, Osiander argues, it could only be accomplished by Christ's divinity. Calvin concurs with him, saying that unless Christ is true God, he could not achieve the atonement for us. For the power of the flesh is too weak to restore the righteousness that was lost through the fall; it cannot bring about a transposition from death to life. Osiander argues that Paul in 1 Corinthians 1:30 and Colossians 2:3 attributes the power of justifying to the eternal Word alone, not to Christ's human nature. He further quotes Jeremiah 23:6, "Jehovah will be our righteousness," to show that justification occurs by Christ's divinity, whereby he imparts to us "essential righteousness."[67] Calvin contradicts his claim by referring the same texts to Christ's humanity, whereby he imputes to us righteousness he acquired via his vicarious obedience and sacrificial death. Timothy Wengert points out that Osiander confuses the origin of righteousness (namely, God—thus Christ's divinity) with the mode of our reception of his righteousness (namely, through the efficacious activities of Christ's humanity). Calvin draws a distinction between the inherent righteousness of Christ's being, which he is in himself, and the acquired righteousness of the cross, which he achieved for us. For him, Christ is our righteousness according to two natures "in his divinity (origin) and through his redemption (mode)."[68] To conceive of Christ as Osiander did, Calvin contends, leads us away from Christ's priesthood and his mediatorial office, the means of acquisition of righteousness, to his "eternal divinity," the origin of righteousness.[69] Osiander's interpretation is "grossly deluded,"[70] Calvin argues, for he undermines the means by which righteousness comes to believers—namely, through Christ's self-humiliation on the cross. Paul's statement recorded in Acts 20:28, that "with his blood God purchased the church for himself," cannot refer to Christ's divinity. If it does, Calvin rebuts, "Who could bear such a foul error?"[71] The Father assigns to the Son the office of expiation: "That he adds the reason—that he is righteous;

66. *Inst.* 1.15.4.

67. *Inst.* 3.11.5, 729n5; *Inst.* 3.11.8.

68. See Wengert, "Philip Melanchthon," 85.

69. *Inst.* 3.11.8 (Beveridge's translation).

70. *Inst.* 3.11.9.

71. *Inst.* 3.11.8.

and that he has lodged the mode and means" in Christ's mediatorial office.[72] "What [Christ] had from the Father he revealed to us, and so what Paul says is referred not to the essence of the Son of God but to our use, and rightly fits human nature."[73] Christ is righteous, as he is of one being with the Father and the Spirit in a differentiated unity. The person of Christ who is true God and the obedient work he came to do in his incarnate life correspond to each other. Calvin says, "We do not divide Christ but confess that he, who reconciles us to the Father in his flesh, is the eternal Word of God, and that the duties of the Mediator could not otherwise have been discharged by him, or righteousness acquired for us, had he not been eternal God."[74] Christ is my righteousness through his incarnation (mode); thus Paul included Christ's human obedience in this righteousness (Rom 5:19). Based on 2 Corinthians 5:21, "Him who knew no sin he made to be sin that we might be the righteousness of God in him," Calvin deduces that "Paul has established the source of righteousness in the flesh of Christ alone."[75]

Osiander's insistence on "essential righteousness," Canlis argues, stems from his failure to appreciate Christ's vicarious obedience as a means of acquiring righteousness.[76] For Calvin, the righteousness that is lost in Adam's disobedience is regained by Christ's obedience. Sin estranges us from God, but righteousness procured by the incarnate Son is credited to us and reconciles us to God. Christ was "made righteous" (1 Cor 1:30) for us not according to his divinity but his humanity. He justifies us when he assumed a servile form and obeyed the Father (Phil 2:7–8), hereby fulfilling the office of justification enjoined on him by the Father. Calvin charges that Osiander mistakenly confuses Christ's two natures with the Trinity, thereby rendering Christ's mediatorial office superfluous. He sees internal inconsistencies in Osiander's system of thought, that

> since Christ is God and man, he is made righteousness for us with respect to his divine nature, not his human nature. Yet if this properly applies to divinity, it will not be peculiar to Christ but common with the Father and the Spirit, inasmuch as the righteousness of one differs not from the righteousness of the

72. *Inst.* 3.11.8.

73. *Inst.* 3.11.12.

74. *Inst.* 3.11.8.

75. *Inst.* 3.11.9.

76. Canlis, *Calvin's Ladder*, 143.

> other. Then, because he was by nature from eternity, it would not be consistent to say that he was "made for us." But even though we should grant that God was righteousness for us, how will this harmonize with what Paul interposes: that Christ was made righteousness by God (1 Cor. 1:30)? This is surely peculiar to the person of the Mediator, which, even though it contains in it the divine nature, still has its own proper designation by which the Mediator is distinguished from the Father and the Spirit.[77]

Christ's priestly function encompasses the "whole course of his obedience."[78] His twofold satisfaction comprises his active obedience through which he fulfilled the law (Phil 2:8), and his death by which he bore the punishment that should have been ours (Gal 3:13). Calvin quotes several passages,[79] such as Romans 3:24–25—"being justified . . . by his grace through the redemption that is in Christ . . ., whom God put forward as a propitiation through faith which is in his blood." To Calvin, Peter's testimony agrees with Paul's: "You were ransomed . . . not with . . . silver and gold, but with the precious blood . . . of a lamb without blemish" (1 Pet 1:18–19). Christ is the "One mediator . . . who gave himself as a ransom" (1 Tim 2:5–6), achieving for us "the forgiveness of sins" (Col 1:14). In Calvin's words, "We are justified or acquitted before God, because that blood corresponds to satisfaction for sin."[80] We plead the merit of the cross where the Son of God in our place really enters the realm of condemnation and offers himself up as "the price of our righteousness." Todd Billings sums up Calvin's insistence on Christ's human nature in which believers participate as essential to justification; they are

> not simply united to a divine nature that is righteous because it is divine or even united to a second Adam who lived a righteous life and hypothetically could have died a natural death. Rather the righteousness of Jesus Christ is the righteousness of the cross—the mystery of the cross connected to the "wonderful exchange" language which is so closely related to imputation—in which the sin of sinners is imputed upon Christ, and the righteousness of Christ is imputed to sinners.[81]

77. *Inst.* 3.11.8.
78. *Inst.* 2.16.5.
79. *Inst.* 2.17.2–5.
80. *Inst.* 2.17.5.
81. Billings, "Double Grace," 61.

The lowliness of the cross wipes out our guilt and his wrath in exchange for his righteousness and mercy. As Colossians 2:14 teaches, "In the cross he canceled the written bond which stood against us."[82] We are received into grace through Christ's act of propitiation by which we escape the wrath of God, and through imputation by which we are reckoned righteous before God.

Faith's very content is none other than Christ and what he has received for us from the Father. It lays hold of Christ so that everything he is (person) and does (work) in his vicarious humanity is ours. As Marcus Johnson notes, "Faith is efficacious for salvation not because it believes in Christ, but because it embraces Christ, who dwells in us through that faith."[83] While Luther compares faith to "a wedding ring"[84] that unites us to Christ and possesses him and all that he has, Calvin compares faith to an empty "vessel" or "pot"[85] through which Christ's righteousness comes to us. Faith, even though it is worthless of itself, can justify us because of Christ. An earthen vessel becomes a treasure, not because of itself but because the precious jewel is hidden in it; likewise, a pot, unworthy in itself, filled with money makes a person rich. Christ (person) must be received in faith before his righteousness (property) is reckoned unto us. Johnson adds, "Faith benefits us only because of *whom* it takes hold of."[86] Faith grasps Christ who first grasps us. Calvin makes use of the language of causality to underscore the connection between the faith *of* Christ and faith *in* Christ: God's mercy is the "efficient" cause of justification, Christ is its "material" cause, and faith is its "instrumental" cause.[87] With regard to the question, "Is salvation through faith?," Calvin's answer is yes, providing that "the Lord Jesus Christ is the object of faith and belief."[88] Then he further clarifies faith as a receiving agent: "Faith is therefore said to justify, because it is the instrument by which we receive Christ, in whom righteousness is communicated."[89] Faith truly receives him as one given to us by the Father. Contrasting faith with works, Calvin writes, "Faith looks at nothing but the mercy of God and Christ dead and risen. All merit

82. *Inst.* 2.17.5.

83. Johnson, "Luther and Calvin," 66.

84. LW 31:352.

85. *Inst.* 3.11.7.

86. Johnson, "Luther and Calvin," 66.

87. *Comm. Gal.* 3:6, *CNTC* 11:50; *Comm. Rom.* 3:22, *CTNC* 8:73; *Inst.* 3.11.7.

88. *SG*, 180.

89. *Comm. Rom.* 3:22, *CNTC* 8:73; *SG*, 342.

of works is therefore excluded from being the cause of the justification when the whole is ascribed to faith."[90] All that opposes life is resolved for those who by faith reap the effects of Christ's mediatorial work: sin blotted out; righteousness bestowed; divine wrath vanished; divine mercy imparted; enmity with God banished; reconciliation with him conferred; divine judgment abolished; divine favor assured.

## CONTRADICTION RESOLVED: GOD'S LOVE AND GOD'S HATRED

Calvin's understanding of atonement must reckon with an apparent contradiction between two assertions: that God "loved us from before the foundation of the world" (Eph 1:4) and hated us simultaneously until he was made favorable to us in Christ (Rom 5:10). We are both enemies and friends of God until Christ dies to appease God's wrath and win God's favor for us. Not until Christ satisfies the justice of God and placates the wrath of God could God love sinners whom God would otherwise justly hate. God's love is eternal, and is prior to our reconciliation in Christ. What God has revealed himself to be corresponds to who he is—namely, love. "Christ is such a shining and remarkable proof of the divine love toward us that, whenever we look to Him, He clearly confirms to us the doctrine that God is love."[91] The love with which Christ loves sinners is identical to the love that the Father shows them. He manifests his benevolence toward sinners, whom he regards as the very objects of his wrath—this he does by banishing sin, the cause of God's hatred, that there might be no impediment to his love. While sin stirs up God's wrath against us, Christ's love, which is identical to God's fatherly love, dissipates God's wrath against us. Christ's expiatory suffering love of the cross banishes the obstacles to God's love for us.[92] The paradox consists in this: The love of God moves God himself to abolish the hatred of God in sinners. God showers his blessings on those whom he also hates, constituting a people no longer under his curse. Calvin's atonement theology has its root in Augustine, who maintains that "God love[s] us even when he hated us."[93] Quoting Augustine at length,

90. *Comm. Gal.* 3:6, *CNTC* 11:50.

91. *Comm. 1 John* 4:9, *CNTC* 5:290.

92. *Inst.* 2.17.2.

93. See Augustine, *John's Gospel* 110.6 (MPL 35. 1923 f.; tr. NPNF 7.411), as cited in *Inst.* 2.16.4, 507n7.

> God's love . . . is incomprehensive and unchangeable. For it was not after we were reconciled to him through the blood of his Son that he began to love us. Rather, he has loved us before the world was created, that we also might be his sons along with his only-begotten Son—before we became anything at all. The fact that we were reconciled through Christ's death must not be understood as if his Son reconciled us to him that he might now begin to love those whom he had hated. Rather, we have already been reconciled to him who loves us, with whom we were enemies on account of sin. The apostle will testify whether I am speaking the truth: "God shows his love for us in that while we were yet sinners Christ died for us" [Rom. 5:8]. Therefore, he loved us even when we practiced enmity toward him and committed wickedness. Thus in a marvelous and divine way he loved us even when he hated us. For he hated us for what we were that he had not made; yet because our wickedness had not entirely consumed his handiwork, he knew how, at the same time, to hate in each one of us what we had made, and to love what he had made.[94]

Though sin has distorted the image of God, God still finds in us something that is lovable. Calvin clarifies, "But because the Lord wills not to lose what is his in us, out of his own kindness he still finds something to love."[95] No matter how deeply sunk we are as sinners, we nevertheless remain his creatures. "God does not hate in us His own workmanship, that is, the fact that He has created us as living beings, but He hates our uncleanness, which has extinguished the light of his image."[96] In as much as God loves us because he created us for life, he too hates us because we fell into sin, until God appeared as Redeemer in the person of his only-begotten Son, through whom we are moved from death to life.[97] Sinners, deprived of righteousness, cannot return to divine favor unless righteousness is reckoned to them. Sin hinders our access to God until God reconciles us to himself by removing it. In Christ, the wrath of God's distance from sinners is replaced by the mercy of God's nearness to them; as Paul says in 2 Corinthians 5:21, "God was in Christ," making Christ "the true Immanuel."[98] In Christ, sin that separates God and humanity is

94. Augustine, *John's Gospel* 110.6, as cited in *Inst.* 2.16.4.

95. *Inst.* 2.16.3.

96. *Comm. Rom.* 3:25, *CNTC* 8:76.

97. *Inst.* 2.16.1.

98. *Comm. 2 Cor.* 5:19, *CNTC* 10:78.

blotted out, hostility with God comes to an end, and communion with God is restored.

The God who loves creatures in eternity becomes wrathful to sinners. But God has pledged himself in the sacrifice of his Son whereby he becomes merciful to them.

> We were loved from before the foundation of the world but not apart from Christ. But . . . the love of God was first in time and in order also as regards God; but, as regards us, His love has its foundation in the sacrifice of Christ. For when we think of God apart from a mediator we can only conceive of him as being angry with us, but when a mediator is interposed between us, we know that He is pacified towards us.[99]

The love that begins in eternity is now manifested in Christ's blood in history, in which God demonstrates his love to sinners, whom he had loved before creation. The free love of God for sinners (Rom 5:8) is the impetus behind the sending of the Son to die. But that alone cannot resolve the impasse of God's love and hatred of sinners except through Christ's expiatory acts. Christ must battle everything opposing reconciliation—sin, wrath, and damnation—to banish them and win for us the blessings of righteousness, mercy, and salvation. "A perpetual and irreconcilable disagreement between righteousness and unrighteousness" has to be resolved, or else sin remains with us, and we remain outside the orbit of God's grace. "Therefore, to take away all cause for enmity and to reconcile us utterly to himself, he wipes out all evil in us by the expiation set forth in the death of Christ."[100] Christ's mediation admits believers into the wonderful exchange in which all cause for hostility with God is wiped out and his reconciliation with us is won. Calvin quotes several passages: "He is the expiation for our sins" (1 John 2:2); "Not that we first loved God, but that he first loved us, and sent his Son to be the propitiation for our sins" (1 John 4:10); "God was pleased . . . through him to reconcile to himself all things . . . making peace in relation to himself by the blood of his cross" (Col 1:19–20). We are "by nature . . . the sons of wrath" (Eph 2:3, cf. Vg.) and cannot escape God's judgment, unless by Christ's sacrifice, which vanquishes God's wrath and secures for us free justification.[101] By Christ's obedience, he truly bestows grace on us, something that he

99. *Comm. 2 Cor.* 5:19, *CNTC* 10:78.

100. *Inst.* 2.16.3.

101. *Inst.* 2.17.2.

has acquired and merited, not for himself, but for us. Of this verse, "We were reconciled, and received reconciliation through his death" (Rom 5:10–11), Calvin explains, "God, to whom we were hateful because of sin, was appeased by the death of his Son to become favorable toward us."[102] This, Calvin notes, is highlighted by "the antithesis": "As by one man's disobedience many were made sinners, so by one man's obedience many were made righteous" (Rom 5:19).[103] Through Adam's disobedience, we are separated from God and fall under God's wrath from which we cannot break free. This condition is rectified by Christ's obedience, through which we are reconciled and return to God's favor. "To declare that by [Christ] alone we are accounted righteous, what else is this but to lodge our righteousness in Christ's obedience, because the obedience of Christ is reckoned to us as if it were our own?"[104]

The atonement by blood was already foreshadowed in the law, where Moses taught: "Iniquity will be atoned for, sin will be blotted out and forgiven" (cf. Exod 34:7; Lev 16:34). All the sacrifices in the Old Testament point to Christ and are realized in him. The prefiguration of the old ceremonies and the experiences of the Israelites anticipate the cross and well attest to, in Calvin's words, "the force and power of Christ's death."[105] Thus Calvin concludes, "It was not in vain that God of old willed, through expiations and sacrifices, to attest that he was Father, and to set apart for himself a chosen people. Hence, he was then surely known in the same image in which he with full splendor now appears to us."[106] Christ appeared in the flesh, who by appeasing God has overcome the impasse between God's love and hatred of sinners. Calvin intimates, "But God's righteous curse bars our access to him, and God in his capacity as judge is angry towards us. Hence, an expiation must intervene in order that Christ as priest may obtain God's favor for us and appease his wrath. Thus, to perform this office, Christ had to come forward with a sacrifice."[107] Christ must be without sin, a pure victim who pacifies us by the atonement of blood. Christ's blood is effective in forgiving sins and, on that basis, satisfies the righteous judgment of God. As John the Baptist

102. *Inst.* 2.17.3.

103. *Inst.* 2.17.3.

104. *Inst.* 3.11.23.

105. *Inst.* 2.17.4.

106. *Inst.* 2.9.1.

107. *Inst.* 2.15.6.

proclaimed: "Behold, the lamb of God, who takes away the sin of the world" (John 1:20).

In ourselves, we hate God and are deprived of communion with God unless that hatred is banished by God's love; God's wrath, about which we cannot do anything, can only be absolved by God's mercy in Christ. "Thus," Calvin affirms, "as far as we are concerned, Christ's grace is the beginning of love."[108] The contradiction between God loving and hating sinners is also resolved through two different ways of knowing God: apart from and in the Mediator. This corresponds to Calvin's distinction between the knowledge of God the Creator in Book 1 and the knowledge of God the Redeemer in Book 2. In Book 1, he states that no sinner can recognize God's fatherly goodness until Christ the Mediator appeared to reconcile him to us.[109] The same content occurs in his transition to the knowledge of God the Redeemer in Book 2; there, Calvin teaches that the whole knowledge of God the Creator would not profit us unless faith follows, setting forth for us the knowledge of God the Redeemer.[110] This transition shows that Christ indeed transforms God's attitude toward us, from hating us as sinners apart from Christ, to loving us in Christ. Adam's sin results in the movement of life to death, which cannot be reversed unless by the righteousness of Christ through which the movement of death to life is made possible. The righteousness of God requires God to be our enemy before he could be our friend by Christ's death. The unrighteousness that deserves God's wrath remains in us until Christ interposes to vanquish it by his death. "Hence, we can be fully joined with God only when Christ joins us with him."[111] Christ's propitiation admits us into the adoption in which what is his by nature (God's Son) is ours by grace, no longer strangers but children of God. We enter into the wonderful exchange in which his righteousness and divine mercy are imputed to us in lieu of our sin and divine wrath. The blessing of God's reconciliation conquers the curse of sin by the intervention of Christ's sacrifice, the foundation which resolves the antinomy between God's loving us and hating us.

108. *Comm. 2 Cor.* 13:14, *CNTC* 10:177.

109. *Inst.* 1.2.1.

110. *Inst.* 2.6.1.

111. *Inst.* 2.16.3.

## THE PENAL QUALITY OF DEATH: RHETORICAL VERSUS REAL

Scriptural language presents God as being moved from wrath to love, from being our enemy to being our friend, by the sacrifice of his Son (Col 1:20). This statement may be seen, as Socinus did, as an accommodation to the weakness of our comprehension so that the awareness of God's wrath causes us to repent and to become more thankful for his loving act in Christ. Calvin asks, "Will not these considerations move him the more deeply, the more strikingly they represent the greatness of our calamity from which he was delivered?"[112] If the scriptural language serves only as a rhetorical device to move us to repent, that would undermine Calvin's atonement theology. So immediately Calvin clarifies, "Although this statement is tempered to our feeble comprehension, it is not said falsely."[113] For God, "the highest righteousness,"[114] cannot leave unpunished the unrighteousness that is in us, that which deserves nothing but God's hatred. "Moved by pure and freely given love," Calvin writes, "the Father goes before and anticipates our reconciliation in Christ."[115] Until the effects of Christ's expiatory death are applied to us, we remain the objects of God's wrath.[116] Calvin quotes Augustine: "For, in some ineffable way, God loved us and yet was angry toward us at the same time, until he became reconciled to us in Christ."[117] God can truly be for sinners only when his wrath against sinners has been placated by the death of Christ and God's mercy has been won for them.

God freely determines with himself Christ's expiatory death as his way of reconciliation.[118] Calvin stresses, "To take away our condemnation, it was not enough for him to suffer any kind of death: to make satisfaction for our redemption a form of death had to be chosen in which he might free us both by transferring our condemnation to himself and by taking our guilt upon himself."[119] Calvin entertains no artificial distinction between guilt and the attribution of punishment, for Christ truly

112. *Inst.* 2.16.2 (Beveridge's translation).

113. *Inst.* 2.16.3.

114. *Inst.* 2.16.3.

115. *Inst.* 2.16.3.

116. *Inst.* 2.16.3.

117. *Inst.* 2.17.2.

118. *Comm. 2 Cor.* 5:19, *CNTC* 10:78–79.

119. *Inst.* 2.16.5.

feels the judgment. Our sins were transferred to Christ, and his suffering entails a penal quality. For love, Christ had to experience the full weight of wrath and vengeance of God against the guilt of our sin. He had to undergo the anguish of separation from God and the pangs of death, for only in this manner could God's wrath be appeased.[120] Calvin argues, "If Christ had died only a bodily death, it would have been ineffectual. No—it was expedient at the same time for him to undergo the severity of God's vengeance, to appease his wrath and to satisfy his just judgment."[121] Hence Calvin interprets the cry of dereliction on the cross by means of Isaiah 53:5, viewing it as the chastisement that vanquishes God's wrath.[122] The merciful God is opposed to sinners, and that opposition remains until Christ's death truly abolishes the enmity between the righteous God and wicked sinners. In our person, and in obedience to the Father's will, Christ willingly enters our place and assumes the punishment we justly deserve and offers satisfaction for our sins. The penalty owed by us is now canceled by Christ's death. "Accordingly, our Lord came forth as a true man and took the person and the name of Adam in order to take Adam's place in obeying the Father, to present our flesh as a price of satisfaction to God's righteous judgment, and, in the same flesh, to pay the penalty that we had deserved."[123] On Galatians 3:13, Calvin writes, "[Christ] took our place and thus became a sinner and subject to the curse, not in Himself indeed, but in us; yet in such a way that it was necessary for Him in act in our name."[124] The Son must become one of us, and "in our name," says Calvin, "fight" against all enemies of life—"the devil's power," "the dread of death," and "the pains of hell"—and finally triumphs over them via his death and resurrection.[125]

Both the Father and Son act as one God in appeasing his wrath against sin, securing for us a righteous standing before God. "The Father destroyed the force of sin when the curse of sin was transferred to Christ's flesh. Here, then, is the meaning of this saying: Christ was offered to the Father in death as an expiatory sacrifice that when he discharged all satisfaction through this sacrifice, we might cease to be afraid of God's

120. *Inst.* 2.16.11.

121. *Inst.* 2.16.10.

122. *Inst.* 2.12.4; 2.16.11.

123. *Inst.* 2.12.3.

124. *Comm. Gal.* 3:13, *CNTC* 11:55.

125. *Inst.* 2.16.11.

wrath."[126] The Son must be God's beloved, or else his death possesses no power of propitiation. "Therefore, just as human sinners are both loved and hated by God," Zachman writes, "so also to free sinners from the impasse of God's love and hatred, Christ himself must not only experience God's vengeance, but must also be loved by God."[127] Zachman's estimation echoes Calvin's:

> He could not be outside God's grace, yet He endured His wrath. For how could He reconcile Him to us if He regarded His Father as an enemy and was hated by Him? Therefore the will of the Father always reposed in Him. Again, how could he have freed us from the wrath of God if He had not transferred it from us to Himself? Therefore He was smitten for our sins and knew God as an angry judge.[128]

If Christ's suffering for sin is real, then where is it located? The person of Christ, Christ's humanity, or Christ's divinity? This is where Calvin makes use of the patristic doctrine of the *communicatio idiomatum* to express the unity of Christ's person.[129] For him, Scripture speaks of this in four separate ways:

> They sometimes attribute to him what must be referred solely to his humanity, sometimes what belongs uniquely to his divinity; and sometimes what embraces both natures but fit neither alone. And they so earnestly express this union of the two natures that is in Christ as sometimes to interchange them. This figure of speech is called by the ancient writers "the communicating of properties."[130]

Calvin cites instances to show his point, but with an emphasis on the divine person—for example, "God purchased the church with his blood" (Acts 20:28), and "the Lord of glory was crucified" (1 Cor 2:8). This does not mean that Christ "suffered anything in his divinity."[131] "Surely God does not have blood, does not suffer," Calvin reasons. "But since Christ, who was true God and also true man, was crucified and shed his blood for us, the things that he carried out in his human nature are transferred

126. *Inst.* 2.16.6.

127. Zachman, "Death of Christ," 79–80. I am indebted to Zachman's observation.

128. *Comm. Gal.* 3:13, *CNTC* 11:55, as cited in Zachman, "Death of Christ," 80.

129. For further discussion of the *communicatio*, see Tylenda, "Calvin's Understanding," 54–65.

130. *Inst.* 2.14.1; cf. 4.17.30.

131. *Inst.* 4.17.30.

*improperly*, although not without reason, to his divinity."[132] Likewise, John says, "No one has ascended into heaven but the Son of man who was in heaven" (John 3:13). Obviously, Christ in his flesh was not in heaven, but "because the selfsame one was both God and man, for the sake of union of both natures he gave to the one what belonged to the other."[133] Calvin's position is not that either nature of Christ possesses the properties of the other nature "essentially or actually";[134] they are, for Calvin, "improperly" attributed to the other nature as an expression of the unity. Helm clarifies, "These [such as God has blood] are permissible modes of speech because they are warranted by the unity of the divine and human natures of the Mediator."[135] The *communicatio* is "improper" when conceived literally; it is "a figure of speech" justified by the union of Christ's dual nature. For Calvin, the *communicatio* is confined to the concrete person of the incarnate Son, and in this case, the suffering of Christ's humanity is not to be predicated of his divinity, but of the person of Christ.

Calvin's point is not that Christ's humanity alone secures our reconciliation with God but rather the actual *person* of Christ, whom the Father sent to perform the work of mediation. As the Mediator, Christ's reality (person) as God-man became a human sinner "in us," suffering and dying in our place, to reconcile us to God. Stephen Edmondson sums up: "Indeed, it is only through the person of Christ that we are brought into intimate relationship with God, so that Christ's person, for Calvin, serves not simply as the ground for his activity as the Mediator of the covenant history but also as the goal of this activity, that through his work as priest, king, and prophet, we are led into fellowship with God as we have fellowship with Christ."[136] The Son of God, who is of one being with the Father, suffers, which, according to the doctrine of *communicatio idiomatum*, means that he suffers not in his divinity, but in his humanity. Calvin's view sets him apart from Luther's view, who supposed the unity of Christ's person allows mutual predication of properties among the two natures in Christ. In Helm's assessment,

> For Martin Luther also the language of *communicatio* is mandated by the singularity of Christ's person. Nevertheless, Luther

132. *Inst.* 2.14.2, my italics.

133. *Inst.* 2.14.2.

134. Edmondson, *Christology*, 216.

135. Helm, *Ideas*, 76.

136. Edmondson, *Christology*, 203.

> goes beyond the scholastics, invoking a minority tradition in the Patristic period (for example, that represented by John of Damascus) in which the properties of divinity are ascribed not only to the divine person, but also to the human nature of Christ, and vice versa. "Because the divinity and the humanity form in Christ one single person, the Scripture attributes to the divinity, on account of this personal unity, everything that concerns humanity, and conversely."[137]

The penal substitution of Christ for sinners is no virtual reality. It has vanquished God's righteous vengeance so that it no longer harms us.[138] Christ's death has achieved for us "the complete fulfillment of salvation": reconciliation with God, the satisfaction of his righteous judgment, the removal of the curse, and the plenary payment for penalty.[139] Christ's death is the culmination of Christ's obedience and legal satisfaction. It must be accompanied by Christ's resurrection, the other side of the same pair.[140] We benefit from the power and efficacy of "the substance of salvation" between Christ's death, through which sin and death are conquered, and his resurrection, through which righteousness and life are restored (1 Pet 1:3).[141] "Just as Christ by his death takes our unrighteousness upon himself," Zachman says, "so by his rising he bestows his righteousness upon us."[142] The "whole of redemption and all its parts" are encapsulated in the cross (Gal 6:14).[143] The cross and resurrection of Christ are so united that the latter does not "lead us away" from the former. Instead, resurrection leads us to the cross, rendering its vulnerability efficacious.[144] The two events—cross and resurrection—constitute a single meaning: a celebration of victory over sin, death, and hell in exchange for righteousness, life, and heaven. Let nothing distract us from glorying in the cross; as Paul exclaims in Galatians 6:14: "God forbid!"

In his discussion of the Apostles' Creed, Calvin belabors that the substance of Christ's expiatory office includes not only his death and

137. Helm, *Ideas*, 74, citing Luther's *Greater Confession of the Eucharist* (1528), itself cited in Wendel, *Calvin*, 221. See Ngien, *Suffering*, ch. 3, for an analysis of some of Luther's texts, showing that properties of one nature can be ascribed to the other nature.

138. *Inst.* 2.16.5.

139. *Inst.* 2.16.13.

140. *Inst.* 2.16.13.

141. *Inst.* 2.16.13.

142. Zachman, *Assurance*, 172.

143. *Comm. Gal.* 6:14, *CNTC* 11:117.

144. *Comm. Gal.* 6:14, CNTC 11:117.

resurrection but also Christ's ascension to the right hand of the Father, where he intercedes for his people, applying to them the efficacy of the cross and resurrection unceasingly.[145] While Christ's priestly role restores our relationship to God by destroying our sinful identity through Christ's death and resurrection, his kingly office enacts that relation by conquering our enemies and sweeping away that which threatens us.[146] The disciples' comfort lies hidden in the treasure and glory Christ's departure to heaven brings; he will receive power from his Father, will be Lord over all, and will bestow on them his Spirit and all his manifold gifts: his power, victory, beauty, magnificence, and wealth.[147]

## PARTICIPATION IN CHRIST'S WORSHIP: IN OURSELVES AND IN CHRIST

Calvin declares, "Christ is the beginning, the middle, and the end,"[148] and "our whole salvation and all its parts (worship included) must be comprehended in Christ."[149]

> If we seek redemption, it lies in his passion; if acquittal, in his condemnation; if remission of the curse, in his cross [Gal. 3:13]; if satisfaction, in his sacrifice; if purification, in his blood; if reconciliation, in his descent into hell; . . . if inheritance of the Heavenly Kingdom, in his entrance into heaven. . . . In short, since rich store of every kind of good abounds in him, let us drink our fill from this fountain, and from no other.[150]

Calvin's view of worship presupposes the basic distinction between "in ourselves," the condition in which we are barred from access to God, and "in Christ," the condition in which we are given a legitimate participation in worship. The purpose of Christ's priestly office is twofold: "not only to render the Father favorable and propitious toward us by an eternal law of reconciliation, but also to receive us as his companions in this great office [Rev. 1:6]."[151] This double emphasis of Christ—reconciliation and

145. *Inst.* 2.16.13.
146. *Inst.* 2.16.16.
147. *Inst.* 2.15.4; 2.16.16.
148. *Comm. 1 Pet.* 1:20, *CNTC* 12:249–50.
149. *Inst.* 2.16.19.
150. *Inst.* 2.16.19.
151. *Inst.* 2.15.6.

intercession—is the locus under which worship is comprehended. "For we who are defiled in ourselves, yet are priests in him, offer ourselves and our all to God, and freely enter the heavenly sanctuary that the sacrifices of prayers and praise that we bring may be acceptable and sweet-smelling before God."[152] This is borne out in Christ's statement, "For their sake I sanctify myself" (John 17:19). The perichoretic interaction of each person of the Trinity is the ground of human faithfulness.

> It is because [Christ] consecrated himself to the Father that his holiness might come to us. For as the blessing is spread to the whole harvest from the first-fruits, so God's Spirit cleanses us by the holiness of Christ and makes us partakers of it. And not by imputation alone, for in that respect He is said to have been made to us righteousness (1 Cor. 1:30); but He is also said to have been made to us sanctification (1 Cor. 1:30), because he has, so to say, presented us to his Father in his own person (*in sua persona*) that we may be renewed to true holiness by his Spirit. Although this sanctification belongs to the whole life of Christ (*ad totam Christi vitam*), it shone brightest in the sacrifice of his death, for he then appeared as the true High Priest who consecrated the Temple, the Altar, all the vessels and the people by the power of his Spirit.[153]

His sanctification is reckoned to us; hence our transgressions and vices no longer hinder us.[154] In us, we could not offer to God true worship; all our gifts are perverted and defiled and do not enter the holy of holies. Christ the Mediator intercedes for us, by whom we present ourselves and what is ours to the Father. Christ's mediation establishes the believer's response to God in the church's worship. Calvin teaches,

> Christ is our pontiff who has entered the heavenly sanctuary [Heb. 9:24] and opens a way for us to enter [cf. Heb. 10:20]. He is the altar [cf. Heb. 13:10] upon which we lay our gifts, that whatever we venture to do, we may undertake in him. He it is, I say, that has made us a kingdom and priests unto the Father [Rev. 1:6].[155]

The object and means of worship are identical: Christ whom we worship is the leader through whom we worship. What we cannot do, God himself

152. *Inst.* 2.15.6.

153. *Comm. John* 17:19, *CNTC* 5:146.

154. *Inst.* 2.15.6.

155. *Inst.* 4.18.17.

provides in Christ, through whom we worship. Torrance expressly writes of Calvin's view, "The mystery, the wonder, and the glory of the gospel is that He who is God the Creator of all things, and worthy of the worship and praises of all creation, should become man and as a man lead us in our worship of God, that we might become the sons of God."[156] Through him, our praise and thanksgiving reach heaven, which the apostle describes as "the fruit of lips confessing His name" (Heb 13:15, Vg.).[157] Christ's mediation not only abolishes the separation between God and us, but it also makes true worship possible: "And that none may be deterred by difficulty of access, we proclaim that a complete fountain of all blessings is opened up to us in Christ, and that out of it we may draw everything we need."[158] Since Christ, our head, has entered heaven "*in our flesh, as if in our name*," we, his members, already possess heaven in him.[159] His entrance into heaven is the presupposition of our entrance into the same place, which allows us to enjoy every good in him, including worship.

Christ is the sacrifice of propitiation and the true priesthood. He is the complete fulfillment of the priesthoods of old: "For Christ is the sole Pontiff and Priest of the New Testament [cf. Heb. 9], to whom all priesthoods have been transferred, and in whom they have been closed and terminated."[160] No priests, except Christ, whose priesthood is heavenly, could intercede efficaciously before God. "Whatever was necessary to recover the Father's favor, to obtain forgiveness of sins, righteousness and salvation—all this was performed and completed by that unique sacrifice of his. And so perfect was it that no place was left afterward for any other sacrificial victims."[161] Commenting on Hebrew 6:19, Calvin writes, "The High Priest has entered the Holy of holies, not in his name only, but also in that of the people . . . so that in the person of one man all entered the sanctuary together . . . our High Priest has entered heaven, not only for Himself but also for us."[162] Christ not only enters our death and rises again in our humanity, he also returns to the Father as our eternal intercessor (Heb 8:1). To enter the sanctuary with efficacy, we must not bypass Christ's humanity and his death, which alone sanctifies what we venture

156. Torrance, "Vicarious Humanity," 70.

157. *Inst.* 4.18.17.

158. Calvin, *The Necessity of Reforming the Church*, in *Tracts*, 147.

159. *Inst.* 2.16.16, my italics.

160. *Inst.* 4.18.14.

161. *Inst.* 4.18.13.

162. *Comm. Heb.* 6:19, *CNTC* 12:87.

to do in worship. In our humanity, and in our name, Christ our head offers a sacrifice once that reaches the holy of holies, and whose efficacy extends to all and is eternal (John 19:30).[163] Calvin opines, "God will not hear us unless He is favorably inclined, and therefore He must first be appeased since our sins have made Him angry with us; and so there must of necessity be a preceding sacrifice for our prayer to have any effect."[164] Access to the heavenly sanctuary is through Christ, who appears before the Father's face as our constant advocate and intercessor (Heb 7:27; 9:11–12; Rom 8:34). Christ ascended in his glorified humanity, opening the way to the heavenly throne that was formerly forbidden us because of Adam's sin. "Since Christ has gone up to the right hand of God to reign graciously in heaven, he is the minister not of an earthly sanctuary but of a heavenly one."[165] Our praise or prayers are rendered void unless Christ as our High Priest sanctifies us and secures for us that grace which admits us into the heavenly sanctuary.[166] Just as we benefit from Christ's intervening sacrifice, through which our prayers can be heard, so we too benefit from Christ's kingly reign through which all forces hostile to God—sin, wrath, the devil, and hell—are ended. Christ turns the Father's gaze to his own righteousness rather than to our sins. He attunes the Father's ears to us, and by his intercession he leads us to the Father's throne.[167] In Christ, the throne of dread, which bars our entrance into the heavenly sanctuary, becomes one of grace, impelling us to offer up our sacrifice of praise to him.

The sacrifice of expiation, upon which faith rests, belongs to Christ alone, for he alone completes it. The sacrifice of thanksgiving and praise, which does not atone for sins but springs from the knowledge of God's benevolence, belongs to the priesthood of believers. In Billings's phrase, "The sacrifice of praise, which includes the whole life of sanctification and 'all the duties of love', has 'nothing to do with appeasing God's wrath, with obtaining forgiveness of sins, or with meriting righteousness.'"[168] The vicarious priesthood of Christ shapes Christian life and inspires worship by constituting us as "participants in his response to the Father and

163. *Inst.* 4.18.13.

164. *Comm. Heb.* 8:3, *CNTC* 12:106.

165. *Comm. Heb.* 8:1, *CNTC* 12:104.

166. *Inst.* 2.16.3.

167. *Inst.* 2.16.16.

168. Billings, "John Calvin's Soteriology," 438; cf. *Inst.* 4.18.17.

companions in this great office."[169] Christ's mediation restores our priesthood and incites human action. "[Christ's] priesthood," John Jansen writes, "is for us in such a way that it recovers our own."[170] Our worship is grounded in what Christ has achieved in the cross and continues to do "in our name" as our great High Priest, the one true minister (*Leitourgos*) of the heavenly sanctuary (Heb 8:2). The efficacy of his vicarious life of worship and intercession before the Father applies to those who are united to him. Yet our worship is a passive response, animated and made efficacious by the double grace accessed through union with Christ, in whom the discord between righteousness and unrighteousness, holiness and unholiness, dissolves, and we are received into God's favor. Our worship, says John Clark, "is our response to the Father's reception of us in Christ; and this response is to be shaped by and reflective of our participation in the sole priesthood of Christ, who gathers up our worship, cleanses it, and presents it to the Father together with his own."[171] Just as God himself pours his gifts upon us in Christ, so we, in return, bring forth praise to his glory through Christ.[172] The continual offering of ourselves, including our prayers, praises, and thanksgivings, is "a reasonable worship" (Rom 12:1).[173] No outward activities reach God unless they are covered by the efficacy of Christ, "the greater sacrifice, by which we are consecrated in soul and body to be a holy temple to the Lord [1 Cor. 3:16]."[174] Our being and all the sacrifices we offer to God must undergo consecration by Christ's holy name so that they may serve his glory. This kind of sacrifice basically expresses our reverence for God's majesty and gratitude for his diverse gifts laid up in Christ's ascended throne. The Spirit lifts us up and places us in Christ from whom flows the heavenly riches from the seat of Christ to his members, as from a head to its body.[175] By the Spirit, we participate in Christ's ascension, the very basis of our ascent to his Father, who by grace is our Father, his God our God (cf. John 20:17). We enter into our adoption through which all heavenly inheritances that wholly belong to Christ are transferred to us, whom he constitutes as "brothers,

169. See Clark, "Principal Point," 82.

170. Jansen, *Work of Christ*, 44. I prefer "restores" to "recovers."

171. Clark, "Principal Point," 83.

172. *Inst.* 3.15.4.

173. *Inst.* 4.18.16.

174. *Inst.* 4.18.16.

175. *Inst.* 2.15.5.

and also fellow heirs with him" (Rom 8:17).[176] Christ went through death to God's right hand, where he through the Spirit "enriched his people, and daily lavishes spiritual riches upon them."[177] By the Holy Spirit, we ascend to the Father through the Son with the sacrifices of praise, thanksgiving, prayers, and service. The whole immensity of the heavenly benefits Christ procured thus becomes for us "the most fruitful occasion"[178] to glorify him.

## THE PARTICIPATIVE POWER OF THE HOLY SPIRIT: CHRIST'S MEDIATION MADE EFFECTUAL

Calvin articulates the pneumatological dynamic of Christ's mediation: "It is by the power of the Holy Spirit which shone out in the resurrection and ascension of Christ that the dignity of Christ's priesthood is to be reckoned."[179] By the Spirit, believers truly feel the power of Christ's vicarious obedience, whereby the opposition between the terror of God's wrath and the consolation of God's mercy is conquered for those who believe. The Spirit's role in the believer's reception of the grace of Christ has its basis in Paul's teaching on our "participation in the Spirit" (2 Cor 13:14).[180] This theme of the Spirit as the testimony and seal of salvation in Christ found expression via Augustine in the Western formulation of the Spirit as the "bond of love"[181] between the Father and the Son, and between the Son and the believer. Calvin builds on this tradition, saying, "The Holy Spirit is the bond by which Christ effectually unites us to himself."[182] Elsewhere, he says, "The bond of this connection is therefore the Spirit of Christ, with whom we are joined in unity, and is like a channel through which all that Christ himself is and has is conveyed to us."[183] Calvin's insistence on the Spirit as the bond of unity leads Wendel to

> justifiably wonder whether the Holy Spirit does not in his view occupy a position, in our relations with the Christ, analogous to

176. *Inst.* 2.12.2.

177. *Inst.* 2.16.18.

178. *Inst.* 2.15.5.

179. *Comm. Heb.* 8:1, *CNTC* 12:104.

180. *Comm. 2 Cor.* 13:14, *CNTC* 10:177.

181. See Augustine, *Trinity*, book 5, 189–204. Discussion of the Spirit as the "bond of love" occurs in *De Trinitate* 6:5; cf. 5:11–12; 7:3; 15:17–19, 26–27.

182. *Inst.* 3.1.1.

183. *Inst.* 4.17.12.

> that of Christ himself in his relation with his Father. . . . Indeed, the Holy Spirit plays the part of an obligatory mediator between Christ and man, just as Christ is mediator between God and man. And in the same way that Jesus Christ is the necessary instrument of redemption, so is the Holy Spirit the no less necessary instrument by means of which this redemption reaches us, in justification and regeneration.[184]

Christology and pneumatology mutually coincide, as both the Son and the Spirit act together as mediators. What God has achieved for us in Christ is what he imparts in us by the Spirit. While the Son mediates between God and us by achieving God's reconciliation with us, the Spirit mediates between Christ and us by applying to us Christ's victory over everything contradicting justification. The Son's mediation reaches its completion in the Spirit's mediation; this is evident in the transition from Book 2, which speaks of union with Christ from whom we receive the benefits of Christ, to Book 3, which speaks of the Holy Spirit from whom "we receive those benefits which the Father bestows on his only-begotten Son—not for Christ's own private use, but that he might enrich poor and needy men [*sic*]."[185] Only when Christ becomes ours and dwells within us could he share with us what he has received from the Father through the Spirit; being incorporated into Christ by the same Spirit, we can partake of Christ and his benefits through faith. W. David O. Taylor writes, "The Spirit is the Go-Between, who, through the Son, takes the gifts of the Father and offers them to creation, while at the same time taking the gifts of creation and, through the Son, offering them back to Father."[186]

The Spirit is called "the Spirit of Christ," not only by virtue of his essential unity with the Father and the Son, but also by virtue of his character as our Mediator. As Jelle Faber explains rightly, "The Spirit bestows on us nothing apart from Christ, and Christ bestows on us nothing but through the Spirit."[187] The Spirit's work and Christ's are not in opposition: Christ works "through" the Spirit, binding us to himself in whom God's favor or grace is found, and the Spirit works "for" Christ, communicating to us the benefits of Christ's mediatorial activity by which we are reconciled to the Father. The dynamic of the Spirit in us thus means that we are no longer governed by ourselves, but by his action and prompting,

184. Wendel, *Calvin*, 239–40.

185. *Inst.* 3.1.1.

186. Taylor, *Theater*, 93.

187. Faber, "Saving Work," 3.

without which all of God's gifts are either perverted or misperceived (cf. Gal 5:19–21). All good things we possess are the fruits of the grace of Christ which the Holy Spirit bestows on us through the vehicle of faith.

Abiding in Calvin's trinitarian dynamic of salvation is a double movement: descent from the Father to the Son by the Holy Spirit, and ascent from the Holy Spirit through the Son to the Father.[188] Since the Spirit binds the redeemed to Christ, they (in Christ) appropriate God's gifts as a parallel movement from the Father, by the Spirit, for his Son's sake.

> God the Father gives us the Holy Spirit for his Son's sake, and yet has bestowed the whole fullness of the Spirit upon the Son to be minister and steward of his liberality. . . . For there is nothing absurd in ascribing to the Father praise for those gifts of which he is the Author, and yet in ascribing the same powers to Christ, with whom were laid up the gifts of the Spirit to bestow upon his people. For this reason he invites unto himself all who thirst, that they may drink [John 7:37].[189]

The double movement of the triune God constitutes the substance of the gospel; both descending (from God to us) and ascending (from us to God) are for *our* benefit, not for God's. Calvin's piety of grace begins with the descent of God to us in Christ, making his benefits available for us through the secret power of the Holy Spirit. It does not culminate there but continues with our ascent to God through the Son by the Spirit. Christ cannot benefit us unless he becomes ours and dwells within us to communicate with us the gifts he has acquired from the Father through the Spirit. The Father descends upon us with extravagant grace through the Son, who gives us the Spirit to raise us up and seat us with the ascended Christ on his throne. The Son's filial status and his response of obedience to the Father are ours by the Spirit of adoption. The Spirit is the dynamic of human response that allows us to share in the Son's faithful response and thus in his Sonship. Our response to God's initiative is created in us by the Spirit, who applies to us the efficacy of the Son's faithful response to the Father. Butin writes, "Its dynamic is the Spirit, who, in perichoretic interaction with the Son, empowers, enables, and authenticates faithful human response to the grace of God that God the Father offers humanity through the renewal of the divine image in

188. Butin, *Revelation*, 82. See Canlis, *Calvin's Ladder*, 89–112, where discussion of the language of descent and ascent occurs.

189. *Inst.* 3.1.2.

Christ."[190] Had the very majesty of God not descended, the whole human race would have perished; we do not possess any power to ascend to God, except through Christ's ascent. Christ's ascension is his homecoming to the Father in a glorified humanity, an upward movement by the Spirit that draws us up as "his companions" into the Son's filial relationship with the Father. By "the Spirit of adoption" (Rom 8), we are exalted to share in the heavenly glory that the Son has with his Father.[191] The upward movement by the Spirit to Christ's ascended position incorporates us into the perichoretic life of the triune God, making us the beneficiaries of his faithful response to, and his reign with, his Father over all things.

Believers are thus given threefold gifts of the one God: the revelation of the Father, redemption in the Son, and human response in the Spirit. We stand in awe as a noble creature before the magnificence of the majestic God, the Father, in gratitude as a forgiven sinner, before the beneficence of a merciful Savior, the Son, and with joy as an adopted child before the sweetness and loving presence of God, the Spirit. The Spirit is the dynamic of human response, the Son's faithful response to the Father is shared with us, and Jesus's Sonship is credited to us; as Calvin says, "What is his is made ours." As the "bond of love," the Spirit incorporates us into the perichoretic life of the Trinity in which the Father's estate is shared with us through union with the Son, the basis of our participation in his faithful response to the Father by faith. Chester expands:

> In responding in faith to the saving divine initiative, believers are reciprocating God's actions for them but can only do so when united with Christ because it is only in Christ that authentic humanity is to be found. For Calvin, there can be no separate human response to an exclusively divine initiative because in the incarnate Christ this divine initiative, and indeed the divine nature, is expressed in perfect humanity. The divine saving work is already itself, in the person of Christ, a human response.[192]

The Spirit's insertion of believers through the Son into the divine life leads to the sanctification of humanity, not its denigration. Objectively, the truth of our identity is not to be sought in us but in Christ. Subjectively, the realization of that true identity-in-Christ is by the Holy Spirit, who sanctifies our humanity by including us into the divine life so that

190. Butin, *Revelation*, 93.

191. *Inst.* 3.1.3.

192. Chester, *Reading Paul*, 291.

we may enter our adoption and enjoy Christ and all his gifts, including his communion with the Father. In Butin's estimation,

> The Holy Spirit is the Spirit of Christ, who is the epitome of humanity and authentic embodiment of the divine image. This Spirit actualized and empowered the incarnate Christ to fulfill genuine humanity. This same Spirit unites believers by faith to that same Christ; authenticating in turn their humanity; not over against God, but rather by incorporation into the divine life.[193]

## CONCLUSION

The images of God as an awesome Creator, a merciful Father, a loving Redeemer in Christ Jesus, and the Holy Spirit as seal are the dynamic of our response of reverence and love, a piety drawn from a right knowledge of God revealed in Scripture. These alluring images of God reflect all aspects of God's activities. In creation, God attracts us by sensuous images in the natural order to a proper contemplation of his deeds wherein his character or nature is located, and from which we reap bountiful benefits for our souls. Just as his creation is his care and concern for us, so is his salvation. In so far as we "learned that our salvation rests with God . . . we are attracted to seek him. This fact is confirmed for us when he declares that our salvation is his care and concern. Accordingly, we need the promise of grace, which can testify to us that the Father is merciful; since we can approach him in no other way, and upon grace alone the heart of man can rest."[194] And in sanctification, the Spirit illuminates our minds and communicates to our hearts the victory of Christ, through which we apprehend God's goodness in creation, and we cling to the God of mercy who conquers the God of wrath, if only we believe this. All of this flows out of Calvin's trinitarian definition of faith: "Now we shall possess a right definition of faith if we call it a firm and certain knowledge of God's benevolence toward us, founded upon the truth of the freely given promise in Christ, both revealed to our minds and sealed upon our hearts through the Holy Spirit."[195] Calvin's piety is trinitarian, as disclosed

193. Butin, *Revelation*, 93.

194. *Inst.* 3.2.7.

195. *Inst.* 3.2.7.

in his reading of Scripture, and in the emphases he places on the way he develops his *Institutes*. Jimmy Boon-Chai Tan sums up well:

> As aspects of trinitarian piety, it possesses a theological focus—depicting a wholesome picture of God the Father, merciful, loving, and benevolent. It possesses a christological focus—pointing the disciple to Jesus and the way of the cross. It retains a pneumatological focus—for it is a piety that integrates the mind and heart through the interior work of the Spirit, progressing beyond intellectual assent into heart-felt apprehension through the faith-producing work of the Spirit.[196]

The trinitarian grammar of salvation is apparent in Calvin's theology. The marvel of the gospel consists of three things. First, that the Supreme Majesty of this universe, worthy of praise, should humble himself in the incarnate Son, so that he might offer himself as the sacrifice of propitiation through which the hostility between God and us is banished, that we might become the sons of God. Second, that the Son of God, who is coequal with the Father and worthy of all creation's worship, should become one of us, so that he as a man could usher us into the heavenly sanctuary without hindrances. Through Christ's priesthood, our being and our earthly sacrifices, unworthy in themselves, become a sweet fragrance of worship. Third, that inculcated in our hearts by the Spirit is this: Christ's mediatorial benefits belong to us in a joyous exchange for our sinful plight and its destructive end. Through union with Christ, which the Spirit effects, we are welcomed into that filial relationship the Son enjoys with his Father, and are equally loved as is the Son by the Father. The Spirit's incorporation of believers through the Son into the perichoretic life of the Trinity leads to the exaltation of humanity, not to its dissolution. Apart from the Holy Spirit, no one can taste either the fatherly love of God or the grace of Christ. The Spirit, the effector of union, creates filial confidence, making God's adoption of us in Christ epistemically real in us. By the Spirit, all that Christ is (person) and has (properties) become ours through the agency of faith: his life is our life; his death is ours; his victory is ours; his righteousness is ours; his heavenly kingdom is ours; his priesthood is our priesthood; his altar is ours; his worship is our worship. We encounter the Trinity backward, beginning with the Spirit through the Son to the Father. Calvin's articulation of the Trinity

196. Tan, *How Then Shall We Guide?*, 174.

is basically economic and soteriological, focusing on the interactive roles the Father, Son, and Holy Spirit play in achieving God's reconciliation with us, in which we participate by faith.

# 3

# Reaping Fruits from the Law

## *Preparative, Preservative, and Restorative*

IN HIS *INSTITUTES*, CALVIN talks about three parts, or uses, of the law: its theological, political, and principal uses.[1] There are two distinct realms—namely, civil and spiritual government—yet there is only one God, one Kingdom, one Mediator, and ultimately one law. The three functions of the law coalesce as a differentiated unity, with different impacts, depending on the state of the sinner, unrepentant or believing. Each has its own domain. Confusion of their distinct functions would result in chaos; severance of any one from the others will also do damage to the unity of the law. Calvin does not relinquish the benefit of civil law, as do the Anabaptists; nor does he reject the law altogether, as do the Antinomians. He espouses a positive view of the law as a norm and guide of the Christian life. Having been freed from the punitive function of the law, Christians find pleasure and sweetness in the law. Once the curse of the law is banished, and works-righteousness expelled, the law is restored to its original function as an expression of the love of God. The epistemic and affective condition undergoes rebirth so that believers begin to relish the commandments as God's gift. They benefit from the law's positive functions in godly living; they are preserved from wandering from the eternal rule of righteousness. They accept the law as God's instrument, which sanctifies their newfound identity so that they may give public expression to the image of God newly ingrained. Believers begin to orient all aspects of their lives toward the bidding of the Holy Spirit, through

1. *Inst.* 2.7.6–12.

whom Christ lives and reigns in us. Joyous obedience for God stems not out of coercion or servile fear, as a slave does with a tyrant, but a filial fear, as a child to a gentle father. Not the spur of the law, however profitable it is for godliness, but God's gentle attraction is the condition of possibility of our cheerful obedience, with hearts filled with gratitude for his mercies.

This chapter aims to achieve a balanced view of the law that incorporates a variety of its uses, both negative and positive. Each usage governs the way humans should live accordingly, in a way that is not incompatible with godliness. Believers who are seized by Christ through the Spirit perceive the law as a salutary doctrine of life and reap from it three distinct fruits or benefits—which David Clyde Jones labels "preparative, preservative, and restorative"[2]—for the formation of their identity. The presentation will focus on the significance of the law in shaping the Christian life under these rubrics: sin, grace, obedience, justification and sanctification, glory, majesty, and the role of the Spirit, as it seeks to navigate through such a complex.

## THE FIRST (PREPARATIVE) USE OF THE LAW: LAW TO GOSPEL

The law is given by God to inform us of the shape he intends for human existence and his claim upon us as well. What God intends for us is already revealed there; it is not something sinners draw from inside themselves.[3] Any attempt to construct a rule of our own is what Calvin calls "the playfulness of the human mind" to dream up various rites with which to shun the obedience God requires.[4] The law is of God; it is good and remains unaltered. There is nothing in the law that would give rise to wickedness and unrighteousness. The blessedness that the law promises is "conditional"[5] upon perfect obedience to it. The nature of the law remains good irrespective of our posture toward it. The function of it changes when it collides with sin. The chief purpose of the law is to quicken faith in the Mediator; it is not to curse, except when it confronts sin. The condemnatory function of the law is "accidental,"[6] not essential.

2. Jones, "Law and the Spirit," 302.
3. *Inst.* 2.8.5.
4. *Inst.* 2.8.5.
5. *Inst.* 2.7.4.
6. See *Comm. Gal.* 3:10, *CNTC* 11:53; Dowey, *Knowledge of God*, 228.

Because our will is not "conformed and composed to obedience to the law," we are stripped of the joy of the blessed life set forth in the law, and incur "mere curse" under it.[7] Victor Shepherd rightly observes the significance of the adjective "mere,"[8] which Calvin uses to differentiate between the function of the law before sin and after sin. Prior to sin, the law had been given for salvation and life; however, when met with the carnal and corrupted nature, it becomes "an occasion for sin and death."[9]

With Luther, Calvin likens the law to "a perfect mirror."[10] Its pedagogical use is perfect because it does not fail to be the agent of exposing God's righteousness and our sinfulness. This mirror remains operative; it holds us guilty of sin, slays us, and places us under God's wrath. "In it we contemplate our weakness, then the iniquity arising from this, and finally the curse coming from both."[11] Only when we are confronted with this mirror do we see ourselves as God sees us. The law awakens us from slumber concerning our sinful condition and its accompanying curse. Using another analogy, only when the law causes us to recognize our sickness would we cling to the gospel for healing. The law acquaints us with the maladies of self-deception, pride, confidence, vanity, covetousness, and self-love, leading us to seek remedy from the heavenly physician.[12]

The reaction to the law differs from person to person. When the law comes upon unbelievers, the effect is detrimental, placing them under the intolerable wrath of God from which there is no relief. Unbelievers fail to see mercy in the law, in which case sin only increases. The more their consciences are aroused and made aware of its sin, the more sin multiplies as they seek to shield themselves by either defending themselves with lies or deceit or pursuing self-chosen expiations to alleviate their guilt. Calvin writes, "For stubborn disobedience against the Lawgiver is then added to transgression."[13] The law "unleashes the thunderbolt of its curse" against those who seek to ground their righteousness in the flesh rather than in the gospel of forgiveness, the basis of our liberation from

7. *Inst.* 2.7.3.

8. Shepherd, *Nature and Function*, 139n66: "The purpose of the law is not to curse—except when the law confronts sin."

9. *Inst.* 2.7.7.

10. *Inst.* 3.18.9; cf. WA 18:677, where we find an example of Luther's talk of law as mirror and the frequent use he makes of Rom 3:20 in his *Bondage of the Will*.

11. *Inst.* 2.7.7.

12. *Inst.* 2.7.6.

13. *Inst.* 2.7.7.

the bonds of the law.[14] To the unbelievers, the law, as Paul taught, is "the ministry of death and condemnation" (2 Cor 3:7). This is the teaching of Augustine: "If the Spirit of grace is absent, the law is present only to accuse and kill us."[15] This applies to the reprobate, who will not and cannot respond, nor avail themselves of the remedy of the gospel.

However, when the law comes upon the faithful, it reveals their iniquity and hopelessness, thus truly preparing them for seeking the remedy of grace which is in Christ. Calvin concurs with Augustine, who, writing to Hilary, exhorts, "The law bids us, as we try to fulfill its requirements, and become wearied in our weakness under it, to know how to ask the help of grace."[16] For the children of God, the law, even in its accusing, death-causing capacity, is not given to suffer them to perish, but so that God may confer upon them mercy as the outcome. Guenther H. Haas writes,

> This awareness [of God's wrath] has the ultimate goal of driving sinners to embrace the grace and mercy of God revealed in Christ. By abandoning any attempts at attaining righteousness by the works of the law, they can be clothed by faith with the righteousness of Christ. Thereby, they have the assurance that in Christ the righteous requirements of the law are satisfied.[17]

In his commentary on John 10:8, Calvin claims, "[No] contradiction [occurs] between the Law and the teaching of the Gospel, for the Law is nothing but a preparation for the Gospel."[18] Commenting on Galatians 3:21, Calvin avers that contradiction between law and gospel occurs only when the power of justifying is transferred to the law. There are not "two opposing methods" of attaining righteousness, but only one, that being placed under the terrifying threat of the law we might cling to the delightful comfort of the gospel.[19] Through the law, God works in us negatively a conviction of our sin, which incurs God's judgment so that he might work in us positively an inclination to seek the consolation of Christ, in whom God's face shines. The law prepares troubled hearts for

14. *Inst.* 2.7.15.

15. Augustine, *On Rebuke and Grace* 1. 2 (MPL 44. 917; tr. NPNF 5. 472), as cited in *Inst.* 2.7.7, 356n11.

16. Augustine, *Letters* 157. 2. 9 (MPL 33. 677; tr. FC 20. 325), as cited in *Inst.* 2.7.9, 357n14.

17. Haas, "Calvin's Ethics," 100.

18. *Comm. John* 10:8, *CNTC* 4:261.

19. *Comm. Gal.* 3:21, *CNTC* 11:64.

an exhilarating experience of being grasped by God, who is nothing but pure mercy.

> [God's children] come to realize that they stand and are upheld by God's hand alone; that naked and empty-handed, they flee to his mercy, repose entirely in it, hide deep within it, and seize upon it alone for righteousness and merit. For God's mercy is revealed in Christ to all who seek and wait upon it with true faith. In the precepts of the law, God is but the rewarder of perfect righteousness, which all of us lack, and conversely, the severe judge of evil deeds. But in Christ his face shines, full of grace and gentleness, even upon us poor and unworthy sinners.[20]

We must maintain the distinction of God's holiness and his grace as surely as we do the distinction of law and gospel. As God cannot be divided, neither can his word. The Spirit through the word both kills and enlivens; he achieves this through law and gospel, which is one word of the same God. The word of the gospel only bestows life on those who have first been slain by the sword of the Spirit and reduced to nothing.[21] This is illustrated by an Old Testament parallel in the story of Hagar, whom God had humbled through affliction, yet "was not reduced to order by stripes only—a heavenly vision was added."[22] Her knowledge of self and her sin did not profit her unless the positive grace of the Spirit was added. For unbelievers, "bare law"[23] works in them condemnation; for believers, both law and gospel work in unity so that while God chastises us with his hand (law), he also consoles us with his Spirit (gospel). The former necessarily leads to the latter.

Calvin relates the distinction between law and gospel to the distinction between "legal" birth and "evangelical" birth. The "legal" birth, which springs from the righteousness of the law, does not make us the beneficiaries of God's inheritance—only the "evangelical" birth, wrought by the righteousness of faith, does this. Only "evangelical" birth is the basis of justification. Correspondingly, "legal repentance" keeps people under the custody of sin and fear of God's wrath from which there is no deliverance, but "evangelical repentance" places them under the canopy of God's mercy, in which they experience deliverance from the misery of sin and terror of God's wrath. "Legal repentance" is "that by which

20. *Inst.* 2.7.8; Wendell, *Calvin*, 199.

21. *Inst.* 3.3.8.

22. *Comm. Gen.* 16:14; CO 23:232, as cited in Hesselink, *Concept*, 265n54.

23. *Inst.* 2.7.2.

stung with a sense of his sin, and overwhelmed with fear of the divine anger, [the sinner] remains in that state of perturbation, unable to escape from it." Conversely, "evangelical repentance" is "that by which the sinner, though grievously downcast in himself, yet looks up and sees in Christ the cure of his wound, the solace of his terror; the haven of rest from misery."[24]

## The Ten Commandments: Threat and Promise

In order to inspire in us love of righteousness and hatred of wickedness, God out of his kindness has added terrifying threats to the promises in the Ten Commandments.[25] Our most merciful Father promises to reward our obedience with present blessings and eternal life; but he will visit the disobedient with present calamities and eternal perdition because he will avenge contempt of his majesty. In these two contradictory activities, God remains "the friend of righteousness and the foe of iniquity."[26] The whole law, which Calvin calls "ten words,"[27] is grouped under two heads: The first table (commandments one to four) particularly instructs us how we may worship his majesty aright. The second table (commandments five to ten) prescribes how we may perform the duties of love toward our neighbor in fear of his name. When discussing the division of the commandments in the *Institutes*, Calvin writes against both Catholics and Lutherans:

> Those who so divide them as to give three precepts to the First Table and relegate the remaining seven to the Second, erase from the number the commandment concerning images, or at least hide it under the First. There is no doubt that the Lord gave it a distinct place as a commandment, yet they absurdly tear in two the Tenth Commandment about not coveting the possessions of one's neighbor. Besides, their division of the commandments was unknown in a purer age.[28]

In the preface of the Decalogue leading into the first commandment—"I am Jehovah, your God, who brought you out of the Land of

24. *Inst.* 3.3.4 (Beveridge's translation).
25. *Inst.* 2.8.4.
26. *Inst.* 2.8.2.
27. *Inst.* 2.8.12.
28. *Inst.* 2.8.12.

Egypt, out of the house of bondage. You shall have no other gods before my face" (Exod 20:2–3)—Calvin accentuates that the identity of God is inseparable from God's operations. God's essence is beyond us; God is to be known in the redemptive act he does for the people of Israel and their posterity. What Luther took as the first commandment, Calvin argues, ought to occupy "the place of the preface" ("I am Jehovah, your God") to the Decalogue.[29] The name "Jehovah" indicates God's authority, rule, and lordship over his creation. The first commandment extols the majesty of God, exalting the Lord as preeminent among his people and as having authority over them. As law, it first underscores God himself as the one who is vested with the right to command and receive obedience due him; as gospel, God draws the people to himself with sweetness by declaring himself as their God, sealed with a promise: "I am their God, and they shall be my people" (Jer 31:33).[30] This preface flows into the first commandment, where God declares who he is, namely, "You shall have no other gods before my face" (Exod 20:3)—meaning he alone is God, whose mighty act of redemption and sweet promise of blessed life is the ground of our sole trust in him.

Calvin then links the first to the second commandment, where he declares how God is to be worshiped. "Therefore in the law, after having claimed for himself alone the glory of deity, when he would teach what worship he approves or repudiates, God soon adds, 'You shall not make for yourself a graven image, nor any likeness' [Exod 20:4]. By these words he restrains our waywardness from trying to represent him by any visible image."[31] God has established for us a proper way to worship him and made us conform to it. True worship thus must adhere to "this principle: God's glory is corrupted by an impious falsehood, whenever any form is attached to him."[32] The proscription of images is closely and causally linked to the human mind, which Calvin describes as "a perpetual factory of idols."[33] From this, Calvin sees the danger in the corrupted mind to construct images and convert them into objects of worship. Calvin is not entirely against images, sculpture, and painting, which he regards as gifts of God. But Calvin warns against using them perversely, saying "only those things are to be sculpted and painted which the eyes are capable of

29. *Inst.* 2.8.12.

30. *Inst.* 2.8.14.

31. *Inst.* 1.11.1.

32. *Inst.* 1.11.1.

33. *Inst.* 1.11.8.

seeing: let not God's majesty, which is far above the perception of the eyes, be debased through unseemly representations."[34] Humanly devised means and superstitious rites are excluded from the spiritual worship ordained by God. Piety is idolatrous if it is directed to anyone or anything except the true God. Calvin cites Isaiah, who "teaches that God's majesty is sullied by an unfitting and absurd fiction, when the incorporeal is made to resemble corporeal matter, the invisible a visible likeness, the spirit an inanimate object, the immeasurable a puny bit of wood, stone, or gold [Isa. 40:18–29 and 41:7, 29; 45:9; 46:5–7]."[35] All visible forms of God are diametrically opposed to his nature; they contradict God's majesty. Every pictorial representation of God, Calvin opines, commits an Athenian error that Paul concedes as a domestication of divine transcendence (Acts 17). Furthermore, not to have strange gods is not to transfer to another that which is rightly his. To properly worship, for Calvin, is to render wholly to God the things that belong to him: "adoration" rendered to God's greatness; "trust," reposing in him and attributing to him all wisdom, righteousness, might, truth, and goodness; "invocation," "the habit of our mind" to resort to his faithful help as our sole support; and "thanksgiving," a heart of gratitude applied to him for all good things.[36]

Both comforting and threatening words are part of Calvin's explanation of the second commandment ("I . . . am jealous, visiting the iniquity of the fathers upon the children, unto the third and the fourth generation of those who hate my name, but showing mercy to thousands of those who love me and keep my commandments"; Exod 20:5–6). God is "jealous," and assumes the character of a true and faithful husband who cannot bear any partner but demands love and conjugal chastity.[37] God emits intensely a burning jealousy when we transfer our allegiance to another. He will vindicate his majesty and glory against the profanation of worship with graven images. Law and promise interplay: The law condemns those who disobey the commandment, placing them under God's wrath for a short period; mercy consoles and is lavishly poured out upon those who obey it for an extended period, just as he promised. The

34. *Inst.* 1.11.12.

35. *Inst.* 1.11.1.

36. *Inst.* 2.8.16. Although Calvin's *Institutes* has established the basic theological framework for worship, the fuller statement is found in the 1543 apologetic treatise *The Necessity of Reforming the Church*, addressed to the Emperor Charles V, where Calvin exhorted all Christians to assume as their primary duty to practice pure worship. See Calvin, *The Necessity of Reforming the Church*, in *Tracts*, 123–234.

37. *Inst.* 1.8.18.

relation between God's wrath and his mercy is succinctly borne out in his commentary on Deuteronomy 5:9–10, where Calvin holds that the glory of God "principally shines" in his mercy that lies hidden in his wrath; this is because God's nature is mercy.

> Now by that he shows what is better explained in other texts of Scripture, that he is slow to anger, inclined toward mercy, patient, and that, if his anger burns for a minute, his loving-kindness is for life and permanent. Thus there you have the true character of God; that he only wants to draw men in all gentleness and does so through his goodness. When he punishes them it is almost [*quasi*] against his nature. Not that it is any more improper for God to punish than it is for him to be gracious, but he wishes to show us that his goodness is much greater, and in brief, that he is not harsh. Rather he only wants to open his heart to us if we will permit him. In fact, he wills to be known as good and merciful; and it is in that that his glory principally shines.[38]

The third commandment—"You shall not take the name of Jehovah your God in vain" (Exod 20:7)—has to do with hallowing the majesty of his name. Our thoughts and words should bear witness to the honor of his sacred name. We must not rashly abuse or defame his holy word, sacraments, or his works. Calvin saw this commandment as having a specific reference to several kinds of oath.[39] First, the false oath is a profanation of God's holy name. When God is despoiled of his truth, God ceases to be God. Second, the needless oath, one that is taken in vain, cheapens God's name and deprives him of its proper glory. Third, the extrajudicial oath or private oath must be made "soberly, with holy intent, reverently, and in necessary circumstances, supported as they are both by reason and by examples."[40] An oath serves to either exalt the Lord's name or edify a brother.

Calvin devotes special attention to the fourth commandment, "Remember to keep holy the Sabbath Day" (Exod 20:8). Most of the early church fathers held that the Jewish Sabbath had been abolished and was replaced by the Lord's Day. This understanding, Calvin argues, only went half way. "We must go deeper"[41]—and he then proposes three purposes for the keeping of this commandment. First, the rest of the seventh day

38. *STC*, 78.
39. *Inst.* 2.8.24–27.
40. *Inst.* 2.8.27.
41. *Inst.* 2.8.28.

refers to the spiritual rest God gave to the people of Israel. Believers abstain from their works and permit God to work in them. Second, God intends a specific day be allotted for worship, meditation, and training in piety. Third, this was also given to servants and those under authority so that they could have some respite from labor. The ceremonial and legal ordinance of the Jews had been abrogated at the coming of Christ.[42] *Christ* is the fulfillment of the Sabbath, not the day Sunday. "The purpose and fulfillment of that true rest, represented by the ancient Sabbath, lies in the Lord's resurrection. Hence, by the very day that brought the shadows to an end, Christians are warned not to cling to the shadow rite. Nor do I cling to number 'seven' so as to bind the church in subjection to it."[43] Calvin does not object using other solemn days for worship and rest, provided that it does not involve superstitious observance. We worship on Sunday, not because this is legalistically required by the fourth commandment, but for the sake of "decorum, order, and peace in the church."[44] The chief point, for Calvin, is that a fixed day or days be set aside for "the hearing of God's word, the administration of the sacraments, and for public prayers."[45]

This commandment expresses the basic pattern of the Christian life that begins in Christ and is completed at the last day. The Sabbath was given as a sign by which Israel may recognize God as "their sanctifier."[46] It is the outward sign of the inward reality—namely, their sanctification. Likewise, God grants us the "blessed rest"[47] from all activities of our own contriving so that he may work in us to restore the image of God through Christ, the substance and fulfillment of this commandment. Meditation on God's work of recreating is not a passive act. We must yield our will, our heart, repudiate all fleshly desires, and allow God to mortify us. In Christ we become increasingly aware of the reality of our having died to the old Adam by being buried with him in baptism. The number seven in Scripture denotes "perfection"; therefore, Calvin argues that the Lord through the seventh day has designed for his people the coming consummation of his Sabbath at the end of time.[48] The rest thus is God's means of

42. *Inst.* 2.8.31.
43. *Inst.* 2.8.34.
44. *Inst.* 2.8.33.
45. *Inst.* 2.8.34.
46. *Inst.* 2.8.29.
47. *Inst.* 2.8.30.
48. *Inst.* 2.8.30.

making them aspire to this completion by a constant meditation on the Sabbath throughout life, until the Last Day when we are filled with the life of God. Here we "begin our blessed rest in him: daily we make fresh progress in it" until we enter the perfect rest, where all warfare with the flesh cease, and God shall be "all in all" (1 Cor 15:28).[49]

Calvin stresses the need to meditate on God's glorious powers in the garment of the world at every moment of their lives, but especially on the Sabbath.

> And certainly God took the seventh day for his own and hallowed it, when the creation of the world was finished, that he might keep his servants free from every care, for the consideration of the beauty, excellence, and fitness of his works. There is indeed no moment which should be allowed to pass in which we are not attentive to the consideration of the wisdom, power, goodness, and justice of God in his admirable creation and government of the world.[50]

Through contemplating the beautiful fabric of the world, we are drawn by its majestic beauty and abundant riches not only to enjoy it, but also increasingly turn to God with reverence, trust, and love.

The dialectical tension between threat and promise occurs in Calvin's explanation of the fifth commandment, "Honor your father and your mother that you may be long-lived on the land which Jehovah your God shall give you" (Exod 20:12). "This is the first commandment with a promise" (Eph 6:2). Yet the promise was given to the whole law, not confined to any particular commandment.[51] Calvin applies majesty to creatures, constituting them as the instruments of divine power for the preservation of the created order. Earthly parents are where God's majesty hides to rule the family; Calvin notes, "But if piety towards an earthly father was a virtue so excellent, and so worthy of praise; with how much greater devotedness of piety ought the sacred majesty of God to be worshipped?"[52] Honoring earthly fathers is "a step toward honoring the highest Father."[53] To ensure that this commandment be carried out, God added a terrifying threat, that an inevitable curse and divine judgment

49. *Inst.* 2.8.30.

50. *Comm. Exod.* 20:8, CTS 4:437.

51. *Inst.* 2.8.37.

52. *Comm. Gen.* 9:23, CTS 1:303.

53. *Inst.* 2.8.38.

would come upon all stubborn and disobedient children. We are to honor the parents or superiors whom God has placed over us. The honor in view comprises three parts: "reverence, obedience, and gratefulness."[54] And the Lord Jesus confirms all aspects:

> The Lord confirms the first—reverence—when he enjoins that one who curses his father or mother be killed [Exod 21:17; Lev. 20:9; Prov. 20:20]; there he punishes contempt and abuse. He confirms the second—obedience—when he decrees the penalty of death for disobedience and rebellious children [Deut. 21:18–21]. What Christ says in Matt., ch. 15, refers to the third kind of honor, gratefulness; it is of God's commandment that we do good to our parents [vs. 4–6].[55]

On the sixth commandment, "You shall not kill" (Exod 20:13), Calvin teaches that God has united all humanity into one so that each person can seek the safety of all.[56] He finds a twofold basis in Scripture of considering this commandment under the rubric of the unity of humanity. First, all humanity is created in God's image, and we are to reverence that image in them, thereby impelling us to hold our neighbors sacred.[57] Second, since all humanity is one flesh, we embrace our flesh in them, and in so doing, we refrain from evil, both in intent and action, and seek only their preservation.[58]

Though this commandment applies universally to all, it finds concrete expression in the special bond among the members of the body of Christ. The sacrament of the Lord's Supper fosters mutual love for each other, since we are made completely one with Christ and are partakers of one body. Accordingly, Augustine often calls this sacrament "the bond of love."[59] The linkage of this commandment to the sacrament of the Lord's Supper means we live not in ourselves but in Christ, from whom we receive many benefits that now flow from us to others. The exhortation to love is a derivative of the soteriological priority of union with Christ through which we have one common father and are members of one body without separation, with whom we share our gifts and powers

54. *Inst.* 2.8.36.

55. *Inst.* 2.8.36.

56. *Inst.* 2.8.40.

57. *Inst.* 2.8.40.

58. *Inst.* 2.8.40.

59. Augustine, *John's Gospel* 26. 13 (MPL 35. 1613; tr. NPNF 7. 172), as cited in *Inst.* 4.17.38, 1415n27.

for the common good of our neighbors.[60] We are to keep this thought in our mind, that whatever is done to any member, whether loving or hating, is done to Christ in him.[61] Self-renunciation is required in order to perform works of love. "Unless you give up all thought of self and, so to speak, get out of yourself, you will accomplish nothing here."[62] The sum of the Christian life consists in being the stewards of all God has given us, by which we are to love all from the heart and apply ourselves to the common upbuilding of the church.

The purpose of the seventh commandment, "You shall not commit adultery" (Exod 20:14), is this: because God commends modesty and purity, we must remove ourselves from all uncleanness, and regulate all aspects of our life with chastity and continence.[63] Marriage has been ordained as "a necessary remedy" to unbridled lust.[64] Calvin cites instances of strengthening the life of modesty and chastity. For example, if one aspires to obedience, he should not let his heart burn with evil lust within, nor should he want his eyes to wantonly run into impure desires. Most importantly, Calvin admonishes his readers not to dwell primarily on the commandment itself, but the Lawgiver, the one who owns us completely and thus rightly demands of us integrity of character and actions.[65]

The eighth commandment, "You shall not steal" (Exod 20:15), enjoins us to strive to protect and promote the well-being and interests of others.[66] Negatively, we are forbidden to crave what is not ours; positively, we are commanded to assist every creature to keep what is his. Theft, fraud, deceit, and all illegal means employed to acquire goods are forbidden. We must be prepared to give up something of our own and extend our abundance to those we see pressed by difficult circumstances. Citizens are to hold all rulers and government authorities in honor and obey the laws and commands. They should conduct their lives with reverential fear toward God, the supreme Judge, to whom they must give an account of their services. The ministers of the gospel must faithfully instruct their sheep both in teaching and living. The flock, in return, receive their shepherds as God's messengers, honor them highly, and

60. *Inst.* 3.7.5.

61. *Inst.* 4.17.38.

62. *Inst.* 3.7.5.

63. *Inst.* 2.8.41.

64. *Inst.* 2.8.41.

65. *Inst.* 2.8.44.

66. *Inst.* 2.8.46.

provide for their necessities. Parents are to nourish their children and embrace them with gentleness and kindness; children owe obedience to their parents. While youth reverences old age, the aged gently guide the younger with their wisdom and experience. Servants obey their masters from the heart; masters must recognize the servants as their brothers and their co-servants under the Lord of heaven. In whatever rank and station God has placed us, whether it be as rulers or citizens, pastors or sheep, masters or servants, parents or children, old or young, we must render our duties of love as if they were done to God.

The ninth commandment, "You shall not be a false witness against your neighbor" (Exod 20:16), enjoins us to affirm the truth and protect the integrity of the name and possessions of our neighbors.[67] What God opposes is not merely evil tongues but also evil intent. This commandment also condemns thoughtless speech, sly suspicion, hateful accusation, exaggerated flattery, and bitter provocation under the pretense of joke.[68] In sum, in true fear and love of God, and by a thoughtful concern for equity and humanity, we do the utmost to keep safe our neighbor's good name by sound judgment.

The tenth commandment, "You shall not covet" (Exod 20:17), enjoins us to "banish from our hearts all desires contrary to love."[69] The rest of the commandments prohibit committing sinful acts, but the disposition to love in this commandment reaches deeper than mere act into the heart that conceives it. Calvin differentiates between "intent" that involves a deliberate "consent" of will, when tempted by lust, and coveting that does not entail such consent, when prickled by perverse objects.[70] In any case, Calvin warns against the destructive power of covetousness, which, if not curbed by the law, "destroys wretched men so secretly that he does not feel its fatal stab."[71] God wills that our whole heart be so filled with arduous love that not one bit of it be given over to ill imaginings. The heart that nurtures covetousness is rid of love. The real point of this commandment, as of all the rest, is simply love as the rule and goal of our motives and actions.

67. *Inst.* 2.8.47.

68. *Inst.* 2.8.48.

69. *Inst.* 2.8.49.

70. *Inst.* 2.8.49.

71. *Inst.* 2.7.6.

## THE SECOND (PRESERVATIVE) USE OF THE LAW: GOD'S PROVIDENCE AND CIVIL GOVERNMENT

The law serves as "a halter to check the raging and otherwise limitlessly ranging lusts of the flesh."[72] Like the first use, the civil use applies to believers in their pre- and post-conversion states. The children of God, before they are called to faith and in so far as they live in the old flesh, are, for fear of divine vengeance, "restrained [by the law] at least from outward wantonness."[73] Calvin differentiates between two kinds of fear: one is filial fear, as a child fears out of love for his beloved father; the other is "a violent fear"[74] that trains people in godliness. In Calvin's assessment,

> Therefore, if [God] does not immediately regenerate those whom he has destined to inherit his Kingdom, until the time of his visitation, he keeps them safe through the works of the law under fear [cf. 1 Pet 2:12]. This is not that chaste and pure fear such as ought to be in his sons, but a fear useful in teaching them true godliness according to their capacity. . . . For all who have at any time groped about in ignorance of God will admit that it happened to them in such a way that the bridle of the law restrained them in some fear and reverence toward God until, regenerated by the Spirit, they began wholeheartedly to love him.[75]

Unbelievers obey the laws of the state, not because of a genuine love of civil righteousness and a concern for the welfare of their neighbors but because of fear of punishment. "All who are unregenerate feel—some more obscurely, some more openly—that they are not drawn to obey the law voluntarily, but impelled by a violent fear do so against their will and despite their opposition to it."[76] They manifest obedience to the law outwardly, but inwardly their hearts are repugnant toward it. Even so, it profits them to experience the violent fear of judgment under the law through which they are trained in obedience, so that "when they are called [to faith], they are not utterly untutored and uninitiated in discipline as if it were something unknown."[77] Lusts would have corrupted

72. *Inst.* 2.7.10.
73. *Inst.* 2.7.10.
74. *Inst.* 2.7.10.
75. *Inst.* 2.7.11.
76. *Inst.* 2.7.10.
77. *Inst.* 2.7.10.

the soul and led it into "forgetfulness and contempt of God" had God the Holy Spirit not opposed it with law, the remedy.[78] The law prevents the lust of the flesh from reigning above the Spirit so that God's righteousness might increase.[79] This restraint thus is an expression of God's providential care, which preserves the created order from utter ruin. Those who are still unregenerate profit from the restraint of the law through which they produce external righteousness. Even pagans recognize the laws of the society are necessary for the preservation of order and peace against the fury of the wicked.

## Natural and Civil Law: Not Effaced but Preserved

Civil law, following natural law, functions positively by promoting true piety toward God and justice among people. In Calvin's estimation, "the moral law is nothing else than a testimony of natural law and of that conscience which God has engraved upon the minds of men. Consequently, the entire scheme of this equity . . . has been prescribed in it. Hence this equity alone is the goal and rule and limit of all laws."[80] Conscience exists in the closest relationship to natural law, which has the sense of equity as its proper content. We all have the natural ability to distinguish sufficiently between just and unjust in such a way that no one can take refuge under the pretext of ignorance. "The recognition of such sense of equity," Helm contends, "is surely strong evidence . . . of his recognition of natural law, . . . which forms part of a person's natural knowledge of God."[81] Like the sense of divinity inscribed in us, the knowledge of the equity and justice is preserved in our conscience and never effaced by the fall.[82] Augustine of Hippo once wrote about the sense of justice, saying, "We have another and far superior sense, belonging to the inner man, by which we perceive what things are just, and what unjust,—just by means of an intelligible idea, unjust by the want of it."[83] The seed of natural restraint, like the natural principle of equity, is implanted in all. Despite the urge to overturn all laws or legal restraints, the "seed of political order" remains

78. *Inst.* 2.7.11.

79. *Inst.* 2.7.11.

80. *Inst.* 4.20.16.

81. Helm, *Ideas*, 363.

82. *Inst.* 2.2.13.

83. Augustine, *City of God*, 11.27.2.

operative, proving that no one "is without the light of reason."[84] This seed achieves, Mary Lane Potter summarizes adequately, four different kinds of restraints—namely,

> the restraint of impiety by the continuing existence of the sense of divinity (*sensus divinitatis*), whereby God assures that the honor due him is maintained minimally in all cultures; the restraint of personal passions by the internal witness of the conscience, whereby God assures that human beings do not descend from the glory of their creation to the level of brute beasts; the restraint of improper familial and social arrangements by the laws of nature, whereby God assures that the yoke of obedience of inferiors to their superiors is not cast off completely; and the restraint of injustice by the natural sense of equity and civil laws, whereby God assures that a certain fairness is preserved among persons in society.[85]

The innate sense of justice is the basis of natural restraints through which all can assent to civil laws. This natural endowment is given to all without distinction, pious or otherwise; it is a free gift of God's beneficence, which safeguards against the collapse of sociopolitical order. Civil law assumes various forms; all of them are comprehended under the natural sense of equity and restraints. It deserves proper regard and must be wholly received with gratitude as "the peculiar grace of God."[86]

Calvin distinguishes between the judicial, ceremonial, and moral laws of Moses. Judicial law in the Torah addresses how Israel as a nation should conduct herself.[87] It may be removed, but the "perpetual rule of love" still remains.[88] Ceremonial laws address how Israel should worship prior to the advent of Jesus Christ. Because Christ fulfilled the shadows in the ancient sacrifices by being the true light, they are no longer operative. "Therefore, as ceremonial laws could be abrogated while piety remained safe and unharmed, so too, when these judicial laws were taken away, the perpetual duties and precepts of love could still remain."[89] Moral law in the Decalogue addresses how people should live in accordance with God's will and character; it still remains in force. The seed of law is

84. *Inst.* 2.2.13.
85. Potter, "Whole Office," 127.
86. *Inst.* 2.2.14.
87. *Inst.* 4.20.15.
88. *Inst.* 4.20.15.
89. *Inst.* 4.20.15.

universal, in that human beings are by nature able to make law, "without teacher or lawgiver."[90] Though every nation is free to make its own laws fitted to itself, these must correspond to the perpetual duty of love, the very purpose of law. Civil law may differ in form, not in purpose; it does not operate on its own but is governed by the moral law, just as is the natural law.

## Two Governments: Civil and Spiritual

Calvin's discussion of civil government falls into three parts: the magistrate, who protects and guards the laws; the law by which he governs; and the subjects, who are governed by the laws and obey their magistrate.[91] The civil magistrates are mandated by God, are holy, and are wholly God's representatives, acting as his vicegerents.[92] Calvin states, "Man is under a twofold government"[93]—civil and spiritual. "Distinction without separation"[94] comprehends the two realms in which God rules. While the former encompasses the earthly government, household responsibilities, all mechanical skills, and the liberal arts, the latter pertains to the heavenly knowledge of God and of his will.[95] The Christian finds herself in each sphere of existence and is obligated to exhibit the shape of Christian's dual membership on earth. The kingdom of God and the kingdom of this world are distinguished; one produces piety and true righteousness, the other produces external peace and prevents evil deeds. Yet the state is no less than the church, as it is an ordained institution through which God providentially cares for the preservation of human life and maintenance of social order. In so far as the magistrate's administration of force and punishment is sanctioned by divine command, it is compatible with piety. Princes and other rulers are ministers through whom God exercises his wrath and very judgments against wrongdoers (Rom 13:4). This is contrary to the Anabaptists, who regarded the magistrate's office as "carnal"[96] and thus rejected its sword and its benefits. On Acts 5:29,

90. *Inst.* 2.2.13.

91. *Inst.* 4.20.3.

92. *Inst.* 4.20.4.

93. *Inst.* 4.20.1.

94. Calvin, "To the Admiral de Coligny" (Geneva, April 16), in *Selected Works*, eds. Beveridge and Bonnet, 7:176–77.

95. *Inst.* 2.2.13.

96. *Inst.* 4.20.2, 1487n7.

"We must obey God rather than men," Calvin counsels that we should render an obedience God requires to the political powers, even when we suffer under the "impious edicts" of ungodly kings rather than compromise our piety before the King of Kings.[97]

> But we must, in the meantime, be very careful not to despise or violate that authority of magistrates, full of venerable majesty, which God has established by the weightiest decrees, even though it may reside with the most unworthy men, who defile it as much as they can with their own wickedness. For, if the correction of unbridled despotism is the Lord's to avenge, let us not at once think that it is entrusted to us, to whom no command has been given except to obey and suffer.[98]

Both civil and spiritual order have the same aim: to reestablish the created order distorted by the fall. Jeannine Olson comments, "Calvin thinks that both church and state" are God's remedy to the fall.[99] Civil authorities and ecclesiastical authorities are complementary; they work together to restrain evil and its vices and restore order. In Calvin's words, "The magistrate ought by punishment and physical restraint to cleanse the church of offenses, so the ministers of the Word in turn ought to help the magistrate in order that not so many may sin. Their functions ought to be so joined that each serves to help, not hinder, the other."[100] Zeal for the kingdom of God does not negate proper regard for civil justice and order. The broken order may be restored either through a crucified life at the personal level or the well-governed state at the sociopolitical level. In any case, the goal is the coming of the kingdom, as in the Lord's Prayer (Matt 6:10). Calvin teaches, "The substance of this prayer is that God would enlighten the world by the light of his Word, would form the hearts of men unto the service of his justice by the inspiration (*afflatu*) of his Spirit, and by his guidance would restore to order whatever has been dispersed (*dissapatum*) in the world."[101] Were God not to govern human schemes and dispositions, there would be complete disorder and chaos. The kingdom of God comes when God's reign takes effect in the lives of

97. *Inst.* 4.20.32, 1520n56.

98. *Inst.* 4.20.31.

99. Olson, "Church and Society," 199.

100. *Inst.* 4.11.3.

101. *Comm. Matt* 6:10, CO 45:197, as cited in Hesselink, *Concept*, 248.

individual people, and when God overthrows his enemies and subjugates them, with Satan as their head, under his authority (Heb 10:13).

If the church is God's remedy to the world's disorder, then it raises a question: "Was there a time when the two kingdoms were not?" Ernest Troeltsch argues that, for Calvin, "the state in particular . . . is never regarded as a mere antidote to the fallen state and a penalty for evil, but is always chiefly regarded as a good and holy institution, appointed by God himself."[102] Along the same lines, John McNeill argues, "In [Calvin's] warm admiration for political government, he does not for a moment regard it as a realm of mere secularity. It is a God-given, a 'benevolent provision' for man's good, and for it men should give God thanks. The function of the magistrate is a 'sacred ministry,' and to regard it as incompatible with religion is an insult to God."[103] Civil authorities are not necessitated by the fall; they are simply part of the creaturely order that works good in human life. Calvin writes, "It behooves us reverently to regard and respect the political order, because it has been appointed by God for the common benefit of mankind."[104] Establishment of the magistrates in itself is, Milner notes, "productive of order."[105] "The notions of tyranny and compulsion," he continues, "must be referred to the fall and its consequences, but government itself, the state, is not made necessary by the fall."[106] Civil kingdom is not a postlapsarian solution to the fall; it coexists with spiritual order from the beginning of the world. It does more than merely restrain all evils; it preserves the people whom God has created. The political order is derived from the *ordinatis Dei*; Calvin writes, "For although even the beasts of the field profit by political order, yet we know government to have been ordained by God for the benefit of man."[107]

The incisive question—"Was there a time when the two kingdoms were not?"—can be resolved depending on the subject to whom civil government is applied, just as the usage of the law is related to the subject to whom it is addressed. In the prelapsarian state, where sin had not occurred, the law was not opposed to the promise. The antithesis between law and gospel occurs in the postlapsarian state; hence the subject to

102. Troeltsch, *Social Teaching*, 613, 898, as cited in Milner, *Church*, 45n1.

103. McNeill, "Introduction," in Calvin, *Political Duty*, ed. McNeill, xiii.

104. *Comm. 1 Pet.* 2:14, CO 55:245.

105. Milner, *Church*, 30.

106. Milner, *Church*, 30.

107. *Comm. Dan.* 4:10–15, CO 40:657, as cited in Milner, *Church*, 30.

whom the law is applied changes—that is, from a righteous person to a sinner. The wicked incur political force against their evil deeds while the righteous are praised for doing right. The dignity of civil order is not derived from its negative function of restraining evil, but from its being a created dispensation appointed by God for the common good of human life. Peace and order proceed from civil governments, just as food does from the earth.[108] This truth is applicable to all governments.

> God appointed the existence of governments (*imperia*) in the world for this purpose—to be like trees, on whose fruits mortals feed and under whose shadow they rest. Hence this ordination of God (*ordinatio Dei*) flourishes, because tyrants, however they are removed from the exercise of just and moderate dominion, whether they wish it or not are compelled to be like trees; for it is better to live under the cruelest tyranny than without any government at all.[109]

## THE THIRD (RESTORATIVE) USE OF THE LAW: ITS PRINCIPAL USE

For Melanchthon, the second, accusatory or theological, use of the law is its "proper and principal use."[110] Likewise, Luther employs the same terminology in his 1535 *Commentary on Galatians*, but further calls it "the true . . . most important and the highest" use of the law.[111] However, for Calvin, the "third use of the law" is its "principal use."[112] The first two functions are basically negative: They either restrain, condemn, or highlight the nature and power of sin. But the third use is positive, and finds its place in those whom God has brought to faith and in hearts already seized by the Spirit of God.[113] Calvin magnifies the third use in his *Institutes*: The chief purpose of the law is "the fulfillment of righteousness to form human life to the archetype of divine purity."[114] God's character is so clearly revealed in the law that if anyone obeys what has been

108. *Comm. 1 Tim.* 2:2, CO 52:266, as cited in Milner, *Church*, 30n4.

109. *Comm. Dan.* 4:10–16, CO 40:657, as cited in Milner, *Church*, 30.

110. Melanchthon, *Loci Communes*, *CR* 21, col. 405.

111. LW 26:91, 310–13, 345, 348; WA 40:168, 481–83, 528, 533.

112. *Inst.* 2.7.12; Hesselink, *Concept*, 251.

113. *Inst.* 2.7.12.

114. *Inst.* 2.8.51.

commanded there, he will reflect God's image newly engraved in the Christian life.[115] The law thus is the instrument of divine power, through which God himself conforms us to his image.

The law comprehends not only the Ten Commandments, which teach us how to lead a godly and righteous life, but also "the form of religion handed down through Moses," which has God as Father to Israel in Christ.[116] The law was added some four hundred years later to the Abrahamic covenant. This addition was, Calvin writes, not "to lead the chosen people away from Christ; but rather to hold their mind in readiness until his coming."[117] The ancient patriarchs embraced Christ just as much as we do. For Christ is reflected twice in the Old Testament, under the "double mirror," as a priest under the tribe of Levi and a king under the Davidic reign.[118] Calvin concedes that the law is intrinsic to God's covenant of grace and is beneficial to those adopted as God's children. The Mosaic covenant is, to borrow Hesselink's phrase, "the cradle"[119] of the law. It is, for Calvin,

> a gratuitous covenant . . . [that] flows from God's mercy; it does not originate in either the worthiness or the merits of men. It has its cause, stability, execution, and completion solely in the grace of God. Whenever God's covenant is mentioned, his clemency, goodness, and inclination to love is also added. . . . God's covenant depends upon and flows from his grace.[120]

The Sinaitic covenant incorporates the law as an integral part of that covenant of grace. Rather than undermining the gracious character of the covenant, the law establishes it, and ratifies it. "For nothing was better adapted to confirm the grace of God than the majesty which was displayed in the promulgation of the law."[121] Thus, law and grace originally are not antithetical but complementary. Just as the gospel is replete with grace, so is the law "graced with the covenant of free adoption."[122] "Bare

115. *Inst.* 2:8.51.

116. *Inst.* 2.7.1.

117. *Inst.* 2.7.1.

118. *Inst.* 2.7.2.

119. Hesselink, *Concept*, 89.

120. *Comm. Dan.* 9:4, CO 41:133–34.

121. *Comm. Deut.* 33:2, CO 25:383.

122. *Inst.* 2.7.2.

law in the narrow sense"[123] is no vessel of grace; it is a dead letter that kills, for it is abstracted from the grace of the covenant of free adoption. Calvin argues that Paul was sometimes compelled to speak of the "bare law" negatively, as that which kills, accuses, or crushes, in order to refute the false teachers who misused the law to attain righteousness.[124] Otherwise, the law is a gift of God. The "whole law" in a broad sense includes not only the commandments, but the whole grace of God as the basis of Israel's adoption.[125] Both the law and the gospel are identical in substance except that the gospel differs from it "in clarity of manifestation."[126] The gospel does not abolish the entire law so as to introduce another way of salvation, but clearly manifests the same Jesus as set forth before Israel. It fulfilled what the law had promised, bringing into clarity what the law foreshadowed typologically. The covenant of law that God once established finally finds its ratification in the covenant of gospel, whose sole foundation is Jesus Christ.

Calvin distinguishes between the use of the law and its effects. He discerns a parallel between how the moral and ceremonial laws change because of the coming of Christ. The moral law is "not abolished in use but in effect," for it no longer binds our consciences to the bonds of the law because of Christ.[127] To the extent we are seized by Christ, to that extent we are free from the curse brought by the law; the former as cause leads to the latter as effect. Helm writes, "So the moral law now no longer condemns us, because of Christ. Though it retains the power to condemn, its use is not to condemn, but to point to Christ."[128] Partee writes, "Ceremonial laws, vain exercises in themselves, [are] now 'abrogated not in effect but only in use.'"[129] This is because Christ is the end of the law for the salvation of every believer (Rom 10:14). The ancient sacrifices of the Old Testament were no "empty show," for "the power of Christ's death and resurrection had . . . been displayed therein."[130] The ceremonies in the old covenant are "a sure pledge of God's fatherly favor," which "would have been but shadow had it not been grounded in the grace of Christ,

123. *Inst.* 2.7.2.

124. *Inst.* 2.7.2.

125. *Comm. Ezek.* 20:12, CTS 12:299.

126. *Inst.* 2.9.4.

127. Helm, *Ideas*, 351.

128. Helm, *Ideas*, 351.

129. Partee, *Theology*, 138; *Inst.* 2.7.16.

130. *Inst.* 2.7.16.

in whom one finds perfect and everlasting stability."[131] The effect thus is not abrogated, because it is one with that of Calvary—namely, the atonement for sins already promised in the ancient sacrifices. The rites of the law are useful before the advent of Christ; their function ceases because Christ, who in abolishing their use by his death has "sealed their force and effect."[132] Christ has brought into clarity what would otherwise be shadowy.

> Consequently Paul, to prove their observance not only superfluous but also harmful, teaches that they are shadows whose substance exists for us in Christ [Col. 2:17]. Thus we see that in their abolition the truth shines forth better than if they, still far off and as if veiled, figured the Christ, who has already plainly revealed himself. . . . Not that the holy patriarchs were without the preaching that contains the hope of salvation and of eternal life, but that they only glimpsed from afar and in shadowy outline what we see today in full daylight.[133]

In David's meditation on the law (Ps 119), Calvin deduces that not only did David grasp in the law "the precepts [commands] but also its accompanying promise of grace."[134] The Mediator he apprehended in the law "sweetens what is bitter."[135] Any abstraction of law from grace converts law into a dead letter, and misery and bitterness are the outcome. In the law, we, like David, apprehend the Mediator, from whom we experience pure delight and sweetness. He shared the same inheritance as we do and a common salvation with us—this is because he, like us, possesses "the grace of the same Mediator."[136] The law is the object of David's veneration. On this theme, Calvin quotes Psalm 119, in which David "proclaims the great usefulness of the law: the Lord instructs by their reading of it those whom he inwardly instills with a readiness to obey."[137] Not that Paul rejects the law entirely—only its ability to bestow righteousness on believers. Paul thus expressly approves of David's praise of the law in Psalm 119, for the prophet David "does not speak of the dead letter that kills those who read it, but he comprehends the whole doctrine of the Law,

131. *Inst.* 2.7.16.
132. *Inst.* 2.7.16.
133. *Inst.* 2.7.16.
134. *Inst.* 2.7.12.
135. *Inst.* 2.7.12.
136. *Inst.* 2.10.1.
137. *Inst.* 2.7.12.

the chief part of which is the free covenant of salvation."[138] David here is not opposing the law to the gospel; instead, he upholds the grace of adoption promised in the law, which was sweeter to him than honey. Calvin writes, "For what would be less lovable than the law, if, with importuning and threatening alone, it troubled souls with fear, and distressed them through fright? David especially shows that in the law he apprehended the Mediator, without whom there is no delight or sweetness."[139]

The third use of the law thus is "a better and more excellent use,"[140] through which the saints attain that goal to which their efforts press forward. Once the "accidental function" of the law is ended, the law's curse and all forms of self-justification are ended too. Consequently, the law returns to its original and proper function of being an expression of the love of God and thus is profitable to Christian growth. The law no longer acts toward us as a rigorous law enforcer who demands absolute satisfaction of the law's requirements.[141] Godly living thus consists in nothing but a constant delight in the law (Ps 1:2). Christ liberates us from the yoke of law so that it no longer holds our consciences in bondage.[142] Believers in Christ are aroused with a disposition toward holiness and obedience through the law, which no longer terrifies or binds us.[143] The inclination to serve God with joyous obedience flows from the freedom with which we had already been furnished. Outside Christ, the law is the constraint of our freedom; in Christ, believers find freedom within the sphere of the law. Peter Wyatt expands,

> The Christian's freedom of conscience is not a freedom from law, excepting the canonical or humanly devised; it is a freedom for law, a freedom for willing and whole-hearted obedience to the One who is the law's giver and the faithful keeper of covenant. Love is the fulfilling of the law because the law commands nothing else than right relationships, relationships in which the aggrandizing self is humbled and remade through encounter with divine grace, and tested through self-denial for the sake of others.[144]

138. *Comm. Ps.* 119:103, as quoted in Potter, "Whole Office," 137.

139. *Inst.* 2.17.12.

140. *Inst.* 2.7.13.

141. *Inst.* 2.7.13.

142. *Comm. Gal.* 5:18, CO 48:351.

143. *Inst.* 3.14.4.

144. Wyatt, *Christ and Creation*, 150.

The law in Deuteronomy 32:46–47 was given to Israel as a guide for life, applicable to every generation. Calvin writes, "Even though the law of the Lord provides the finest and best-disposed method of ordering a man's life, it seemed good to the Heavenly Teacher to shape his people by an even more explicit plan to that rule which he had set forth in the law. Here, then, is the beginning of this plan: the duty of believers is 'to present their bodies to God as a living sacrifice, holy and acceptable to him,' and in this consists the lawful worship of him [Rom. 12:1]."[145] Only the justified, to whom righteousness has been given through faith, enjoy a freed conscience. Only through union with Christ can the justified serve God in willing obedience. Wyatt reflects, "Only incorporation into Christ (conformity to Christ through adoption) can issue in conduct on the pattern of Christ's obedience (conformity to the image of Christ)."[146] The law is "one everlasting and unchangeable rule to live by," and offers "a perfect pattern of righteousness."[147] And that "one everlasting and unchangeable rule" is nothing other than Jesus Christ, whose character is replicated by the Spirit in those who are seized by the sweetness of the Mediator apprehended in the law. David Clyde Jones sums up the matter well:

> The Lawgiver expresses his personal will by way of precepts or commandments, which in turn are reflective of who he is and his ideal purpose for human beings in their calling as his vicegerents in creation. Since God has delineated his own character in the law, it is unthinkable that it should not be observed by those whom he has graciously adopted as his children. Jesus is the full and final expression of the character and will of God; the law is thus personalized in Christ, the Mediator. Character is ultimately Christlikeness and is formed by the Holy Spirit through the means of grace and the practice of the truth.[148]

## Sanctification and the Law: The Work of the Holy Spirit

Regarding the grace of sanctification, the law occupies a normative function of shaping the believer in whom Christ's Spirit reigns. The emphasis on the positive activity of the law in the faithful is a direct implication of Calvin's doctrine of sanctification. The gospel "must penetrate the inmost

145. *Inst.* 3.7.1.

146. Wyatt, *Christ and Creation*, 150.

147. *Inst.* 2.7.13.

148. Jones, "Law and the Spirit," 313–14.

affections of the heart, take its seat in the soul, and affect the whole man a hundred times more deeply than the cold exhortations of the philosophers," so as to effect transformation of believers "into itself that it may not be unfruitful for us."[149] The Christian life is marked by a continual exercise on "godliness, for we have been called to sanctification."[150] Karl Barth, following Calvin, asserts, "We are not dealing with a second divine action which either takes place simultaneously with [justification], or precedes or follows it in time."[151] The Protestant view of justification by faith alone, for Calvin, does not lead to denying the holy life of the Spirit; for the two are one, as Christ is one. Those who are in Christ are sanctified by the Spirit that they may cultivate a life of purity through the law, "the perpetual rule of a good and holy life."[152]

Calvin considers repentance as "a singular gift of God."[153] Repentance flows from faith, as fruit from a tree. "Now the hatred of sin, which is the beginning of repentance, first gives us access to the knowledge of Christ, who reveals himself to none but poor and afflicted sinners, who groan, toil, are heavy-laden, hunger, thirst, and pine away with sorrow and misery."[154] The desire to live a holy life arises from being united to Christ, and as a result, he dies to himself that he may live for God. "For from 'mortification' we infer that we are not conformed to the fear of God and do not learn the rudiments of piety, unless we are violently slain by the sword of the Spirit and brought to nought. As if God had declared that for us to be reckoned among his children our common nature must die!"[155] Though sin ceases to reign in us, it never ceases to reside in us.[156] The old flesh continually produces vices, just as the furnace continually emits sparks.[157] Our corrupt nature needs continual purification by the law. Sanctification consists of a double process: the mortification of the old Adam, whereby we put to death all fleshly vices, and the vivification of the new person, whereby we are restored in the image of God, which

149. *Inst.* 3.6.4.

150. *Inst.* 3.19.2.

151. Barth, *CD*, 4/2:502.

152. *Comm. Gal.* 4:4, *CNTC* 11:74.

153. *Inst.* 3.3.21.

154. *Inst.* 3.3.20.

155. *Inst.* 3.3.8.

156. *Inst.* 3.3.11.

157. *Inst.* 4.15.11.

Paul understood as "true holiness and righteousness" (Eph 4:24).[158] These simultaneous activities are performed by the Holy Spirit, who works through the instrument of the law. Both happen to us by Christ's Spirit, who is not only "the Spirit of sanctification" (2 Thess 2:13), setting us apart from the world, but also "the root and seed of heavenly life in us," arousing in us the hope of a complete renewal.[159] Calvin conceives of the Christian life as a race or in terms of growth toward which we aspire. The weakness of the flesh may impede the progress of the new creature. But even our most heinous sins do not render our justified status in Christ ineffectual. In this regard, justification is "the main hinge on which religion turns."[160] Calvin's approach embraces the paradox of believers being saints and sinners simultaneously; as Van Vlastuin contends, "Christians continue to live from the absolute righteousness *extra nos* (outside us) of faith, and that focus on the contrasting aspect of the *in nobis* (in us) is always secondary and dependent on *extra nos*."[161]

The Christian has the law as our rule and the Holy Spirit as the source of power, by which she makes progress toward the goal.[162] By the Spirit, God inculcates in our hearts the love and cultivation of righteousness, daily making them anew; by his word, he bestirs in them a desire to seek after godliness, attaining the same renewal. A Christian seized by Christ's Spirit humbly confesses, "We are not our own: in so far as we can, let us therefore forget ourselves and all that is ours. . . . But the Christian philosophy bids reason give way to, submit and subject itself to, the Holy Spirit so that the man himself may no longer live but hear Christ living and reigning within him [Gal. 2:20]."[163] The Spirit who acts upon believers is "the helper," assisting them to act aright. We are acted upon by the Holy Spirit, so we act in accordance with God's will. Human agency is not removed from the movement of the Holy Spirit. From the word "help," Calvin infers that we must also act when God acts. Calvin quotes Augustine: "To will is of nature, but to will aright is of grace."[164] Calvin repudiates the concept of "co-operating grace," in that the human

158. *Inst.* 3.3.9.

159. *Inst.* 3.1.2.

160. *Inst.* 3.11.1.

161. Van Vlastuin, "Kuyper's Spirituality," 532.

162. *Inst.* 3.14.9.

163. *Inst.* 3.7.1.

164. Augustine, *Sermons* 156.9.9; 11.11–12 (MPL 38.855f.; tr. LF *Sermons* 2.769), as cited in *Inst.* 2.5.14, 335n29.

will in itself is cooperative; rather, he insists that the human will is deprived of powers to do good and freedom to choose the good, unless by the "operating grace" of the Holy Spirit.[165] Calvin acknowledges that "we have a will from nature; but as it is evil through the corruption of sin, it begins to be good only when it has been reformed by God."[166] The genuinely human response is not autonomous, totally independent of divine enablement. Human response is a gifted kind, contingent upon

> the rule of the Spirit to direct and regulate man's will. The Spirit cannot regulate without correcting, without reforming, without renewing. For this reason we say that the beginning of regeneration is to wipe out what is ours. Likewise, he cannot carry out these functions without moving, acting, impelling, bearing, keeping.[167]

All these actions arise from grace, and are wholly divine. Yet, Calvin adds, quoting Augustine, "Grace does not destroy the will but rather restores it."[168] Grace converts the will, directs it toward the good, and causes it to continue in the good. The same human action is at once that of God's grace, in the primary sense, and of human beings, in the derivative sense.[169] "Appealing to the work of the Holy Spirit," Partee writes, "God's action within human action is simultaneously that person's action."[170] God acts in us but in such a way that does not eradicate our will but empowers it, making our response authentically human. Calvin concludes, "We ourselves are fitly doing what God's Spirit is doing in us, even if our will contributes nothing of itself distinct from his grace. . . . For any mixture of the power of free will that men strive to mingle with God's grace is nothing but a corruption of grace. It is just as if one were to dilute wine with muddy, bitter water."[171] Our "doing," says Chester, is

165. *Inst.* 2.2.6.

166. *Comm. Phil.* 2:13, *CNTC* 11:254.

167. *Inst.* 2.5.15.

168. See Augustine, *On Grace and Free Will* 20.41 (MPL 44.905; tr. NPNF 5.461), as cited in *Inst.* 2.5.15, 335n30.

169. See Partee, *Theology*, 213, where he summarizes Butin's view: "Where Christian believers are concerned, there is no intrinsic incompatibility between attributing the same human actions primarily and fundamentally to God's grace, and yet concurrently (in a second and wholly derivative sense) to human beings." Cf. Butin, *Revelation*, 93, 127, 15–16, 76, 83, 78, 43, as cited in Partee, *Theology*, 213n44.

170. Partee, *Theology*, 213.

171. *Inst.* 2.5.15.

not to be identified as "meriting."[172] To clarify this distinction, Calvin, commenting on Philippians 2:13, writes, "This is the true artillery for destroying all haughtiness; this is the sword for killing all pride, when we hear that we are utterly nothing, and can do nothing, except through the grace of God alone. I mean supernatural grace, which comes forth from the Spirit of regeneration."[173] "Divine indwelling" is the ground of "human empowering"—both are of the same Spirit.[174] The Spirit indwells us to empower us that we might render obedience and glory to God.

> We confess that while through the intercession of Christ's righteousness God reconciles us to himself, and by free remission of sins accounts us righteous, his beneficence is at the same time joined with such a mercy that through his Holy Spirit he dwells in us and by his power the lusts of the flesh are each day more and more mortified; we are indeed sanctified, that is, consecrated to the Lord in the true purity of life, with our hearts formed to obedience to the law. The end is that our especial will may be to serve his will and by every means to advance his glory alone.[175]

In Christ, the rigor of the law is abolished, and those who are governed by the Spirit undergo the transformation of the epistemic perception of the law. "Then we now realize how agreeable Christ's yoke is, and how light His burden" (Matt 11:30).[176] "Our delight in the law," says Potter, "is directly proportionate to the gracious gift of the Spirit, which sanctifies our minds and makes them capable of relishing the taste of heavenly wisdom presented to us in the law."[177] The Spirit offers a new affective condition in which we find delight in the law and "long to obey God."[178] Through rebirth, "the hearts of the pious are so effectively governed by God that they follow Him with unwavering intention."[179] The Spirit creates a new inclination of the heart, and nourishes a constancy in the pursuit of righteousness. As justifying faith is not by works, yet not

172. Chester, *Reading Paul*, 294.

173. *Comm. Phil.* 2:13, *CNTC* 11:253–54.

174. Partee, *Theology*, 213: "The work of the Holy Spirit provides both divine indwelling and human empowering."

175. *Inst.* 3.14.9.

176. *Comm. Acts* 15:10, *CNTC* 7:41.

177. Potter, "Whole Office," 137.

178. *Inst.* 2.7.12.

179. *Inst.* 2.3.10.

without works, so also it is not by love, but through love. Calvin writes, "It is faith alone that first engenders love in us," not the reverse.[180] Faith, the action of the Spirit, has changed our affections and actions. We are moved by the abundant sweetness of grace to love God in return.

> But can the mind be aroused to taste the divine goodness without at the same time being wholly kindled to love God in return? For truly, that abundant sweetness which God has stored up for those who fear him cannot be known without at the same time powerfully moving us. And once anyone has been moved by it, it utterly ravishes him and draws him to itself.[181]

The appropriate conative condition is given so that we by the Spirit can restrain our will, not permitting its natural inclination to reign, but disposing it to godliness. We welcome the teaching of the law as not only "tolerable, but also pleasing and agreeable; and we must not refuse the bridle which restrains us gently, but does not drive us further than is expedient."[182] Believers profit from the law "that newness [contained in it] by which his image can be restored in us."[183] They embrace the law as "the best instrument," by which they are tutored with truth and confirmed in that truth so they might make fresh progress into the will of the Lord to which they aspire to obey.[184] Sin can so easily deceive and stealthily destroy us that we no longer feel its destructive force. Hence the Christian requires the law, by which she is made aware of sin's eroding effects and not be swayed by the evils of covetousness.

Calvin uses several negative images (bridle, spur, whip, sting) to speak of the law as the instrument of conformity to God's will. Quoting Calvin, "The law, so far as it is a rule of life, is a bridle which keeps us in the fear of the Lord, a spur to correct the slackness of our flesh, in short, so far as it is profitable for teaching, correcting, reproving, that believers may be instructed in every good work, is as much in force as ever, and remains intact."[185] "The law is to the flesh like a whip to an idle and balky

180. *Inst.* 3.2.41.

181. *Inst.* 3.2.41.

182. *Comm. Acts* 15:10, *CNTC* 7:41.

183. *Inst.* 3.6.1.

184. *Inst.* 2.7.12.

185. *Comm. Gal.* 3:25, *CNTC* 11:67.

ass, to arouse it to work."[186] The law remains a "constant sting"[187] that does not allow the believer to remain idle but incite him to obey it and remain on the path of holiness. A frequent meditation upon the law yields these benefits: "to be aroused to obedience, be strengthened in it, and be drawn from the slippery path of transgression."[188]

## Motives of Obedience: Gentle Attraction and Joyous Obedience

Calvin speaks of the motives of obedience to the law. First is the creature's obligation to divine majesty, to whom we are deeply in debt. Since our being and all that is ours come from him, God justly claims his supreme dominion over us and has the perfect right to be obeyed.[189] God by right occupies the place of the Father and the Lord to whom we not only owe our existence, but also glory, reverence, love, and fear. So, "we must obey out of natural obligation."[190]

The second motive for obeying is nothing but gratitude. This is already inherent in the preface to the entire law, where Moses recounts the marvelous benefits and memorable greatness of deliverance from bondage. The recital of manifold benefactions serves two purposes: Positively, it animates a heart of gratitude; negatively, it annihilates the despicable vice of ingratitude.[191] Moses exhorted the redeemed people to "give evidence of their gratitude by obeying the law.... The sum is that there was good reason why they should observe all the precepts of the law by which God intended that his people, after their redemption, should praise his benefits."[192]

The third motive is reward for obedience; as Calvin writes, "For because the eye of our mind is too blind to be moved solely by the beauty of the good, our most merciful Father out of his great kindness has willed to attract us by sweetness of rewards to love and seek after him."[193] In his commentary on Deuteronomy 7:9, Calvin teaches that because God's

186. *Inst.* 2.7.12.

187. *Inst.* 2.7.12.

188. *Inst.* 2.7.12.

189. *Inst.* 2.8.4; 2.8.13.

190. *Inst.* 2.8.2.

191. *Inst.* 2.8.15.

192. *Comm. Deut.* 6:20, CO 24:225.

193. *Inst.* 2.8.4.

mercy establishes God's claim, it changes the attitude with which we treat God's claim. The claim does not come from an imperial emperor who demands absolute satisfaction, but a merciful father who gently allures us by the sweetness of his promises. God's promise is prior to God's claim; it becomes effective in the form of a kind invitation rather than compulsion from fear; as Calvin writes,

> The promise stands first because God chooses rather to invite his people by kindness than to compel them to obedience from terror. The word *mercy* is coupled with the *covenant*, that we may know that the reward which believers must expect, does not depend on the merit of their works, since they have need of God's mercy.[194]

By a gentle persuasion, as a loving father does to his beloved child, we are impelled to obey, because the law is acknowledged as sweeter than honey; it is more attractive, no longer irksome. In his commentary on Exodus 20:1, Calvin reinforces what he teaches in his *Institutes*:

> Moses adds, that He is the peculiar God of the Israelites; for it was expedient, not only that they should be alarmed by the majesty of God, but also they should be gently attracted, so that the law might be more precious than gold or silver, and at the same time sweeter than honey; for it would not be enough for men to be compelled by servile fear to bear its yoke, unless they were also attracted by its sweetness, and willingly endured it.[195]

"The fear of the Lord," for Calvin, is "reverence compounded of honor and fear."[196] The shape of joyous obedience consists in this: that we obey God not as servants, fearing if we have ever fulfilled the exact measure; rather we serve him as children, trusting that our obedience and service will be accepted by our loving Father, even though we fail to fully express our adoption. We serve God, not with abject terror of a servile kind, but with a filial fear, like a child has toward his beloved father out of love and reverence for him. Our works are no longer measured by the rigorous standard of perfect righteousness, but a gentle attraction of boundless grace. Believers are free from the anxiety of self-torment and agonizing about whether God is continually angered by the remnants of sin, manifested in imperfect or defective service.

194. *Comm. Deut.* 7:9, *CF* 3:225.
195. *Comm. Exod.* 20:1, *CF* 1:339.
196. *Inst.* 3.2.26.

The old flesh constantly needs the stab of the law to keep us on the path of holiness, the benefit for which we ought to be grateful. However, too much of the law's stabbing might convert the law into a bitter experience. The law may become repulsive, causing us to flee or even hate God, and eventually lapse into sheer despair from which there is no remedy. The bridle, however gently it restrains us, may not arouse in us a piety of voluntary obedience. The spur of the law, however expedient it is for the attainment of holiness, may not be readily endured, though we need it to curb the lust of the flesh. By contrast, the sweet promise of reward from our kind Father more readily moves us to obedience. The Father's gentle attraction is the dynamic of cheerful obedience. This is evident in Calvin's *Sermons on the Ten Commandments*, where he holds that "the beginning of obedience, as well as its source, foundation, and root," is God's love.

> This love cannot exist until we have tasted the goodness of our God. For as long as we conceive of God as being opposed to us, of necessity we will flee from him. . . . Then we must realize that he is our Father and Savior, that he only wants to be favorable to us. Thus once we have tasted his mutual love which he reserves for us, then we will be motivated to love him as our Father. For if this love is in us, then there will be no doubt that we will obey him and that his law will rule in our thoughts, our affections, and in all our members.[197]

We are so denuded of love that we of ourselves cannot love God unless by his love that is imparted in us. Bound to God's mercy, we are totally free, free to love, to obey and to submit to God's will without doubting whether God is offended or honored by our works. Put trinitarianly, hearts that are captured by God's mercy in Christ through the Spirit willingly and cheerfully turn toward God, extolling him as the author of their freedom, and embracing the lawgiver who by right claims them for Godself. As all things originate with God, they should in turn orient their end to him.[198]

## CONCLUSION

The Spirit works through the gospel to produce faith in us but also works through the law to govern us. The law in its civil usage promotes justice and order in society. In its theological usage, the law works in a sinner

197. *STC*, 76.
198. *Inst.* 2.8.15.

a recognition of his sorely lost and miserable condition. However, this recognition and humility does not cause one to seek God's grace, unless one is consoled by the sweetness of God's sheer mercy. Calvin regards the law of Moses not only as that which establishes a righteous way of living but also as the form of religion God communicated through Moses that declares God as Father to Israel in Christ in the twin image of priest and king. Calvin considers "the Ten Commandments not as prior to, but as already contained within, the self-revelation of God the Father in Jesus Christ."[199] Unlike the Antinomians who want to abolish the law, Calvin stresses the Ten Commandments as they apply to the Christian life. Benjamin Farley highlights the contrast between Luther and Calvin as this: "Calvin's purpose in the sermons [on the Ten Commandments] was not to hail the removal of the Law's curse, as Luther so powerfully did in his *Lectures on Galatians*; rather, it was to persuade men that God's Law is 'the true and eternal rule of righteousness,' even for Christian believers. The Decalogue is precisely this because it continues to call men from self-deception and self-reliance and confronts them with God's rule for their lives."[200] In the same vein, Beeke sums up the basic difference between Luther and Calvin: "For Luther, the primary purpose of the law is to help the believer recognize and confront sin. For Calvin, the primary purpose of the law is to direct the believer to serve God out of love."[201]

Calvin, in stressing the third use of the law, could potentially be charged with servile legalism.[202] However, such a charge is unfounded, because Calvin's teaching on the law as a guide for the believer occurs strictly in the context of the covenant of grace in Christ. The law is, as Zachman states, "both rooted in and bearing witness to the covenant of adoption fulfilled in Jesus Christ."[203] Calvin includes the law as part of the covenant of grace, thus recognizing the significance the third use of law has in the hearts where Christ's Spirit dwells and reigns. Calvin does not set the law in opposition to the gospel; thus what is in view is not the contrast between the merits of works and the righteousness of faith.

199. Zachman, *Assurance*, 144.

200. *STC*, 26.

201. Beeke, "Calvin on Piety," 133.

202. See Wendel, *Calvin*, 204–5, which states, "We can hardly deny that there is a certain legalism about this, tending to efface the antinomy between the Law and the Gospel upon which Luther had been so insistent. But in reality, this is only from . . . the standpoint of the unbeliever. To the believer . . . the Gospel, far from being in any sense reduced to the Law, assimilates the latter to itself."

203. Zachman, *Assurance*, 145.

For him, writes Hesselink, when the law "is seen in the light of the new covenant where it is written on the heart by the Holy Spirit, then the law should be welcomed by the believer and used in gratitude for the gift already received. That gift . . . is the Mediator who must be 'apprehended' in the law."[204]

Luther uses the law to instruct through its negative condemnation of sinful actions and its positive expressions of God-pleasing behavior. But the law itself cannot cause things to happen; it does not motivate us to please God, which faith itself does. God approves of works done in faith; otherwise, they are sin. Truly God-pleasing conformity to the commands of God proceeds from faith but is instructed by the law. There is a subtle difference in emphasis in the Reformers.[205] The faithful person, for Luther, is one who fears, loves, and trusts in God above all things, and new obedience emerges as a fruit of that trust. The impetus to do good works lies in trusting God when we hear his declaration, "You are forgiven and thus my righteous child." "True and living faith," Luther asserts, "arouses and motivates good works through love."[206] Apart from trust, the law becomes a moral code against which we evaluate ourselves; our conformity to the law is then converted into another form of self-establishment as lord. For Calvin, the Christian law is "a perpetual rule" of life; it guides us and keeps us on the path of sanctification. Believers benefit from "the proper purpose" of the law, that through it they may be inspired to obey, strengthened in it, and kept from stumbling into sin.[207] A life devoted to God is characterized by a mind turned wholly toward the tables of the law and the actions therein. Quoting Titus 2:11–14, Calvin sums up all actions of piety under three parts: soberness, righteousness, and godliness. When united by an inseparable bond, these will spur us toward perfection.[208]

204. Hesselink, *Concept*, 255.

205. See Ngien, *Grace and Law*, 42.

206. LW 27:30; WA 40:2.37.

207. *Inst.* 2.7.12.

208. *Inst.* 2.7.3.

# 4

# The Spirit, Faith, and Prayer

## *Christ, an Overflowing Spring*

In discussing prayer in the *Institutes*, Calvin begins with a transitional statement—"The Way We Receive the Grace of Christ"—that links back to his teaching on what the cross of Christ has achieved for us. That transitional statement forms a natural bridge to the subject at hand, where he stresses prayer as a vehicle through which believers receive the treasures of Christ's grace.[1] "The Trinitarian portrait of prayer's significance," Todd Billings observes, governs the way Calvin develops his theology of prayer.[2] Union with Christ and the Spirit are where he begins his chapter on prayer. "Destitute and devoid of all good things," the Christian "must go outside himself" and seek fulfillment in the revelation of Christ by faith through the Holy Spirit. In Calvin's own words,

> For in Christ he offers all happiness in place of our misery, all wealth in place of our neediness; in him he opens to us the heavenly treasures that our whole faith may contemplate his beloved Son, our whole expectation depend upon him, and our whole hope cleave to and rest in him. This, indeed, is that secret and hidden philosophy which cannot be wrested from syllogisms. But they whose eyes God [the Spirit] has opened surely learn it by heart, that in his light they may see light. . . . The Spirit of adoption, who seals the witness of the gospel in our hearts [Rom. 8:16], raises up our spirits to dare show forth to God their

1. Parker, *Biography*, 41.
2. Billings, *Participation*, 110.

> desires, to stir up unspeakable groanings [Rom. 8:26], and confidently cry, "Abba! Father!" [Rom. 8:15].[3]

Calvin inculcates in believers the necessity of prayer and offers four rules to shape their disposition to prayer: reverence God's majesty; acknowledge the need for God's mercy; abandon all self-reliance; and cling to God with a confident hope that he hears our prayers. We pray by God's command, his precepts, and his "kindly invitation."[4] The motif of "kindly invitation" or "gentle" attraction by the "sweetness" of his promises looms large in Calvin's theology of prayer. As God invites us to trust in him, so he invites us to request of him what he promises to offer. God's command must be accompanied by the faithfulness of his promise through which God trains us and "gently attracts"[5] us to entreat him. Prayer does not coerce God to act; rather it is God's vehicle through which we receive all good things that are buried in Christ. For whatever we need and lack is in Christ, "an overflowing spring,"[6] from which we are bidden to "dig up"[7] by prayer inestimable treasures. Prayer draws believers into communion with God "by which, having entered the heavenly sanctuary, they appeal to him in person concerning his promises in order to experience . . . that what they believed was not in vain."[8] Just as God speaks "in person" to us in Scripture, the children of God too instinctively engage "in person" in an intimate conversation with him and unburden their cares into his bosom. Calvin understands prayer, Wendel notes, "as a sort of verification of faith."[9] True faith cannot be idle or indifferent about calling upon God. Calvin discerns a proper order in the apostle's teaching: "Just as faith is born from the gospel, so through it our hearts are trained to call upon God's name [Rom. 10:14–17]."[10] Faith finds expression not only in love but also in prayer, which Calvin regards as "the chief exercise of faith."[11] To pray fruitfully is therefore to "embrace with both arms"[12] the assurance of receiving what we ask, which God enjoins with his word.

3. *Inst.* 3.20.1.
4. *Inst.* 3.20.13.
5. *Inst.* 3.20.13.
6. *Inst.* 3.20.1.
7. *Inst.* 3.20.1.
8. *Inst.* 3.20.2.
9. Wendel, *Calvin*, 253.
10. *Inst.* 3.20.1.
11. *Inst.* 3.20.1.
12. *Inst.* 2.20.18.

## GOD'S WORD: COMMAND AND PROMISE

Calvin frames his theology of prayer within the command and promise of God.[13] God has enjoined his people to call upon him and has promised to shower them with his bountiful treasures. When these two things—command and promise—are established, it is certain that those who refuse to call upon God are not only impiously obstinate but also convicted of unbelief for distrusting his promises. God's threats and promises are two distinct ways in which God's word is heard. Whenever only the negative aspect of the command is heard, we encounter terror at the hands of God who imposes punishment for our disobedience; when the negative aspect is heard alongside the positive aspect, it leads us to seek grace by prayer. God commands his people to ask of him all that he has promised, and it would be folly of us to disdain God's word in either form. The faith that gives rise to prayer is God's creation by his word; it is ever nourished and sustained by God's creative word. The word of God remains the ruling principle by which our prayers are governed and restrained. Rather than following the dictates of our minds or wishes, our prayer must be, in Ronald Wallace's words, "in compliance with what God has commanded, making our prayers an echo in our hearts of His promises, and not allowing ourselves to seek anything more than he has promised."[14]

Calvin acknowledges three essential elements of public worship: preaching, prayer, and the administration of the sacraments.[15] But in the *Institutes*, Calvin considers the office of prayer the "chief part of worship."[16] Those who despise God's precept and ignore his gracious invitation to pray defraud him of honor. For God "to be called upon" in the hour of need, Calvin notes, is "highest and precious above all else" (Ps 50:15).[17] The importuning of God by believers constitutes a sacrifice of worship, which not only is rightly due him, but is also conducive to their own profit.[18] The believer receives the benefit of prayer, the promises of God's immense sweetness, which would otherwise remain in the "treasure house of heaven." Don Garlington writes, "Apart from prayer, the promises of God remain locked up in his Word; and although for the

13. *Inst.* 3.20.13.
14. Wallace, *Christian Life*, 278.
15. Calhoun, "Prayer," 359.
16. *Inst.* 3.20.13.
17. *Inst.* 3.20.13.
18. *Inst.* 3.20.3.

believing mind the promises are sure and irrevocable, *prayer is the divinely appointed means by which the faithful experience the benefits of their salvation*, which otherwise would simply reside in the treasure house of heaven."[19] Hence, the more confidently we extol God's benefits, the more we are keenly aroused to ceaselessly lay our desires before God, lest our faith be idle or sluggish.[20] As proof, Calvin cites Elijah, who, after he has promised rain to King Ahab (so he is certain of God's will), still earnestly prays and sends his servant seven times to look (1 Kgs 18:42). He does this simply because he was fulfilling his duty to pray and exercising his faith in a way that profits him.[21]

God anticipates our calling upon him, in his word: "Call upon me in the day of affliction; I will deliver you, and you shall glorify me" (Ps 50:15). Bidding us to pray by the precept itself does not move us to come, unless a promise is added, as is necessary. We would flee from God if he does not promise to be "easily entreated and readily accessible."[22] To accommodate our weaknesses, God gently invites us, rather than coercing us, to pray. God induces us by means of the noble titles or sweet names of God, from which "we may taste how gently God attracts us to himself."[23] For instance, Psalm 65:1–2 says, "O God . . . thou who hearest prayer! To thee shall all flesh come"; and Psalm 145:18 reads, "The Lord is near to all who call upon him, who call upon him in truth." Calvin extols, "For what is more lovely or agreeable than for God to bear this title, which assures us that nothing is more to his nature than to assent to the prayers of the suppliants?"[24] The reality of the fulfillment of prayer lies in the infallible promise of God, which assures us that he acts efficaciously for us, not against us.[25] The inducements of God's noble titles or names form "the sweetness of the melody" by which all self-inducements, idleness, or indifference are subdued; and we are motivated to follow him, not to fear him.[26] By "the steps of the promises,"[27] the suppliants in their self-abasement but with elated confidence climb upward to God, the fountain

19. Garlington, "Doctrine of Prayer," 22, italics original.
20. *Inst.* 3.20.3.
21. *Inst.* 3.20.3.
22. *Inst.* 3.20.13.
23. *Inst.* 3.20.13.
24. *Inst.* 3.20.13.
25. *Inst.* 3.20.14.
26. *Inst.* 3.20.13.
27. *Inst.* 3.20.14.

of living waters, rather than digging out for themselves dry cisterns (Jer 2:13). Believers' hearts are raised by God's sheer generosity freely given them so that they may cease from wandering through mazes looking for relief. Failure to pray is, therefore, the result of our unwillingness to be earnestly motivated and rightly empowered by the promises of God. Calvin writes, "We receive this singular fruit of God's promises when we frame our prayers without hesitation or trepidation; but, relying upon the word of him whose majesty would otherwise terrify us, we dare call upon him as Father, while he deigns to suggest this sweetness of names to us."[28] David, for one, has implemented this rule, claiming for himself the sweet promise given him that he may obtain by prayers. "Thou . . . O God, hast revealed to the ear of thy servant . . . ; therefore thy servant has found courage to pray" (2 Sam 7:27). Prayer includes meditating intently on God's attributes and God's acts upon us: God's power, his goodness, and the constancy of God's promises. Such meditation on God's creative and providential actions infuses new vigor into languishing spirits.[29]

## THE NECESSITY OF PRAYER: SIX REASONS

If God has determined everything that comes to pass according to his immutable will, some argue, this would make prayer useless. Why do we ask for that which will inevitably occur, or ask for what cannot obtain? God does not need to be reminded of what we need, as though he slumbers until awakened by our cries; nor does he require the petition of some creaturely beings to bring about a particular action.[30] So they consider prayer superfluous. Calvin retort, "But they who thus reason do not observe to what end the Lord instructed his people to pray, for he ordained it not so much for his own sake as for ours."[31] To foster communion with God, Calvin adduces six purposes for petitionary prayer:

1. that our hearts may be "fired with a zealous and burning desire ever to seek, love, and serve him," and become accustomed to rely on him, "a sacred anchor";

28. *Inst.* 3.20.14.
29. *Inst.* 3.20.13.
30. *Inst.* 3.20.3.
31. *Inst.* 3.20.3.

2. that our hearts become trained not to entertain any wishes that render them ashamed before God, but to pour out all our desires before God;
3. that our hearts be prepared to receive his blessings "with true gratitude and thanksgiving," knowing that every blessing comes from God;
4. that having obtained by prayers, we should be impelled to meditate upon his goodness more ardently in granting our desires;
5. that we may "embrace with greater delight those things which we acknowledge" as having been obtained by prayer; and
6. that our "use and experience [of being granted that for which we petition God]" may confirm divine providence, through which we know God's unfailing promises, and that he "ever extends his hand to help his own, not wet-nursing them with words but defending them with present help."[32]

Nonetheless, our merciful God may appear unresponsive to our petitions. God gives such an impression in order to train us to entreat him and enjoy the benefits of prayer.[33] "So our petitions are both ordained by God," Oliver Crisp relates, "and yet also an obligation that is enjoined upon all believers, by an exercise of faith."[34] We pray—not to help God, but to help ourselves. Prayer is an occasion for the exercise of faith, by which we are cleansed of indolence. Through it, we also attest God's providential care in granting the benefits that flow from his voluntary liberality. Through impetration, we call upon God to "reveal himself as wholly present to us."[35] As a result we meet him wholly and vividly "in person,"[36] from whom flows into our conscience extraordinary peace and satisfaction amid insecurities and turbulences that assail us relentlessly. The aforementioned six points "overlap and reinforce one another," David Calhoun writes, "bringing to [God] our love and our concerns, with

32. *Inst.* 3.20.3; cf. Beeke, "Calvin on Piety," 139, which summarizes the six purposes of prayer: "To fly to God with every need, to set all our petitions before God, to prepare us to receive God's benefits with humble gratitude, to meditate upon God's kindness, to instill the proper spirit of delight for God's answers in prayer, and to confirm his providence."

33. *Inst.* 3.20.3.

34. Crisp, *Retrieving Doctrine*, 149.

35. *Inst.* 3.20.2.

36. *Inst.* 3.20.2.

thanksgiving for his kindness, with delight in his goodness, and with confidence in his faithfulness."[37]

## THE PERFECT RULE: FOUR AIDS

Calvin develops four aids to constitute "the perfect rule" of prayer.[38] He weaves into them several theological elements—God's majesty, law and gospel, grace, faith, reverence, repentance, words of God, justification, sanctification, the Spirit, God's wrath, and his mercy—to cultivate piety in prayer. This rule is "the general attitude required of the faithful rather than precise and clearly-distinguished rules."[39] With "reverence and moderation," this attitude keeps us on the path that leads nearer to the "perfect rule."[40]

### Rule One: A Heartfelt Reverence for God

Piety, for Calvin, is "that reverence joined with love of God which knowledge of his benefits induces."[41] Accordingly, prayer must be framed duly with a reverential disposition of "keenness of mind" informed by the knowledge of God's benefits, and of "affection of heart" moved by the love of God.[42] This rule is tightly linked to Calvin's trinitarian definition of faith: "*a firm and certain knowledge* of God's benevolence toward us, founded upon the truth of the freely given promise in Christ, both revealed to our *minds* and sealed upon our *hearts* through the Holy Spirit."[43] Gripped by the truth of the gospel, the mind rises beyond itself to a pure contemplation of God's character; touched by the love of God, the heart turns to God with gratitude for his abundant provision. Both the mind and the heart are required for a pious and intimate conversation with God. For nothing is more ineffectual than the prayer that proceeds from a mind that is occupied with idols and a heart that is cold. To shape reverence for God, two things must be avoided: impropriety for the mind

37. Calhoun, "Prayer," 353.
38. *Inst.* 3.20.15.
39. Wendel, *Calvin*, 254.
40. *Inst.* 3.20.16.
41. *Inst.* 1.1.1.
42. *Inst.* 3.20.5.
43. *Inst.* 3.2.7, my italics.

to flit about hither and thither, and impiety to mix sacred with profane. Nothing is more repugnant to reverence than letting an excess of frivolity affect us and deprive us of awe of God. Dullness, inertia, and slothfulness, to which we all are prone, are contrary to reverence; they can be conquered by the aid of the Spirit. The affections of the regenerate remain trapped in darkness until the Spirit's light shines. The Spirit "affects our hearts in such a way that these prayers penetrate into heaven itself by their fervency."[44] Consequently, the mind aspires to rise beyond carnal cares and vain thoughts, by which we are led astray, to a life of purity, by which we are established.[45] Whoever engages in prayer must apply our minds and efforts zealously to godliness, focusing on God's majesty.[46] The harder we contemplate God's majesty and grandeur, the more we are raised outside of ourselves and freed from captivity to evil thoughts and fleshly cares that still abide on earth.

## Rule Two: A Sincere Sense of Want and Repentance

The constancy in prayer flows from a knowledge of who we are before God—namely, beggars in perpetual need of God's mercy.[47] Just as we groan to seek all that we desperately need, so we strive with passion to attain that for which we seek.[48] Reciting prayers habitually or asking without thinking are inappropriate for a pious conversation with God. Some pray out of a confused or vague sense of their need, which does not arouse them to seek its remedy rightly.[49] To illustrate this, Calvin mentions those who ask pardon for sins while either thinking they are not sinners, or not thinking they are.[50] Unquestionably, this is to make mockery of God. When we request anything from God for our own need, we are to "yearn for it with sincere affection of hearts" and "with no less ardor and eagerness" as if it were done only to God's glory.[51] It robs God

44. *Comm. Rom.* 8:26, *CNTC* 8:178.
45. *Inst.* 3.20.4.
46. *Inst.* 3.20.5.
47. *Inst.* 3.20.7.
48. *Inst.* 3.20.6.
49. *Inst.* 3.20.6.
50. *Inst.* 3.20.6.
51. *Inst.* 3.20.6.

of his honor if we refer every cause and every needy situation for which we pray to some other source than God himself.

Assaults from outside and anxieties from within could divert our minds from a right and pure contemplation of God. The temptations that continue to assault us signal our lack of resources within ourselves and our need of God's provision outside ourselves. In us is emptiness and poverty, causing us to seek outside ourselves for aid; in God is fullness and satisfaction, causing us to seek God alone for fulfillment. Commenting on Romans 8:28, Paul, says Calvin, sees God's hand in adverse situations, which cannot be met by human resources.[52] Effectual prayer is based on the word, which bestirs us to approach God with delight. But our flesh exclaims that, since our afflictions remain, even after fervent prayer, and our adversities appear to hinder our salvation, God does not care for us. "Hence the Apostle anticipates this [exclamation] and says, that though God does not immediately succor his people, he yet does not forsake them, for by a wonderful contrivance he turns those things which seem to be evils in such a way as to promote their salvation."[53] There may be a season, as for David, in which our existential condition demands prayer. We may not be motivated with equal measure to pray, and yet our needs do press us to pray. Scripture commands us to pray constantly (1 Thess 5:17) and exposes our laziness or lack of attentiveness to it. Failure to seek God in times of necessity, says Calvin, is tantamount to "reproaching him for poverty, or want of means, or cruelty and excessive rigor."[54] Those who trivialize this rule would be exposed to "hypocrisy and wily falsehood," which otherwise would have been removed from a life given to constancy in prayer.[55]

Those whose hearts are closed to God will find God's ears closed. Callous hearts feel only God's severity, the effect of coming under the intolerable threat of law.[56] Fruitful prayer must be accompanied by the sweet promises of the gospel, which soften the obstinate heart and cause it to seek remedy in God. Only contrite and sincere worshipers will feel God conciliatory toward them, the effect of coming under the consolation of gospel. In preparation to pray, Calvin advises that we place ourselves under the negative light of law, through which we are exposed of the sins

52. *Comm. Rom.* 8:28, CTS 19:314.

53. *Comm. Rom.* 8:28, CTS 19:314.

54. *Inst.* 3.20.36.

55. *Inst.* 3.20.7.

56. *Inst.* 3.20.7.

(including slackness in prayer) that still cling to us and incur God's wrath unless we repent of them.[57] Subsequently, through the positive light of the gospel, we are received into God's mercy, which admits us into intimate conversation with God. The punitive function of the law is curative, not an end in itself, as it inspires in us an awareness of our own emptiness, causing us to be filled with God's goodness through the vehicle of prayer. Inherent in this rule is a double knowledge: the knowledge of our utter lack, and the knowledge of God's sheer mercy. The knowledge of such want is causal, and causally useful if it causes us to move outside ourselves and cling to God's mercy as the remedy to our needs.

## Rule Three: Humility Before God

As in the second rule, believers approach God as beggars, yielding all self-confidence, and trusting in God's mercy alone for things spiritual and temporal. They give glory completely to God and give up all thoughts of their own. "The beginning, and even the preparation," of an efficacious prayer, for Calvin, is the infallible mercy of God, not some soteriological resources within us.[58] We are full of uncleanness and unrighteousness, which banish us from God's presence. Only when divine wrath is appeased do we find God propitious. Sin is removed only when his anger has been dissipated. We cannot benefit anything from God until we are freely reconciled to him; neither is God resolved to be kindly disposed to anyone other than those he has forgiven.[59] Our minds are aroused by free mercy, resulting in a sincere confession of sin; our callous hearts are softened by it, resulting in an earnest plea for God's forgiveness. Hence, as often as we pray, we must always remember not only our individual sins, the symptomatic aspect of depravity, but also our corrupt nature before God, its systemic aspect (Ps 51). The primary concern is not with the removal of "the effect" but "the cause."[60] Wallace writes,

> We must remember always in our praying that our true need before God is for forgiveness. Though we may have many other urgent needs, "the thing which we must principally and particularly request is that he will have mercy upon us, which is

57. *Inst.* 3.20.7.
58. *Inst.* 3.20.9.
59. *Inst.* 3.20.9.
60. *Inst.* 3.20.9.

> the source of every other blessing." The penitent man of faith before God will implore the cure of his sin and will "beware of imitating foolish patients, who, anxious about curing accidental symptoms, neglect the root of the disease."[61]

Calvin concedes that in Scripture the saints refer to their own righteousness in calling on God for help, as did David in Psalm 86:1: "Keep my life, for I am good."[62] This expression "I am good," Calvin writes, "is nothing else but that by their regeneration itself they are attested as servants and children of God."[63] It is not an assertion of the merits of achievements of which one may boast; rather, it is that of one's desire of guilelessness and innocence of which God approves (cf. Pss 34:14; 33:16). Corresponding to God's promise to answer the prayers of the godly (1 John 3:22) is the saints' attestation, in which they mention their purity, in order that they, like all servants, may feel certain that their righteous services have indeed reached God, thus proving true of God's favor. The godly thus enjoy a pure conscience, the promises with which God consoles and strengthens his people having been confirmed in themselves.

## Rule Four: Confident Hope

The utter helplessness and unworthiness we feel within ourselves might cause us to flee God. So Calvin counterbalances it with an exhortation, that we should approach God with a sure hope that our cries will be heard. Believers may find themselves so harassed by blind unrest that they almost lose their senses—until faith comes to their rescue.[64] They, unlike unbelievers, still rest upon God's immeasurable goodness that outweighs the perplexity of their predicament. Here Calvin brings the relation of faith and repentance to bear upon prayer. The two, though distinguished, are inseparably one: while one "terrifies" us, the other "gladdens" us.[65] Quoting Psalm 5:7—"I through the abundance of thy goodness will enter thy house, I will worship toward the temple of thy holiness with fear"—Calvin intimates, "Under God's goodness [David] includes faith,

61. Wallace, *Christian life*, 281; cf. *Comm. Ps.* 119:58, CO 32:239–40; *Inst.* 3.20.9.

62. *Inst.* 3.20.10.

63. *Inst.* 3.20.10.

64. *Inst.* 3.20.11.

65. *Inst.* 3.20.11.

meantime not excluding fear."[66] On the one hand, we should pray confidently—not with abject terror, but with reverential fear of God's majesty, which constrains us to abandon all self-reliance. On the other hand, we should pray in faith, boldly grasping God's manifold goodness, which alone raises up those oppressed by all misfortunes.[67]

Godly prayer arises from the groans caused by fears, and our groaning lays them in God's lap. Under the weight of various assaults, believers groan with weariness along with fear, while at the same time praying to God to extend his helping hand.[68] Those who call upon God, wavering in their own minds whether they will be heard or not, will obtain nothing. Here Calvin reinforces the first rule. "Any use of true prayer"[69] presupposes faith—"a firm and certain knowledge of God's benevolence toward us"[70]—without which God cannot be rightly called upon (Rom 10:14).[71] We do not pray by chance, but in true faith, being persuaded of the knowledge of divine favor for us. For "no one can well perceive the power of faith unless he feels it by experience in his heart."[72] The insensate conscience of unbelief will not feel or see God. Only those who have learned of God's mercy from the gospel feel the power of faith, through which they approach the heavenly throne with confidence and boldness (Eph 3:12). Where the assurance of hope is absent, prayers vanish into thin air.[73]

Though God at times answers prayer that is not framed according to the rule of his word, Calvin argues this does not abrogate "a universal law."[74] "Faith grounded upon the word is the mother of right prayer."[75] Any deflection from God's word will corrupt prayer. From Scripture, Calvin recognizes that God is ready to prove his care toward unbelievers whose prayers are uttered with the same intensity of mind and sincerity of heart as those of believers (cf. Ps 107:6, 13, 19). Prayer of this type obtains effect for the purpose of highlighting God's mercy. By comparison,

66. *Inst.* 3.20.11.
67. *Inst.* 3.20.11.
68. *Inst.* 3.20.11.
69. *Inst.* 3.20.12.
70. *Inst.* 3.2.7.
71. *Inst.* 3.20.12.
72. *Inst.* 3.20.12.
73. *Inst.* 3.20.12.
74. *Inst.* 3.20.15.
75. *Inst.* 3.20.15.

it induces in the godly the assurance that, if the defective prayer of the unbelievers is not without effect, how much more would they profit from imploring God's aid! God hearkens to ungodly wailings, not to approve them, but to "prove" by doing so how much more he will hearken to godly groans, simply because the godly are his elect.[76]

Greater problems, however, emerge from those defective prayers offered by Christians. Abraham, for example, prayed for Sodom without a word from God on the subject (Gen 18:23); and Jeremiah prayed for the deliverance of the city of Jerusalem from God's judgment (Jer 32:16–25). But, says Calvin, it is not as though their prayers are done without faith. "Relying upon the general principles by which God bids us and bestows mercy even upon the unworthy, they did not utterly lack faith, although in this particular instance their opinion deceived them."[77] Then, drawing insight from Augustine, Calvin argues that the saints in view were not praying against God's decretive will—"that hidden and unchangeable will"—rather that they based their supplications on "the will that he inspires in them, that he may hearken to them in another way as he wisely decides."[78] Calvin expands, "For he so tempers the outcome of the events according to his incomprehensible plan that the prayers of the saint, which are a mixture of faith and error, are not nullified."[79] All of this, however, neither excuses the saints nor venerates such prayer as an example for imitation. Therefore, where no "certain promise" is attached, we must pray "conditionally."[80]

In private prayer, the action of the tongue without the kindling of the mind displeases God. "Besides, the mind ought to be kindled with an ardor of thought so as far to surpass all that the tongue can express by speaking." The tongue is no longer required, except when the inner feeling is too weak to arouse itself, or it has been powerfully aroused to do what the tongue does.[81] When the mind is aroused by the wondrous grace of God, the tongue spontaneously breaks forth into speech, followed by bodily gestures;[82] raising our hands in prayer, for example, aids in raising our thoughts on high (Pss 25:1; 24:1). Individual private prayer

76. *Inst.* 3.20.15.

77. *Inst.* 3.20.15.

78. See Augustine, *City of God* 22.2.1–2, as cited in *Inst.* 3.20.15.

79. *Inst.* 3.20.15.

80. *Inst.* 3.20.15.

81. *Inst.* 3.20.33.

82. *Inst.* 3.20.33.

must be learned and nourished so that the church's corporate prayer may grow. By this corporate piety, the "unity of the faith" is strengthened so that "the prayers of the church are never ineffectual."[83]

Singing, which is part of prayer, kindles our mind with pondering on God's magnificence and keeps it attentive. Our ears must not pay more attention to the melody than our minds to the meaning hidden in the words. "When the melody is added [to a word], that word pierces the heart much more strongly and enters within. . . . Singing has great power and vigor to move and inflame our hearts."[84] Congregational singing creates desire for God, leading worshipers into the affective experience of God. However, the gift of music can be easily abused. "It is true that every evil word corrupts morals, as St. Paul says, but when melody is with it, this evil penetrates much deeper into the heart and enters within. Just as through a funnel the wine is poured into the vase, so also the poison and corruption is instilled in the depth of the heart by the melody."[85] Songs that appeal "only" to the "sweetness and delight of the ear" are most repugnant to God.[86] To incite reverent worship, Calvin suggests having "songs not only decent, but also holy which should act as spurs to incite us to pray and to praise God, to meditate upon his works so as to love, fear, honor, and glorify him."[87] The melody must bear "the weight and majesty appropriate to the subject."[88] Calvin finds a treasury of holy music in the "Psalms of David which the Holy Spirit dictated and gave to us."[89] Ross J. Miller argues that "Psalm-singing, indeed, had extraordinary potential for penetrating the affective center of the worshipper where the Spirit began its work of sanctification."[90] Singing, if it exalts

83. *Inst.* 3.20.29.

84. Translation by Ford Lewis Battles, in "John Calvin: The Form of Prayers and Songs of the Church, 1542, Letter to the Reader," *Calvin Theological Journal* 15.2 (1980), 163, as quoted in Lane, *Ravished by Beauty*, 80.

85. Calvin, "'Preface' to the Psalter," OS 2:17, as cited in Miller, "Music and the Spirit," 51.

86. *Inst.* 3.20.33.

87. Calvin, "'Preface' to the Psalter," OS 2:17, as cited in Miller, "Music and the Spirit," 51.

88. Calvin, "'Preface' to the Psalter," OS 2:17, as cited in Miller, "Music and the Spirit," 51.

89. Calvin, "'Preface' to the Psalter," OS 2:17, as cited in Miller, "Music and the Spirit," 51. For further discussion of Calvin's usage of Psalm-singing, see Miller, "Psalm-singing," 35–48.

90. Miller, "Music and the Spirit," 51.

God's majesty, "both lends dignity and grace to sacred actions and has the greatest value in kindling our hearts to a true zeal and eagerness to pray."[91] "Voice and song, if interposed in prayer," must spring from the stirring of the heart, and not only from the moving of the lips; otherwise, they provoke God's wrath, because this is to defame God's holy name and to scorn his majesty.[92]

No one has ever achieved the "perfect rule" of prayer; this reality leads Calvin back to the third rule, reflecting further on God's mercy or pardon. Admitting our worthiness or bankruptcy before God is the condition of possibility of experiencing the double grace accessed through union with Christ: Christ's righteousness and holiness cover our sinful prayers. Believers united to Christ are freed from terror before God because their adoption to sonship is sealed by "the Spirit of adoption" and not vitiated by imperfect prayers. "Thus, even though believers cannot perfectly express the adoption received," Billings writes, "they can be repeatedly encouraged to enter into this adoption through the Spirit by bringing all of their burdens and thanks before the generous Father."[93] This leads to the next section, the Trinity as the dynamic of prayer.

## THE TRINITARIAN STRUCTURE OF PRAYER

Calvin follows this ascriptive pattern of the Trinity: "To the Father is attributed the beginning of activity, and the fountain and wellspring of all things; to the Son, wisdom, counsel, and the ordered disposition of all things; but to the Spirit is assigned the power and efficacy of that activity."[94] He applies this doctrine to his understanding of prayer. Of this, Joel Beeke writes, "Prayer originates with the Father, is made possible by the Son, and is worked out in the soul by the Spirit, through whom it returns via Christ to the Father."[95] Prayer evinces a trinitarian framework, beginning with praying to the Father, through the Son, and by the Holy Spirit. All three persons are involved as one God in the dynamic of prayer. Ivan Mesa writes,

91. *Inst.* 3.20.32.

92. *Inst.* 3.20.31.

93. Billings, *Participation*, 112.

94. *Inst.* 1.8.18.

95. Beeke, "Communion with God," 36.

> In summary fashion, it is the Father who initiates prayer, requires faith, and encourages believers to pray by His promises; it is the Son's mediatorial work that grounds prayer and, because of believers' union with Christ, their prayers are joined with Christ Himself; and the Spirit helps believers in their weakness, enables them to strive in prayer, and binds them to His Word.[96]

The trinitarian structure informs Calvin's exposition of the Lord's Prayer. Prayer is addressed not with a generic reference to God, but with a specific reference to "our Father," the origin of prayer. Trinitarianly, each person relates to believers in his distinct manner: The Father initiates us, the Son provides for us, and the Spirit enables us. The Father encourages believers, and teaches them through his beloved Son that they ought to pray to him. We are given the privilege to commune with God, not by any prior action or worth of ours, but by the gift of adoption that distinguishes us as God's children. As it is rashness for mortal souls to call God Father without his invitation, so it is folly for them to presume upon the title of sonship without his adoption. The Father's initiatory activity is mediated through the Son, whose voice alone we are to hearken. The Lord's Prayer is an ideal form he prescribes for his children "to seek of him, all that is of benefit to us, all that we need ask."[97] The only begotten Son of God "supplies words to our lips,"[98] with which we pray to God and receive his blessings. The Spirit enables us to open our mouths before God, as he instructs us to pray rightly (Rom 8:26). All three persons work together as one God, who sweeps believers up into salvation, and stirs up in them the desire to commune daily with their Lord in prayer. The grace of our triune God not only stimulates our prayer of response but also shapes our praying. Prayer that reaches the Father's throne lies not in anything we bring, but in Christ's mediatorial work made available to us by the effective agency of the Holy Spirit.

## Pray to the Father: The Beginning of God's Activity

Calvin ascribes to the Father "the beginning of the activity," apart from which nothing of consequential necessity would occur. The Father is "the fountain and wellspring" from which all heavenly blessings proceed.

96. Mesa, "Trinitarian Theology of Prayer," 180.

97. *Inst.* 3.20.34; 3.20.48.

98. *Inst.* 3.20.34.

Prayer begins with the Father, who invites us to come by his promise. "Our most Gracious Father will not cast out those whom he not only urges, but also stirs up with every possible means, to come to him."[99] In his treatment of the Lord's Prayer, Calvin's rendering of the address "Father" evokes warmth and intimacy. The God who calls himself Father and allows us to so address him possesses "great sweetness"[100] not to be found elsewhere. The Father is the abundance of immense sweetness, from which flows a great "feeling of love" that "frees us from all distrust."[101] God's boundless love is attested with a sure proof that his "feeling of fatherhood"[102] is moved by the tears and groans of his children, even as their wounded hearts are moved by his affection, that than which no greater or more excellent can be found, to take refuge in his protection. When we appeal to God "in person" as a child does to his dear father, he appears to us "in person" with an abundance of his fatherly compassion, which only his beloved can experience. Fortified by the sweet and stirring titles with which God invests himself in his word, the suppliants gladly submit themselves to his safekeeping, and without hesitation implore the assistance that his sweet name inspires. The promises of God motivate us to access by prayer the riches laid up for us with the Heavenly Father (Ps 119:76).

The God who urges us to pray is not some remote or aloof deity but the heavenly Father, whose words are endearing and moving. Commenting on Joel 2:32, Calvin writes, "The only stronghold of safety is in calling upon [God's] name."[103] This passage is inexhaustible in application, especially in light of what Calvin teaches on the mind, "a [ceaseless] factory of idols,"[104] to which we naturally run for safety rather than to God, a ceaseless storehouse of treasures, from which we draw aid. This brings into focus the import of the first commandment, "Thou shall not have other gods," that God alone is God, ever Lord of all. And this God is also the Father of the first article of the Creed, who provides all goods so that we are never without want. Hence God is extolled preeminently as "the Lord and Father."[105] Prayer is a practical implementation of the

99. *Inst.* 3.20.14.

100. *Inst.* 3.20.36.

101. *Inst.* 3.20.36.

102. *Inst.* 3.20.36.

103. *Inst.* 3.20.2.

104. *Inst.* 1.11.8. The translations use "perpetual."

105. *Inst.* 1.14.22.

first commandment, honoring God as God. Prayer that originates from the first commandment takes us back to it. Any slackness in prayer or thoughts of deferring prayer dishonors God and distances us from God who wishes himself alone to be our God, to whom we should flee for all good. By calling upon God, we declare not only the significance of God to us, that he is majestic above all and worthy of trust and praise, but also our significance before him, that we are his beloved children whose prayers the heavenly Father promises to hear.

## Pray in the Son: The Mediatorial Activity

Prayer is ineffectual apart from the name of Christ. Calvin writes, "In calling God 'Father,' we put forward the name 'Christ.'"[106] Mesa writes, "This is shorthand for the mediatorial work of Christ."[107] Christ, through his death, acquires for us access to an otherwise awesome and frightful deity. By faith, believers are endowed with the honor of sonship on account of the grace of Christ. By nature, Christ is a true Son, whose divinity is one with the Father. He is now given believers as brothers so that what is true of him by nature is ours by adoption. As adopted children, we are given the same privileges as is Christ, the natural Son; the former is found pleasing to God through the latter. As soon as the believer contemplates the majesty of God, he is made aware of his unworthiness, and thus he recoils in fear and shrinks by that knowledge from approaching God for anything. To encourage believers to pray, Calvin eagerly commends Christ as the only mediator, who "appears in our name and bears us upon his shoulders and holds us bound upon his breast so that we are heard in his person; further, that our prayers are cleansed by sprinkled blood."[108] The title of sole Mediator is uniquely Christ's, bestowed upon him by the Father. To transfer it to another is to "obscure the glory of his birth, and make void the cross; in fine, they strip and deprive of its praise all that he has done or suffered!"[109] God's fatherly promises hidden in the Son become ours by prayer, as Christ is given to be ours by faith. As God counts "the height of dishonor"[110] those who abuse God's holy name, so

106. *Inst.* 3.20.36.
107. Mesa, "Trinitarian Theology of Prayer," 182.
108. *Inst.* 3.20.18.
109. *Inst.* 3.20.21.
110. *Inst.* 3.20.7.

he counts "the height of stupidity"[111] those who are intent on accessing God through other means, thereby removing themselves from Christ, apart from whom no entry into the holy of holies lies open. They receive nothing from God except wrath, judgment, and terror.

The expiatory work of Christ on the cross sustains and renders our prayer effectual at every moment. Niesel summarizes aptly, "It is not simply that He has once by His sacrifice interceded between God and sinful humanity; it is rather that His intercession with the Father on our behalf continues day by day."[112] The prayers we bring before God are not vitiated, as Christ's prayer is not. Yet to pray, says Parker, "is not simply a matter of praying through Christ, but rather *with* Christ, of our prayers being united with his intercession for us."[113] On account of the believers' union with Christ, their prayers are united with his. Horton relates, "We are not Christ, but we are one with him—even on our knees."[114] Through the Spirit, we are united to Christ, who alone gathers up all the petitions of the people and makes them effective before God.

## Pray by the Holy Spirit: The Efficacy of Activity

Our whole faith consists in contemplating God's beloved Son, the source of our happiness and hope. "This," Calvin argues, "is that secret and hidden philosophy which cannot be wrested with syllogisms."[115] Only those whose eyes the Spirit opens are impelled to dig up by prayer the heavenly treasures buried in the Son.[116] The Spirit of adoption seals the witness of the gospel in our hearts, causing us to embrace with both hands the promises of God hidden in Christ. The pile of treasures remains useless should it remain outside us; it does not profit us unless it is made ours by praying in the Spirit. The Spirit does not replace our praying but confers on us Christ's benefits, which we receive by praying. He "arouses in us *assurance, desires, and sighs*, to conceive which our natural powers would

111. *Inst.* 3.20.20.
112. Niesel, *Theology*, 154.
113. Parker, *Calvin*, 110, italics original.
114. Horton, *Christian Life*, 164.
115. *Inst.* 3.20.1.
116. *Inst.* 3.20.2.

scarcely suffice."[117] These three gifts flow from being united to Christ, which the Holy Spirit communicates to our hearts by faith.

First, the Spirit generates in us an inexhaustible *assurance* of God's unconditional love when assailed by doubt or insecurity. Believers' hearts are so narrow that they can neither contain nor comprehend God's boundless favor. So the Father sets before them not only Christ as "the pledge and guarantee of adoption," but also the Spirit as "witness to us of the same adoption" through which he may embolden them to pray.[118] As Gerald Bray writes, "The proof of [sonship] is the presence of the Holy Spirit in our hearts. The Holy Spirit makes our sonship effective and allows us to claim the promises made to Abraham and fulfilled in Christ."[119] The Spirit surges over us with an assurance that is far from cold and abstract, but is saturated with the sweetness or feeling of fatherhood, proving to us the certainty of God's adoption into sonship despite appearances to the contrary (Gal 4:6; Rom 8:15). Believers belong to the family of God because they have God as their Father and Christ as their brother.[120] The Spirit is given them as a witness, that God abounds with great devotion toward his children, confirming in them that he is by far "the best and kindest"[121] father of all, though they are unworthy of such. The Spirit we encounter in our prayer is not some mysterious force that makes us aware of God; rather it is the Spirit through whose action God draws us to himself, to taste of the sweetness of his name for the sake of Christ.

However, the assurance of which Calvin speaks is not one completely without anxiety. Calvin's "extravert character of faith," as Van Vlastuin notes, means "faith can also be opposite to inner feelings, and is never without unbelief and doubt."[122] Calvin paints a vivid picture of the feeble heart that is in conflict and varies between two opposites.

> Therefore the godly heart feels in itself a division because it is partly imbued with sweetness from its recognition of the divine goodness, partly grieves in bitterness from an awareness of its calamity; partly rests upon the promise of the gospel, partly trembles at the evidence of its own iniquity; partly rejoices at the

117. *Inst.* 3.20.5, my italics.

118. *Inst.* 3.20.37.

119. Bray, *Galatians, Ephesians*, 132.

120. *Inst.* 3.20.21; 3.20.36.

121. *Inst.* 3.20.37.

122. Van Vlastuin, "Kuyper's Spirituality," 530.

> expectation of life, partly shudders at death. This variation arises from imperfection of faith, since in the course of the present life it never goes so well with us that we are wholly cured of the disease of unbelief and entirely filled and possessed by faith.[123]

The assurance of our adoption is firm when our faith is weakened by trials. For "even weak faith is real faith" that pleases God. "When even the least drop of faith is instilled in our minds, we begin to contemplate God's face, peaceful and calm and gracious toward us. We see him afar off, but so clearly as to know we are not at all deceived."[124] Calvin compares a life of faith to a person locked in a prison, surrounded by darkness everywhere, but who can still see the rays of the sun breaking in through a narrow window, though obliquely and obscurely.[125] A life of faith is not one that is exempted from troubles or assaults but one that falls beneath God's safekeeping, even when we are not in perfect repose. Those who are profoundly "tossed about by various doubts" will find themselves profoundly sustained by nothing other than the goodness of God promised and hidden in life's calamities.[126] Commenting on Ephesians 3:12, "through whom we have boldness," Calvin reinforces the instrumental causality of faith, that it grasps God's unwavering promises through which we remain calm and bold amidst life's trials:

> First confidence and then, as its result, boldness, are begotten of faith. Thus there are three steps to be taken. First, we believe the promises of God; next, by resting in them, we conceive confidence, so that we have a good and quiet mind. From this follows boldness, which enables us to banish fear, and to entrust ourselves courageously and steadfastly to God.[127]

The second gift that flows from being united to Christ is that the Spirit creates in us an unquenchable *desire* for God's boundless mercy, when molested by sin and terrified by God's wrath. Everything we do, including the manner and motive, is tainted with radical depravity. The godly may feel the depths of sin within themselves and terror of divine wrath against their hideousness. They feel the crushing weight of the law, but not so that it might impede the power of faith in prayer; rather, by

123. *Inst.* 3.2.18.

124. *Inst.* 3.2.19.

125. *Inst.* 3.2.19.

126. *Inst.* 3.20.11.

127. *Comm. Eph.* 3:12, *CNTC* 11:164.

the Spirit, the law impels them to cast themselves beneath God's mercy, which frees them to pray in confidence that he hears them, even where he sees "neither perfect faith nor repentance."[128] Hence, the more ardently believers present themselves to God, the more strenuously they should cling to Jesus Christ, the true intercessor, who transforms "the throne of dreadful glory to the throne of grace."[129] Suffused with the Spirit, the suppliants feel the power of Christ's sole mediatorial activity through which the Father is made propitious and easily entreated. Faith flees from the inscrutable majesty that terrifies us; it clings to the mercy of God in Christ that consoles us. God remains the divinely unapproachable and dreadful majesty before whom we would be annihilated if we do not place our confidence in the mercy of God that has appeared in Christ. The knowledge of God's wrath, which the Spirit discloses, can be useful as it causes us to "especially"[130] desire the fruit of the gospel, that in Christ's cross God's mercy has triumphed over his wrath, whereby our hearts are mitigated and led to pray in true spontaneity before God. Calvin asserts, "No one can give himself cheerfully to prayer until he has been softened by the cross and thoroughly subdued."[131] The epistemic perception of the greatness of Christ's love by the Spirit is useful; it raises us above ourselves and the world so that our sole desire is the expiatory suffering love of God, "the highest wisdom" to which the pious must aspire.[132] Calvin asserts, "Beyond it there is nothing solid, nothing useful, nothing in short, that is right or sound."[133]

The third gift the Spirit stirs in us is an ineffable *sigh*—that is, a salutary knowledge of our emptiness, which can be filled by asking what God promises to offer. By the Spirit, we are lifted out of ourselves and pour out our thoughts and desires before God with unspeakable groans, and confidently cry, "Abba! Father!" (Rom 8:15). Not by merits or intercession of the saints but by the Spirit does the yearning of our hearts reach God. God moves toward us through the Son in the Spirit in order that we might be moved toward him through the Son by the Spirit. We pray by the Spirit who knows us profoundly in love, and who presents our prayers with sighs too deep for words. When tormented by unfathomable

128. *Inst.* 3.20.16.

129. *Inst.* 3.20.17.

130. *Inst.* 3.20.9.

131. *Comm. Ps.* 30:9, CO 31:297, as quoted in Wallace, *Christian Life*, 280.

132. *Comm. Eph.* 3:18, *CNTC* 11:168–69.

133. *Comm. Eph.* 3:18, *CNTC* 11:168–69.

thoughts of evil, the believer reaches the limit of human language but finds solace in the Spirit, the comforter who directs his life toward God. The Spirit inculcates in the godly the paradoxical work of God under the appearance of contraries, that hope begins, and comfort is no less real, when words end. When confronted with brokenness and fragmentation, which often escape analysis and articulation, God's promise of his providential care remains intact and whole. When the troubled conscience suffers turmoil of laments, frustration of regret, and harassment of guilt, the Spirit confirms in our hearts that God remains our "Abba! Father!" into whose bosom we can unload our cares. We sigh, knowing that God's help is not far off but near, hidden in a situation that seems hopeless. Words are replaced by sighs, and these will capture God's ears because it is the Spirit's stirring in the hearts that yearn for relief.

Commenting on the groaning of which Paul speaks in Romans 8:22, Calvin writes, "The meaning is that creatures are not content in their present state, and yet that they are not so distressed that they pine away without a prospect of a remedy, but that they are as it were in travail; for a restoration to a better state awaits them."[134] So the godly do not sigh perpetually; rather it is a phase in the life of faith in which they, by the Spirit, make a transposition from the sighing of hurt to relinquishing it, moving from grief to relief. Groaning thus is not without effect; for in due course it will yield joy, a blessed fruit of the Spirit.

Spirit-actuated sighing is the language of faith's discourse with God. Godly or genuine sighing is trust's wrestling with God, who has promised to meet us, even when physical eyes fail to perceive it. Sighing is a vehicle through which the one assailed receives the plenitude of God's treasures. In his nude and helpless condition, he flees to God with sighs, compelling the divine majesty to respond. Sighing thus is the result of a pious encounter with God, not a preparation for it. It is not to be understood as a sort of preexistent salvific material that prepares us to receive grace; rather it is a sign of the absolute nothingness within us that leads us to "forget ourselves and all that is ours"[135] and find fulfillment in God alone. Sighing causes us to leave the self so that we might cleave solely to God for satisfaction. As our sighing orients our lives, our sighs acquaint us with our salvation, and we live by the Spirit, through whom we become aware of God's consolation.

134. *Comm. Rom.* 8:22, CTS 19:306.

135. *Inst.* 3.7.1.

## THE LORD'S PRAYER: THE MASTER'S RULE

The Lord's Prayer, Christ's own words that we invoke, is God's gift, and intended to stir our hearts to pray with content that befits chiefly his glory and secondarily our needs. We pray through Christ's mouth the very words that proceed from the lips of the second person of the Trinity. "In order to be a genuine exercise of faith," Ronald S. Wallace writes, "prayer must be controlled, formed and inspired by the Word of God."[136] The words of the Lord are not to be strictly followed, for in Scripture, there are various prayers that use different words, but are of the same Spirit.[137] As regards this, Elsie McKee notes, "Calvin himself did not hesitate to paraphrase the text [of the Lord's Prayer] for Sunday worship, to enable the people to understand better what they were asking."[138] Prayer may vary in words but not in the sense or content contained in Jesus's prayer.[139] The suppliants must comply with the thoughts, whereby their minds are kindled with an ardor toward God and freed from wavering. The Lord's Prayer is so perfect that God's glory, God's will, God's wisdom, and our needs are contained in it. True prayer must bind to the "Master's rule,"[140] which Tertullian calls "the lawful prayer."[141] We pray, allowing God's word to guide and reign over our own desires, not adding to or subtracting from it; such practice "rightly accords with fear, reverence, and solicitude."[142]

To shape our hearts for God, Calvin advises that we set aside certain hours of the day for prayer. He specifies four times a day: in the morning when we wake up, before we begin our daily work; at mealtimes; and in the evening at bedtime.[143] This pattern, however, is not to be used as a superstitious observance of hours, but as a tutelage to counteract our weaknesses.[144] At those times when we are hard pressed by adversity, the pattern moves our hearts to implore God's mercy; and at the times when

136. Wallace, *Christian Life*, 276.

137. *Inst.* 3.20.49.

138. McKee, "Teaching," 94.

139. *Inst.* 3.20.49.

140. *Inst.* 3.20.48.

141. See Tertullian, *On Flight in Persecution* 2. 5 (CCL Tertullian 2. 1138; tr. ANCL 11. 359), as cited in *Inst.* 3.20.48.

142. *Inst.* 3.14.20.

143. *Inst.* 3.20.50.

144. *Inst.* 3.20.50.

we are blessed with prosperity, the same pattern stimulates our hearts to express praise and gratitude for benefits received.

Calvin cautions against both the temptation to bring God's way of working into conformity with our own circumstances, and any intention to prescribe law or impose conditions on God to come through for us. When, what, where, and how our prayers are answered is taken out of our control and placed wholly in God's hands. By nature, we are self-centered, more concerned about our own needs and advantage than we are about God's glory. For Calvin, the whole of the Lord's Prayer gives "chief place"[145] to God's glory, though the first three petitions focus on the consideration of that glory. The second set of petitions highlights the generosity of God, from whom flows a promise of God's abundance for human needs. Yet Calvin warns that regardless of our need or want, the honor of God occupies first and foremost importance to which all else is subordinate. For the goal of the Christian life is the glory of God, which must reign above self-fulfillment.

Under the name "Father" is set before us that prayerful ascent to God that, with sure faith, is through the only-begotten Son, the image in which God presents to us. The name "Father" is effective in curbing idolatry, as it diverts our minds away from some false idols of our own making; it also engenders trust in God's fatherly heart of the sweetest and greatest affection for us. The phrase "in heaven" arouses our confidence in God, who creates the inscrutable universe, and rules it by his providence and might. Our thoughts are raised upward and above the place of sense perception that we might behold nothing more sublime and majestic than the God of infinite greatness, boundless might, and everlasting wisdom.[146]

Christ introduces us to call God "Our Father," a form of address that includes fellowship with all the people of God. By the same right of mercy, we are made God's children of one father common to us all. We are to love one another with the same zeal and affection with which we love our heavenly Father. We are to pray with the whole community of faith—the gathered and the scattered—in mind; we relate with special affection to those of the household of faith, thereby fulfilling the law of love (Gal 6:10).

145. *Inst.* 3.20.35.

146. *Inst.* 3.20.40.

Our prayer must be done in conformity to God's holy name, "Hallowed be Thy name"—that is, our words or thoughts must "breathe pure glory."[147] We pray this, so that God might vindicate his holy name of all dishonor, and subdue all humanity to revere it. The second entreaty, "Thy Kingdom come," is "almost identical"[148] to the first. Calvin acknowledges two parts to this kingdom: that God by his Spirit might crush the prompting of the old flesh, and that he might shape all our thoughts to voluntary obedience to God.[149] This occurs "when he manifests the working of his word through the secret inspiration of his Spirit in order that it may stand forth in the degree of honor that it deserves."[150] God's kingdom is fulfilled when the subjects demonstrate obedience to his rule zealously by mortifying the flesh and sacrificially bearing the cross so that righteousness increases.[151] And yet God's kingdom cannot thrive apart from God's will; thus we pray the third petition, "Thy will be done on earth as in heaven." We submit our will to God, allowing it to be restrained by him as by "a bridle"; it relinquishes its control of God and regards him as "the arbiter and director of all its entreaties."[152] Our desire for the good is still tainted with residual sins; it tends to yield deformed fruits. By this prayer, our minds and hearts are renewed (cf. Ps 51:20), our faith is exercised, and the vilest desires of our flesh are subdued. Prayer forms us to self-denial, causing us to forget ourselves but follow the Spirit, the inward teacher who governs our hearts so that we may set our affections on things that please God, and shun those that displease him. Consequently, all wishes or feelings that oppose God's will are rendered futile and have no control over us.[153]

The fourth petition beckons us to ask for "our daily bread," that we may rest content with what the Heavenly Father has deigned to dispense to us, and that we need not obtain these things by unlawful means.[154] The word "our" stresses that the abundance of God's generosity "is made ours by title of gift."[155] Our labors are in vain unless God blesses them

147. *Inst.* 3.20.41.
148. *Inst.* 3.20.42.
149. *Inst.* 3.20.42.
150. *Inst.* 3:20.42.
151. *Inst.* 3.20.42.
152. *Inst.* 3.20.50.
153. *Inst.* 3.20.43.
154. *Inst.* 3.20.44.
155. *Inst.* 3.20.44.

and causes them to flourish. For Calvin, these words—"today," "day by day," and "daily"—accentuate the immediacy with which we by prayer conquer the unbridled passion for fleeting things, from which sprouts evils.[156] We ask God only to provide sufficiently for our needs daily, but with this assurance that God who provides for us today will not waver tomorrow. Daily, we testify to "a singular proof"[157] that God is our sole help and rescue in times of crises; and that he sustains us through the creaturely means he provides for us. As is evident in 1 Timothy 4:8: "Godliness holds promise not only for the life to come but also for the present life." Here the order of emphasis, for Calvin, is from the present life to the future life. Christ gives priority to the earthly nourishments—"the inferior things"—not so that our identity may be defined by them but that through them he might gradually lead us to the heavenly life. This is a "far more important" thing than the creaturely provisions taught in the two remaining petitions.[158]

In his explanation of the fifth petition, "forgive us our debts," Calvin combines christological and pneumatological grace to draw us to God. "Here Christ begins with forgiveness of sins, then presently adds the second grace: that God protect us by the power of his Spirit and sustain us by his aid so we may stand unvanquished against all temptations."[159] This petition calls sins "debts," thereby revealing our stance before God: We are debtors. Purely by God's free mercy, our debts are wiped out, payment from us exonerated, and satisfaction made on our behalf in Christ, who once for all gave himself as a ransom (Rom 2:24). The Spirit imparts to us the fruit of Christ's death, God's mercy through which we entreat God; and to do otherwise is to incite his judgment. To pray this petition is to avail ourselves of his prevailing grace: that God deigns forgiveness as a necessary remedy to the residual stains in us. Consequently, God gradually restores his image in us through prayer.

The conditional clause—"as we forgive"—Christ adds is not so that, by the forgiveness we render to others, we merit his forgiveness. There is nothing in the gospel but forgiveness offered as a gift. This clause has a pedagogical purpose: "partly," as an aid to the weakness of our faith, the Lord "has added this as a sign to assure us he has granted forgiveness to us, just as surely as we are aware of having forgiven others. . . .

156. *Inst.* 3.20.44.

157. *Inst.* 3.20.45.

158. *Inst.* 2.20.44.

159. *Inst.* 3.20.45.

Also, partly by this mark that the Lord excludes from the number of his children those persons" whose hearts are saturated with hostility, hatred, and revenge against others. "This the Lord does that such men dare not call upon him as Father."[160] By forgiving others, we show ourselves to be truly God's children. This petition encourages us to ask for God's forgiveness, recognizing that we too must forgive others. Any presumption that we could beseech God for forgiveness while our hearts foment enmity against the wrongdoers has no place in the Christian life.

With the ancient writers, Calvin joins the sixth and seventh petition together. He renders, "Do not allow us to be oppressed by temptation but rather bring help for our weakness, and deliver us from falling."[161] Calvin argues that the Lord's Prayer consists of six petitions rather than seven. It is because "by inserting the adversative 'but' the Evangelist seems to have meant to join those two members together."[162] God provides us with the grace of the Spirit through which our hearts are softened and our will is inclined toward God. Calvin indicates two sorts of temptation that war against us, one aroused by the inordinate desire within and the other instilled in us by the devil's guile without. We pray for his power, through which we may overcome vilest desires of our flesh and conquer the wicked thoughts of our mind. The pious do not shun temptation, by which they are aroused so that they may not remain sluggish and eventually fall prey to evil. Both God and Satan try us, but with a different purpose: "Satan tempts that he may destroy, condemn, confound, cast down," so that there is no escape, "but God, that by proving his own children he may make trial of their sincerity, and establish their strength by exercising it," eventually preparing a way out of it.[163] In prosperity, we pray that we may not be smug; in adversity, we pray that we will not despair; in perversity, we pray that we will not yield. We pray this petition, for the filling of the Spirit and more of God's grace, to gain victory over all evil—"the devil or sin."[164]

The Lord concludes his prayer with "Amen," so that, with "the warmth of desire,"[165] we can receive what we have prayed for. "Prayer

160. *Inst.* 3.20.45.

161. *Inst.* 3.20.35. See note 71, where he cites Pseudo-Chrysostom, *Homilies on Matthew* (incomplete work), hom. 14 (MPG 56. 715).

162. *Inst.* 3.20.35.

163. *Inst.* 3.20.46.

164. *Inst.* 3.20.46.

165. *Inst.* 3.20.47.

without faith," Mesa says, "is a vain exercise of moving lips with an empty heart of unbelief."[166] Just as he encourages prayer by his promises, he too urges that we pray in sure faith, grasping what God has furnished for us in Christ (Jas 1:6). Faith must be present for the command, promise, and the words of prayer to be effective. It is summed up in our willingness to utter "Amen," believing that our prayers will surely be heard. The confidence of being heard stems not from our own worth or merits, but solely from God's nature—namely, the God who never lies, but who does deliver his promises. God often tests the faith of believers by keeping them longer in their grief before he offers them any relief. Perseverance and hope in prayer stem from the conviction that God is not "a deaf God," and will eventually receive the fruits of this "chief exercise of faith": patience in poverty, consolation in affliction, and solace in turmoil.[167]

## CONCLUSION

True piety consists in reposing in God alone. For no one can ever be moved to pray unless by the gospel of grace, just as no one can believe unless it moves them. Sinful and mortal souls cannot of themselves ascend to God. But God prepares a way of ascent to God by giving us his Son, who is the Way himself. Prayer is God's ordained means through which believers by the Spirit lay hold of God's treasures buried in Christ. Prayer takes on a personal and communal dimension. Prayer does not earn but receives God's grace, even as we offer praise to God and plead for his faithfulness. While the Spirit enables a subjective reception of Christ's benefits that proceed from the expiatory suffering of the cross, prayer acquires a subjective reception of the blessings that proceed from the agency of the triune God. So, what is invoked in prayer is not the soteriological resources within us, which we do not possess, but the abundant gifts of the triune God that are stored up in heaven. The gifts of the triune God in the gospel become ours through faith, expressed in prayer, especially the Lord's Prayer. Grounded in the word of God, prayer declares with earnestness the superlative character of God, "the only stronghold of safety," in whom we hide, despite appearances to the contrary. The saints' prayers are far from perfect, often fraught with hideous sins. They suffer defects, which only God's mercy can heal. Their

166. Mesa, "Trinitarian Theology of Prayer," 182.

167. *Inst.* 3.20.51; 3.20.52.

prayer is animated by the reliable character of God, a treasure house of promises, from which they obtain help. Through the Spirit, believers find filial confidence in Christ, "an overflowing spring," from which flows the greatest feeling of love of the best father, and through which they are drawn into his bosom to place their burdens there. Manifest trials and afflictions of all sorts inspire an awareness of our inherent lack; thus they steer us away from seeking peace and satisfaction within ourselves, and lead us to receive the benefit of prayer that whatever we need and lack finds fulfillment in God. Through active and serious engagement in prayer, we become closely bound to Christ, in whose name we pray, and through the Spirit we enjoy intimate communion with God in Christ, the wellspring of abundant sweetness. God is revealed, wholly and "in person," to those who confess their emptiness and desire the filling of God's sweet abundance. Their prayers reach God, not because they twist by force the hands of the Almighty God through some penitential actions; not because they have a natural inclination toward God; and not because of a remnant desire for good; but simply because God, despite their flagrant faults, remains theirs, persuading them that his grace is ever ceaseless, even when human resources cease.

# 5

# The Church as the Vehicle of Grace

## *Its Ministerial, Not Magisterial, Role*

Our whole salvation is achieved by Christ's sole priesthood, a magisterial role Christ exhausts on our behalf. The mediatorial benefits Christ has achieved for us are now conveyed not through just anything, but particularly through the church's administration of word and sacrament, the two inviolable marks of a true church.[1] In stressing the ministerial role of the church, Calvin introduces Cyprian's maternal imagery. Calvin alludes to Cyprian favorably: "You cannot have God for your Father unless you have the church for your Mother."[2] For him, outside the Christian church, there is no salvation. God as Father extends his compassion by constituting the church as our mother so that we know where to seek help for the flourishing of our faith. "Since, however, in our ignorance and sloth (to which I add fickleness of disposition) we need outward helps to beget and increase faith within us, and advance it to its goal, God has added these aids that he may provide for our weakness."[3] To portray the parental nature of God's love, Calvin uses the mother metaphor as a pedagogical tool to highlight the significance the church plays in the formation of believers' identity as God's children, serving as a continual support of their faith.

1. *Inst.* 4.1.9.

2. *Inst.* 4.1.1, 1012n3, citing Cyprian, *On the Unity of the Catholic Church* 6 (CSEL 3.1.214; tr. LCC 5. 127 f.).

3. *Inst.* 4.1.1.

> For there is no other way to enter into life unless this mother [the church] conceive us in her womb, give us birth, nourish us at her breast, and lastly, unless she keeps us under her care and guidance until, putting off mortal flesh, we become like the angels [Matt. 22:30]. Our weakness does not allow us to be dismissed from her school until we have been pupils all our lives. Furthermore, away from her bosom, one cannot hope for any forgiveness of sins or any salvation.[4]

The word is the principal mark of the church, to which all other means of grace are subordinate. God was truly present in them, yet he remains distinct from the earthly elements, the perfecting cause of the saint's faith. The word in the forms of preaching and sacraments truly accomplishes what it says—sometimes despite appearances, due to the mystery of the remnant of sin and evil in the lives of the faithful. In the Old Testament, symbols are "intermediaries" that God uses to "introduce Himself in a familiar way to slow men, until step by step, they ascend to heaven."[5] So also in the New Testament, word and sacrament are God's accommodated mode of delivering his heavenly goods, which we obtain by faith. Human ministers and the creaturely signs are imperfect and frail, and cannot accomplish anything, unless the Holy Spirit is added, making these ministries effective as part of God's work of regeneration. The church is the locus of the Spirit's sanctification; it is where the Spirit distributes the gifts of the head to his members in that union. Any growth or increase of faith is ascribed not to the creatures but to the Holy Spirit. Sacraments bear the word of promise as the content, the strengthening of faith as the intent, and the Holy Spirit as the effector, without whom what we hear and see remain outside us and do not affect us within. As in preaching, so also with the sacraments: The Spirit manifests his power, making us receive the sacramental benefits, even as we discover Jesus Christ in them. The symbols are God's gracious invitation extended to those who come by faith to the banquet and enjoy him in his wholeness. Sacraments have their effectiveness among us when we receive in true faith the riches of God's grace offered there. Sacraments not only point to God's grace so that faith can grasp it but also deliver grace to those who receive it with faith in the power of the Spirit.

4. *Inst.* 4.1.4.

5. *Comm. Acts* 17, *CNTC* 7:114.

## THE ORDER OF THE CREED: GRACE AVAILS IN THE CHURCH

For faith to flourish, God "deposited" the gospel in the church.[6] The word "deposit" does not mean the church possesses or owns the gospel; rather the church is a faithful servant of it. The gospel constitutes the church, yet the gospel cannot be known apart from the church. The article in the Creed should read "I believe the church," rather than "in" the church, simply because the church that exercises maternal or ministerial care for the family of believers is not the object of our faith; only God is. The preposition "in" is to be used exclusively of God, in whom our whole being rests for safety.[7] "We testify that we believe *in* God because our mind reposes in him as truthful, and our trust rests in him."[8]

"The communion of saints" expresses what the church is—namely, the saints who are gathered into the society of Christ. Since God is their common Father and Christ the common head of all united in love, they naturally would share the benefits of God with one another.[9] The church thus is called "catholic," or "universal," because Christ cannot be divided. Calvin extols the word "communion" from which we, as members, might reap a wealth of comfort and hope; it firmly binds us to the society of God where our faith increases. As part of the benefits of the communion of the saints, Calvin introduces the power of the keys, the ministry of reconciliation given to the church. The Lord has invested his mercy in the word of absolution whereby our sins are continually forgiven. There are three factors to the power of the keys in binding and loosing sin (Matt 16:19; 18:9–18; John 20:23), which work for our benefit.[10] First, no matter how great we excel in holiness, we remain sinful, in perpetual need of forgiveness. Second, this benefit cannot be enjoyed unless we remain in communion with the church. Third, it is mediated to us through the ministers and pastors of the church. Their office has been committed to strengthen godly consciences by the gospel of forgiveness, but it does not usurp the place of him who alone can forgive. Against the fanatics, Calvin propounds that God conveys the grace of forgiveness, not through the secret working of the Spirit, but through the physical, external word

6. *Inst.* 4.1.1.
7. *Inst.* 4.1.2.
8. *Inst.* 4.1.2.
9. *Inst.* 4.1.3.
10. *Inst.* 4.1.22.

spoken by human beings in Christ's name. Luther extends the power of the keys to the laity, that a word spoken by a layperson is as fully effective as that spoken by the clergy in the stead of Jesus Christ.[11] But Calvin binds the power of the keys to the professional clergy. In both Reformers, the efficacy lies in the word, which assures us that nothing, neither death nor the devil, will sever us from God. Whether privately or publicly administered, faith is required to benefit from the instrumental character of the priest's absolution.

Not sinlessness but forgiveness admits us into the society of church by the sign of baptism and God's kingdom. The Lord not only receives us into favor and incorporates us once for all into the church, but also, by the same means, preserves and protects us there. This accounts for the logic of the order of the Creed, in which we are taught that grace avails ceaselessly in Christ's church. "For once the church has, so to speak, been established, forgiveness of sins is added to it."[12] No matter what the numbers are—small or great—Christ's church will not perish on account of this: "I believe in the forgiveness of sin," which is a fruit of Christ's mediatorial activity the Spirit daily communicates to us who have been grafted into the body of the church.[13] Thus "Christ's death is fruitful,"[14] despite the seeming fruitlessness at times of the church's ministry.

The church can "neither totter nor fall," for two reasons.[15] First, she stands by God's election, as certain as is his eternal providence. Second, having been united to Christ, the head, we remain within the bosom of the church, for his steadfastness will not allow his members to be estranged from him. These promises hold true for them: "There will be salvation in Zion" (Joel 2:32); and "God will abide in the midst of Jerusalem forever, that it may be never be moved" (Ps 46:5).

## THE "TOUCHSTONE": SCHISM AND UNITY

Calvin offers two defining marks of a true church: "Wherever we see the Word of God purely preached and heard, and the sacraments administered according to Christ's institution, there, it is not to be doubted,

11. See LW 69:313–436 (Eastertide sermons).
12. *Inst.* 4.1.27.
13. *Inst.* 4.1.21.
14. *Inst.* 4.1.2.
15. *Inst.* 4.1.3.

a church of God exists (cf. Eph 2:20)."[16] These two marks constitute "a touchstone"[17] by which the validity of a church is tested. The preaching of the word and the observance of the sacraments can never be without fruits, though they do not have immediate results. Wherever they are received, they manifest their effectiveness. These two inviolable marks are sufficient pledge and guarantee that a true church, however defective, abides. Calvin's definition is crucial, not only in what it explicitly accepts, but also in what it excludes. McGrath writes,

> Calvin's definition is significant as much for what it does *not* say as for what it does explicitly affirm. There is no reference to the necessity of any historical or institutional continuity with the apostles, or with any institutionalized concept of the church—most notably, the medieval church. For Calvin, institutional continuity was not sufficient to guarantee intellectual and spiritual fidelity. It was more important to teach what the apostles taught than to be able to show an unbroken line of institutional continuity with them.[18]

Even when one may find faults in the administration of doctrine or sacraments, this in no way means we should renounce the communion of the church or remain in it to create uproar and disturb its order. Not all the articles of true doctrine are of equal importance. Some are disputable; others are essential, to be held by all as "the proper principles of the faith."[19] Calvin specifies at least three essentials: "God is one; Christ is God and the Son of God; our salvation rests in God's mercy; and the like."[20] As long as the cardinal doctrines are maintained, there is no ground for schism. But Calvin finds grounds for departing from the Roman Catholic Church, for in it "the sum of necessary doctrine is overturned, and the use of sacraments is destroyed."[21] Calvin distinguishes between *church* and *churches*. Calvin believes that the church as an institution has corrupted the true church through idolatry, superstition, and unbiblical doctrine, and thus has to be rejected.[22] Though Calvin does not categorically concede to the papists "the title of *the* church," he does not deny

16. *Inst*. 4.1.9.

17. *Inst*. 4.1.11.

18. McGrath, *Reformation Thought*, 189, italics original.

19. *Inst*. 4.1.12.

20. *Inst*. 4.1.12.

21. *Inst*. 4.2.1.

22. *Inst*. 4.2.2.

that there are churches or a remnant of God's people among the papacy.[23] He offers two reasons. First, the Lord preserved baptism as evidence of his inviolable covenant, which, consecrated by his lips, retains its power despite human impiety. Second, there are traces of the church under the papacy, which the Lord permits by his own providence to remain, that the church might survive the destruction.[24]

Against the Donatists of Augustine's time, Calvin holds that the church is not a pure body of believers, besmirched with no blemish; with Augustine, he maintains that it is a mixture of saints and sinners. They stay together like wheat and tares until the harvest (Matt 13:24–30). The church's task is not to separate them out but to gather them, as the net gathers all kinds of fish (Matt 13:47–58), until the day of judgment.[25] Both the Corinthian and Galatian churches abound in heinous misdeeds—and yet Paul did not forsake them. Neither is stripped of the title "church," simply on account of the ministry of word and sacrament, which remain firm and unrepudiated.

## PREACHING, A "SINGULAR PRIVILEGE": THE VOICE, FACE, AND HEART OF GOD

For Calvin, edification is central to the office of preaching. "For God will have his people edified. . . . When we come together in the name of God, it is not to hear merry songs and to be fed with wind, that is, with vain and unprofitable curiosity, but to receive spiritual nourishment."[26] The preaching of the heavenly gospel has been enjoined upon pastors in order that believers can mature under the education of the church. They are to be governed and guided by teachers appointed to this maternal function of nurturing. There is no greater help for believers than public worship, through which God strengthens his own flock gradually. Calvin elevates the office of preaching above all else, for it is "the most excellent of all things."[27] The church is "built up solely by outward preaching."[28] She is not built on human judgments or the priesthood, but on the teaching of

23. *Inst.* 4.2.11.
24. *Inst.* 4.2.11.
25. *Inst.* 4.1.13.
26. Calvin, *Mystery*, 56; cf. DeVries, "Calvin's Preaching," 110.
27. *Inst.* 4.3.3.
28. *Inst.* 4.1.5.

the apostles and prophets (Eph 2:10). The emphasis on the apostolic contents in Calvin marks a decisive break with the Catholic insistence that the authenticity of the church is to be measured by the apostolic succession. God is not bound to the means he has selected; he remains entirely free to communicate his grace, albeit by means of pastors, to whom we as the pupils are bound to receive help. Whoever abolishes this order established by Christ, that he works through insignificant or frail ministers, is aiming at the ruin and demise of the church. Preaching, Dawn DeVries sums up well, "serves as a bond of union between believers, knitting the church together into a cohesive community. . . . God joins all believers together into one who is appointed pastor to teach the rest, and the benefits of salvation are communicated to the many through the service of one. The ministry of the Word, then, is like a sinew that binds tissue and bones together in one body."[29]

John Leith describes Calvin's view of preaching as "sacramental": "In preaching, the Holy Spirit uses the words of the preacher as an occasion for the presence of God in grace and in mercy," and thus, "in this sense the actual words of the sermon are comparable to the elements in the sacraments."[30] Preaching is not, in the sense of a visible sign, a sacrament. It is the instrument that the Holy Spirit uses as his own tongue and lips to do the recreative speaking that effects faith and thus saves. Calvin elaborates, "When the prophet says, *by the breath of his lips*, this must not be limited to the person of Christ; for it refers to the word which is preached by his ministers. Christ acts by them in such a manner that he wishes their *mouth* to be reckoned as his *mouth*, and their *lips* as his *lips*."[31] Quoting him again, "The voice which in itself is mortal, is made an instrument to communicate eternal life."[32] In this regard, preaching cannot be reduced to teaching, a pedagogical function in which there is merely an impartation of information; it is chiefly a saving event in which Christ and all his benefits are imparted to us through the proclaimed word. Preaching is both a human work (instrumental) and a divine work (effectual). Preaching is where God hides in human speech, and is active in preaching through human voice. Leith elaborates, "The justification for preaching is not in its effectiveness for education or reform. . . . The

29. DeVries, "Calvin's Preaching," 108.

30. Leith, "Proclamation," 210–12.

31. *Comm. Isa.* 11:4, CTS 7:381.

32. *Comm. 1 Pet.* 1:25, *CR* 55:231, as cited in Wallace, *Word and Sacrament*, 85.

preacher, Calvin dared to say, was the mouth of God."[33] Such perspective is closely linked to Calvin's understanding of the effective, not just instructive, nature of God's word; as Brian Gerrish writes, "God's word, for Calvin, is not simply a dogmatic norm; it has in it a vital efficacy."[34] Gerrish's assessment concurs with that of Stephen Webb, who writes, "God's Word accomplishes what it commands. It is covenantal speech, active and full of life. Even in its stuttering, it has the power to give what it asks. God's Word called the world into being, and it continues to uphold the world through the speech of the Spirit-filled church."[35] As in John L. Austin's speech act theory, language is creative, not descriptive. Preaching does not merely describe but accomplishes. To speak is to do, creating a new reality that corresponds to itself. God's actions occur through the word, and preachers are the instruments God consecrates for conveying life-changing, recreating messages. Calvin teaches,

> This is the manner of fulfilment: through the ministers to whom he has entrusted this office and has conferred the grace to carry it out, he dispenses and distributes his gifts to the church; and he shows himself as though present by manifesting the power of his Spirit in this his institution, that it be not vain or idle.[36]

Calvin affirms the trinitarian dynamic of preaching in which God himself speaks through his appointed servants: "God breathes faith into us [by the Spirit] only by the instrument of his gospel, as Paul points out that 'faith comes from hearing' [Rom. 1:16]."[37] Proclamation is "dead and useless, unless the Lord gives effective power to it by His Spirit."[38] God is "the author of preaching, joining his Spirit with it, promises benefits from it."[39] Entirely free, God has nonetheless bound himself to this ordinary office of teaching to meet us.[40] Nothing is "more notable or glorious" than the preaching ministry of the word, through which the Spirit conveys Christ's righteousness and blessedness to us.[41] The conversion of Lydia in Acts 16:14, for Calvin, is an instance of the Spirit's work, where the

33. Leith, "Proclamation," 210–12.

34. Gerrish, *Grace and Gratitude*, 85; cf. *Inst.* 2.10.7.

35. Webb, *Divine Voice*, 159.

36. *Inst.* 4.3.2.

37. *Inst.* 4.1.5.

38. *Comm. 1 Cor.* 3:7, *CNTC* 9:70.

39. *Inst.* 4.1.6.

40. *Inst.* 4.1.5.

41. *Inst.* 4.3.3.

Spirit opens her mind and creates in her reverence for his word, which otherwise would not take root in her heart.[42] In his *Institutes*, Calvin highlights the affective encounter with the Spirit, who makes effectual the proclaimed word in the hearts of the hearers:

> It now remains to pour into the heart itself what the mind has absorbed. For the Word of God is not received by faith if it flits about in the top of the brain, but when it takes root in the depth of the heart that it may be an invincible defense to withstand and drive off all the stratagems of temptation. But if it is true that the mind's real understanding is illumination by the Spirit of God, then in such confirmation of the heart his power is much more clearly manifested, to the extent that the heart's distrust is greater than the mind's blindness. It is harder for the heart to be furnished with assurance than for the mind to be endowed with thought. The Spirit accordingly serves as a seal, to seal up in our hearts those very promises the certainty of which it has previously impressed upon our minds; and takes the place of a guarantee to confirm and establish them.[43]

God's word must reign supreme in worship—if not, the majesty of God is robbed; as Calvin avers, "It is the same as though its despisers attempted to thrust God from heaven."[44] The servants of the word of God "cannot firmly execute their office except they have the majesty of God before their eyes."[45] Calvin warns against placing confidence in preachers rather than in God's majesty alone. "[God] shows how great is the power of truth when he works through it by the secret influence of his Spirit. God sometimes connects himself with his servants, and sometimes separates himself from them: when he connects himself with them, he transfers to them what never ceases to dwell in him; for he never resigns to them his own office, but makes them partakers of it only."[46] Those who have God's majesty before their eyes know that they are given the privilege to preach but have no power to accomplish; for "all power of action resides in the Spirit himself, and thus all praise ought to be entirely referred to God alone."[47]

42. *Comm. Acts* 16:14, *CNTC* 7:73.
43. *Inst.* 3.2.36.
44. *Comm. Jer.* 5:13, *CJL* 1:280.
45. *Comm. Jer.* 1:9–10, *CJL* 1:44.
46. *Comm. Mal.* 4:6, CTS 15:629.
47. *Comm. Ezek.* 2:2, CTS 11:109.

God proves his compassion for our weakness by meeting us in human manner through teachers, this familiar way through which he gently attracts us to himself, rather than appearing on the scene with lightning and thunder, surrounded by myriads of angels, which drives us away. Preaching is a form of divine accommodation, in which the faithful, freed from the terror of God's majesty, truly feel the benefit of God coming near to them. Quoting Calvin, "Indeed, from the dread with which God's majesty justly overwhelms them, all the pious truly feel how much this familiar sort of teaching is needed."[48] Preaching is the means through which the word of God comes to visible expression in the worship of the gathered community. The majesty of God is hidden in preaching so that we truly meet him in our midst. Calvin maintains,

> It is certain that if we come to church we shall not hear only a mortal man speaking but we shall feel (even by His secret power) that God is speaking to our souls, that He is the teacher. He so touches us that the human voice enters into us and so profits us that we are refreshed and nourished by it. God calls us to Him as if He had His mouth open and we saw Him there in person.[49]

The belief in God's majestic presence in preaching leads to Calvin's high regard on the pulpit. He writes, "The office of preaching is committed to pastors for no other purpose than that God alone may be heard."[50] In preaching, we hear his ministers speaking "just as if" God himself speaks.[51] To clarify, Calvin's phrase *just as if* is not to imply a lack of certainty in the office of preaching's efficacy; it could mean *just as*, without the *if*, God himself speaks, albeit through pastors. Simply put: Whoever hears the preacher hears God (Luke 10:16). Elsewhere, Calvin does not include *if*; for instance, on John 10:4, "They know His voice," Calvin intimates, "Although He is here speaking of ministers, He wants not so much them, as God speaking through them."[52] Divine majesty hides in the appointed ministers to meet us. In Rebekah Earnshaw's words, "When God speaks, it is as if a king steps unmistakably into the room, even in the persons of his messengers. The unmistakable element for Calvin is

48. *Inst.* 4.1.5.
49. Calvin, *Epistle to the Ephesians*, 42.
50. *Comm. Isa.* 2:3, *CI* 1:95.
51. Calvin's phrase "just as if" is found in *Inst.* 4.1.5.
52. *Comm. John* 10:4, *CTNC* 4:260.

divine majesty. Yet Calvin's God remains unlike idols, he remains without creaturely form."[53]

God has spoken personally, and definitively, in his incarnate Son. "For just as in men speech is called the expression of the thoughts, so it is not inappropriate to apply this to God and say that He expresses Himself to us by His speech or 'Word.'"[54] In preaching, it is God who speaks "in person" through his appointed instruments, and by his voice, we are summoned into communion with God. Calvin avers, "There is no other way of raising up the Church of God than by the light of the word, in which God himself, by his own voice, points out the way to salvation."[55] Those who spurn godly prophets and pastors efface "the face of God which shines upon us in teaching."[56] As often repeated in ancient times under the law, believers were commanded to assemble at the sanctuary where "God's face" shines (Pss 27:8; 100:2; 105:4; 1 Chr 16:11). For the patriarchs, the teaching of the law and the prophets were nothing but "a living image of God";[57] likewise, Paul's preaching is nothing but "the glory of God [shining] in the face of Christ."[58] God himself appears in our midst, as he did to the holy patriarchs in "the mirror of his teaching."[59] God is truly present in the tabernacle, "the place of God's name" (Exod 13:20), but transcends the limitations of the earthly sphere, for "God dwells not in temples made with hands" (Acts 7:48; Isa 66:1–2). As God hides in the voice of the incarnate Son to address us, so he hides in the voice of the preacher to converse with us. The treasures of God's true character and all his gifts are communicated through the voice of the preacher, a significant aspect of the ministerial role of the church. Among all the noble gifts with which God has adorned the human race, the Lord bestows on preachers "a singular privilege":[60] that he deigns to consecrate their mouths and tongues for his service so that his voice may be heard again, his face be seen, and his heart be felt.

53. Earnshaw, "Usefulness," 191.

54. *Comm. John* 1:1, *CNTC* 4:7.

55. *Comm. Mic.* 4:1–2, *CTMP* 3:257.

56. *Inst.* 4.1.5.

57. *Inst.* 4.1.5.

58. *Inst.* 4.1.5.

59. *Inst.* 4.1.5.

60. *Inst.* 4.1.5; 4.3.3.

## THE WORD IN SACRAMENTAL FORMS: SEVEN CONSTITUENTS

Calvin defines a sacrament as

> *an outward sign* by which the Lord *seals* on our consciences the *promises* of his good will toward us to support *the weakness of our faith*; and we in turn *attest our piety toward him*, in the presence of the Lord and of the angels as well as before men.[61]

This simple definition comprises five major elements: a sacrament as an outward sign; God's act of sealing his promises of good will; the promises themselves; our weakness of faith; and the attestation of our piety. It is Calvin's basic presupposition that the efficacy of the sacraments is supplied by the Spirit in connection with the word. Sacraments have no intrinsic power to effect anything, but, "as agencies of the Holy Spirit and in association with the Word," they deliver "the clearest promises" of God which faith apprehends.[62] Hence Calvin's theology of sacraments comprises seven elements, including faith and the Spirit.

### An Outward Sign and Inward Reality

Calvin explicitly endorses Augustine's concept of a sacrament as "a visible sign of a sacred thing" or "a visible form of an invisible grace."[63] Ever since the beginning of the world, God governed the holy patriarchs through tangible and material signs so that they could recognize him visibly.[64] Through these natural things, or miracles, God has caused his people to be more certain and confident of the truth of his promises. For examples, Isaiah went naked to demonstrate that Palestine was to be plundered (Isa 20:2–4); God set the rainbow for Noah and his descendants as a token that he would not destroy the earth (Gen 9:13–16); God showed Abraham a light in a smoking fire pot (Gen 15:17); as a promise to Gideon of victory, God watered a wool fleece with dew while the earth around it remained dry (Judg 6:37–38). These symbols act as vehicles, by which we, like the patriarchs, might rise upward with faith from the visible symbols on earth to the invisible God in heaven.

61. *Inst.* 4.14.1, my italics.
62. *Inst.* 4.14.5; 4.14.7.
63. *Inst.* 4.14.1.
64. *Inst.* 4.14.4.

As in the Old Testament, where God's people were given signs of God's presence, so in the New Testament, believers are given sacramental signs so that we know where to take hold of him. "There is only one difference: the former foreshadowed Christ promised while he was as yet awaited; the latter attest him as already given and revealed."[65] Whatever we receive today in ours, they also apprehended in theirs. Both share the same content: God's fatherly goodness and the graces of the Spirit are given us in Christ, except that in ours the attestation is "clearer and brighter." Both deliver Christ and his riches, but "in ours more richly and fully."[66] The sacraments instituted by Christ may be "fewer in number [than those celebrated by the Roman Catholic Church, but they remain] more majestic in signification, [and] more excellent in power."[67]

The sign is visible and physical; the thing signified is invisible and spiritual. The sign points to the reality it signifies: Christ, the "matter" or the "substance" of the sacraments.[68] The sign is not a simple reminder; it is an effective sign, as it conveys the reality that is signified in it. However, the union of the sign and the reality does not collapse their distinction so that what belongs to one may not be attributed to the other.[69] Sacramental elements possess value only as God's instruments through which he accomplishes his purpose. Calvin warns against two vices that render sacraments worthless:[70] the first is to receive the signs as though they are useless and vain figures, empty of the truth of God's grace they signify; the second is to be so fixed on signs that we attribute to them the glory that rightly belongs to Christ, who lies hidden in them. "And [Christ's benefits] are conferred through the Holy Spirit, who makes us partakers in Christ; conferred, indeed, with the help of outward signs, if they allure us to Christ."[71]

65. *Inst.* 4.14.20.

66. *Inst.* 4.14.26.

67. *Inst.* 4.14.26. See, e.g., *Inst.* 4.18.19 for Calvin's affirmation of only two sacraments.

68. *Inst.* 4.14.16.

69. *Inst.* 4.14.15.

70. *Inst.* 4.14.7; 4.14.16.

71. *Inst.* 4.14.16.

## The Word Added to the Sign

With Augustine, Calvin asserts that a material sign without an accompanying word is empty. He adds the word of promise to the outward sign to constitute a sacrament. "The existence of the sacraments," Wendel writes, "depended, in [Calvin's] view, upon a prevenient divine promise."[72] Without promise, the sign is devoid of meaning or power: "The sacrament requires preaching to beget faith."[73] The reference to promise in Calvin's definition accentuates the Protestant Reformation priority of God's word, the vehicle of God's presence, and that the sacrament has validity only in connection with it. The sign without God's word is a "bare sign."[74] For example, the rainbow God set before Noah was an ordinary thing, but, inscribed by God's word, it acquired a new form, different from what it was previously.[75] By this symbol of the rainbow, we apprehend God's promise that the earth will never be swept away by flood. On Calvin's analysis of the symbols of the cloud and pillar of fire in Genesis 13:21, Zachman writes, "The presence of God is truly exhibited by the symbol, even as God is not attached to or confined within the symbol."[76] God's presence via the symbol, in Calvin's words, "is a sacramental mode of speaking, wherein God transfers the name to visible figures; not to affix to them his essence, nor to circumscribe his immensity, but only to show that he does not deceitfully expose the signs of his presence to men's eyes, but that the exhibition of the thing signified is at the same time conjoined with them."[77] The cloud and pillar of fire represent God's presence; they help the Israelites' ascent to God. Though God was truly present in these symbols, we must not collapse God into the earthly elements, thereby either reducing the invisible God to the material level or subjecting his infinite glory to the finite signs of ignobility.

So when we hear the "sacramental word," we hear the promise, proclaimed by a minister, whereby we are led to where the sign directs us—namely, Jesus Christ. "Accordingly," Calvin asserts, "when we hear mention of the 'sacramental word,' we must understand the promise, which, when proclaimed in a clear voice by the minister, leads the people

72. Wendel, *Calvin*, 313.

73. *Inst.* 4.14.4.

74. *Inst.* 4.14.4.

75. *Inst.* 4.14.18.

76. Zachman, *Image and Word*, 208.

77. *Comm. Exod.* 13:21, CTS 3:236.

by the hand to where the sign aims and where it directs us."[78] In the new covenant, God institutes two sacraments, baptism and the Lord's Supper. The gifts set before us in the sacraments are bestowed not on account of the virtue of them being water, bread, and wine, but of their being consecrated by God as the instrumental causes of his grace. Earthly elements are the appointed signs in which the word of God is hidden, and to which the promise of his presence is attached.

## God's Seal as Confirmation

The seal by which God assures believers of his promises is analogous to the official stamp that authenticates an important document and confers authority upon it. The word delivers God's grace and summons hearers to respond in faith in Christ. The sacraments make certain that grace in the believer's heart in a visible and tangible way. This makes preaching indispensable, for without it the seals are void. The seals inculcate upon us the authority of the preached word.[79] Between the preaching of the word and the sacraments, Calvin prioritizes the former and calls the latter "a sort of appendix" of the word.[80] Calvin, as Avis argues, apparently intends to collapse the sacrament into the word.[81] This in no way means that he devalues the sacraments. Both preaching and sacraments share the same function: they bestow "Christ and, in him, the treasures of heavenly grace."[82] "But the mode of impact is different. The sacraments supplement the Word in a way that makes the Word somehow more real and immediate."[83] Kolb and Trueman write,

> By physical elements and liturgical action, the sacraments represent to us what the Word brings when read and preached: Jesus Christ and his grace. Therefore the sign speaks to us precisely because it is placed in the context of proclamation. The sacraments are thus not equal to the Word nor independent of it. While there can be proclamation without the administration of the sacraments, there can be no sacraments without proclamation of the Word. Indeed, for Calvin as for Luther, the Word

78. *Inst.* 4.14.4.

79. *Inst.* 4.14.5.

80. *Inst.* 4.14.3.

81. Avis, *Church*, 31.

82. *Inst.* 4.14.17.

83. Kolb and Trueman, *Between Wittenberg and Geneva*, 166; *Inst.* 4.14.6.

must be proclaimed before the sacraments, because otherwise they are just meaningless, dead symbols.[84]

## Accommodating the Weakness of Faith

God's word itself is firm, not in need of any extraneous confirmation. But our faith is feeble and unstable, in need of strengthening by means outside itself. God, out of his infinite kindness, "condescends to lead us to himself by these earthly elements and to set before us in the flesh a mirror" of gifts hidden in them.[85] "Because we are of flesh," sacraments appear "under things of the flesh" as an act of his adaptation to our dull capacity. This is "to lead us by the hand as tutors lead children" to perceive those deep mysteries beneath the physical elements.[86] Knowing our difficulty in receiving his promises, God supplements the word with visible and tangible signs of his favor. Sacraments are "mirrors in which we contemplate the riches of God's grace."[87] They are "pillars" that sustain faith, which has the word as its ultimate "foundation": "For by them he manifests himself to us . . . and attests his good will and love toward us more expressly than by word."[88] Sacraments set forth truly God's promises in the word in such a tangible way, as "a picture," that we are as certain of them as if they were before our eyes.[89]

## God's Action and Human Attestation

Calvin affirms both the causative character of a sacrament, which confirms and seals God's promises in the earthly elements, and its declaratory character, in which believers make confession of their faith and love before God and the public. Calvin's briefer definition of a sacrament includes "mutual attestation of our piety toward him."[90] With Zwingli, Calvin accepts the ceremonial or corporate dimension of church life in which the declaratory character of the sacraments has its rightful place.

84. Kolb and Trueman, *Between Wittenberg and Geneva*, 165.

85. *Inst.* 4.14.3.

86. *Inst.* 4.14.6.

87. *Inst.* 4.14.6.

88. *Inst.* 4.14.6.

89. *Inst.* 4.14.6.

90. *Inst.* 4.14.1.

Sacraments are ecclesial events, where a public attestation of our allegiance to Christ is made, similar to the oath of allegiance to the commander taken by a recruit to the army.[91] In regard to God, sacraments are testimonies of God's grace by which our faith is nourished; in regard to us, they are marks of profession by which we openly declare our faith, binding ourselves to him in obedience. Drawing on Chrysostom, Calvin speaks of sacraments as "covenants" by which God pledges himself to us, and we in turn pledge ourselves to him, in mutual concord.[92] He elaborates,

> For as in them the Lord promises to cancel and blot out any guilt and penalty contracted by us through our transgression, and reconciles us to himself in his only-begotten Son, so do we, in turn, bind ourselves to him by this profession, to pursue piety and innocence. Hence you can rightfully say that such sacraments are ceremonies by which God wills to exercise his people, first, to foster, arouse, and confirm faith within; then, to attest religion before men.[93]

Sacraments do not cause faith but merely provide the occasion by which faith, drawn from God's word, may be publicly demonstrated. Sacraments, therefore, are primarily God's actions that "serve our faith before God," and only secondarily our response that serves "our confession before people."[94]

## Faith as a Vessel

The whole force of the sacrament lies in the word, which evokes faith, not in the material elements, which of themselves possess no validity. While preaching begets faith, sacraments assure us more of the reliability of God's word. "God works through his Word, even in the sacrament. But God does not do this *ex opera operato* ['through the work that is worked'] as in the Roman Mass, whereby the sacramental action itself is efficacious. For Protestants, the attachment of the sign to the Word is crucial. It is the Word that makes the sign potent."[95] "The sacramental word is

91. *Inst.* 4.14.13.
92. *Inst.* 4.14.19.
93. *Inst.* 4.14.19.
94. *Inst.* 4.14.13.
95. Kolb and Trueman, *Between Wittenberg and Geneva*, 165.

not an incantation," Gerrish explains, "but a promise" whose reality is grasped only through faith.[96] A sacrament is therefore not efficacious in being celebrated but in being believed. With Augustine, Calvin teaches that "the efficacy of the Word is brought to light in the sacrament, not because it is spoken, but because it is believed."[97] Christ and his grace hidden in word and sacrament profit nothing unless received instrumentally through sure faith, without any works or powers or merits of our own.[98] Calvin likens faith to a "vessel," which receives the varied instances of graces of God represented in word and sacrament.[99] "As with wine or oil or some other liquid, no matter how much you pour out, it will flow away and disappear unless the mouth of the vessel to receive it is open; moreover, the vessel will be splashed over on the outside, but will still remain void and empty."[100] Faith abandons all other causes of righteousness, which human ingenuity may fashion for itself, but holds fast to the promise of Christ. God's promise remains firm, and its own force does not suffer due to the weakness of our faith. Godrey writes, "Faith does not create the promise nor cause the Spirit to act. But only faith receives the blessing of the promise and the Spirit."[101] When receiving the sacraments, believers do not contribute anything to deserve praise; they merely receive God's gifts hidden in them. As such, it is merely a "passive" act on our part, so that all human merits are excluded.[102] The passive character of faith underscores God's causative action in such a way that all forms of works-righteousness are expelled from the doctrine of justification.

The promise is valid because God is speaking it, quite apart from faith. Unbelief fails to benefit from it, but the promise still is God's. As the word of God remains what it is, even when met with unbelief, so the integrity of the sacraments remains as they are, even when received by unbelievers, for God's institution stands inviolable. The efficacy of the sacraments suffers no defect, even when an immoral person receives them, yet without benefit to himself. Calvin quotes Augustine favorably: "If you receive carnally, it does not cease to be spiritual, but it is not so

96. Gerrish, *Grace and Gratitude*, 139.

97. *Inst.* 4.14.7.

98. *Inst.* 4.14.16.

99. *Inst.* 4.14.17.

100. *Inst.* 4.14.17.

101. Godfrey, "Sacraments," 377.

102. *Inst.* 4.14.26.

for you."[103] Furthermore, the efficacy of the sacraments lies not in the merit of him who administers. So long as "the handwriting and seal in a letter are sufficiently recognized," Calvin writes, it makes no difference who delivers it; likewise, it suffices to recognize "the hand and seal of our Lord in his sacraments," even if they come through impure and apostate priests.[104]

## Sacramental Content and Intent: The Holy Spirit as the Effective Agent

Sacraments possess the word of promise as the content, and the confirmation of faith as the intent. Both content and intent do not affect us, unless accompanied by the Holy Spirit, the effective agent, whose work is to "begin, sustain and consummate faith."[105] As God himself is present in preaching by the power of the Spirit, so he is present in the external symbols by the same Spirit. There is a divine scheme in which "the one blessing of God" differentiates into three. First, the Lord teaches us by the word; second, he confirms it by the sacraments; and third, he illuminates our minds by the light of the Spirit and opens our hearts for an entrance of word and sacrament, which otherwise remain outside us.[106] "God acts by his own intrinsic power"[107] through the created means to deliver what he promises, engraving on our hearts the reality of his bountiful goodness extended by the sacraments. "God therefore truly executes whatever he promises and represents in signs; nor do these signs lack their own effect in proving their Author truthful and faithful."[108] The Holy Spirit makes us partakers of Christ's benefits with the help of outward signs. Consequently, the knowledge of the good will of our Heavenly Father set forth in word and sacrament is vivified in our hearts.

103. Augustine, *John's Gospel* 27.6 (MPL 35.1618; tr. LF 9.419), as cited in *Inst.* 4.14.16.

104. *Inst.* 4.15.16.

105. Butin, *Revelation*, 104. See also *Inst.* 4.14.8.

106. *Inst.* 4.14.8.

107. *Inst.* 4.14.17.

108. *Inst.* 4.14.17.

There is no "secret force"[109] or "hidden power"[110] attached to the sacraments by which they of themselves could justify and confer grace. The only function divinely imparted to them is ministerial—to attest and ratify God's benevolence toward us.[111] "They do not bestow any grace of themselves, but announce and tell us, and (as they are guarantees and tokens) ratify among us, those things given us by divine bounty. The Holy Spirit . . . is he who brings the graces of God with him, gives a place for the sacraments amongst us and makes them bear fruit."[112]Any increase or confirmation of faith through word and sacrament must not be ascribed to creatures, but solely to the Holy Spirit. "Neither ought our confidence to inhere in the sacraments, nor the glory of God be transferred to them."[113] Without the Spirit, "the power to act," the ministry of sacraments alone is empty, and accomplishes nothing more than the brightness of the sun shining upon blind eyes, or a sound falling on deaf ears.[114] "But sacraments properly fulfill their office only when the Spirit, that inward teacher, comes to them, by whose power alone hearts are penetrated and affections moved and our souls are opened for the sacraments to enter in."[115] Just as the eyes cannot see unless by illumination, just as the ears cannot respond to any sound unless by being created for the hearing, so also the heart cannot receive unless it is fitted to receive.[116] The word that strikes our ears (hearing) and the sacraments that appear before our eyes (seeing) do not "affect us within" (receiving) unless the Spirit "makes it effective."[117] Calvin sums up:

> For, that the Word may not beat your ears in vain, and that the sacraments may not strike your eyes in vain, the Spirit shows us that in them it is God speaking to us, softening the stubbornness of our heart, and composing it to that obedience which it owes the Word of the Lord. Finally, the Spirit transmits those outward words and sacraments from our ears to our soul.[118]

109. *Inst.* 4.14.9.
110. *Inst.* 4.14.17.
111. *Inst.* 4.14.17.
112. *Inst.* 4.14.17.
113. *Inst.* 4.14.12.
114. *Inst.* 4.14.9.
115. *Inst.* 4.14.9.
116. Inst. 4.14.9.
117. *Inst.* 4.14.8; 4.14.10.
118. *Inst.* 4.14.10.

## BAPTISM: INITIATION, PURPOSES, AND PROMISES

Baptism is "the sign of the initiation" by which God engrafts us into the society of his church and makes us his own by adoption.[119] This initiation serves first "our faith before God," and second, "our confession before people."[120] Baptism consists of three specific promises—first, forgiveness of sins. The virtue of baptism lies not in water, which without the word bears no efficacy. We receive from this sacrament the knowledge and certainty of God's benevolence. Baptism promises purification via the sprinkling of Christ's blood symbolized by the water of washing: "He saved us . . . in virtue of his own mercy, through the water of regeneration and of renewal in the Holy Spirit" (Titus 3:5). The grace of baptism is not obliterated by postbaptismal sin. Calvin's insistence runs contrary to the medieval order of salvation in which the gifts of baptism are forfeited by subsequent sins and renewed by the sacrament of penance. For Christ's purity has been granted us in baptism; it buries and blots out all defilements. Baptism, though administered once in a lifetime, has a perduring effect for Christians, as the power of baptism is extended throughout the entire course of regeneration. The word "initiation," Parker writes, "has not only a backward reference, in forgiving the past, but also a future."[121] Therefore, our troubled conscience finds relief by recalling the memory of our baptism, from which we obtain the assurance of the continuing cleansing that is offered in Christ's blood.[122]

Baptism conveys another promise—namely, mortification of the old Adam, and renewal of the new person. As Paul taught, "We have been baptized into his death, . . . buried with him into death, . . . that we may walk in newness of life" (Rom 6:3–4). Union with Christ in baptism means union with his death and resurrection; "these two are inseparably connected, [so that] our old man is destroyed by the death of Christ so that His resurrection may restore our righteousness, and make us new creatures."[123] Perversity always dwells within us, as long as the old nature abides. In a lifelong and tedious fight against sin, baptism conveys

119. *Inst.* 4.15.1; 4.18.19.

120. *Inst.* 4.15.1.

121. Parker, *Calvin*, 151.

122. *Inst.* 4.15.4.

123. *Comm. Rom.* 6:4, *CNTC* 8:122.

a promise to the faithful that God is at work in renewing them; this also encourages them to press on because sin does not rule over them.[124]

The third promise of baptism is that we are so engrafted into Christ that we reap all his benefits by faith.[125] To baptize in Christ's name is to baptize in the name of the Father and of the Spirit as well. The triune God is the agent in baptism: God by the Spirit conveys through baptism to us the gifts that are laid up in Christ. The Father is the "cause," the Son "the matter," and the Spirit "the effect."[126] The Trinity is the dynamic of accomplishment of God's gifts for us: The merciful Father (cause) reconciles us with him through the cleansing of the Son's blood (matter) offered in baptism, which is applied in us by the Spirit (effect). In Calvin's estimation:

> For we are cleansed by his blood because our merciful Father, wishing to receive us into grace in accordance with his incomparable kindness, has set this Mediator among us to gain favor for us in his sight. But we obtain regeneration by Christ's death and resurrection only if we are sanctified by the Spirit and imbued with a new and spiritual nature.[127]

The force of baptism rests not on the worth of the priests; nor is the sign voided by the impurity of the ministers. The promise remains firm and inviolable, by virtue of Christ's institution. The promise that had been proffered in baptism benefits those who receive it in faith. Yet faith does not create God's promise; it merely receives these salutary benefits hidden in baptism:[128] that he has forgiven our sins, triumphed over Satan, and made us partakers of Christ's death and resurrection.[129] The outward representation and inward bestowal are one, for God effectively brings to us by the baptismal sign the clear testimony of God's goodwill.

## INFANT BAPTISM, CIRCUMCISION, AND CONFIRMATION

Calvin draws a parallel between baptism and circumcision. The covenant God established with his people in circumcision is ever effectual, and

124. *Inst.* 4.15.11.
125. *Inst.* 4.15.5–6.
126. *Inst.* 4.15.6.
127. *Inst.* 4.15.6.
128. *Inst.* 4.15.6.
129. *Inst.* 4.15.14.

restoration into God's covenant is not by a second circumcision but by repentance, "the sole condition." "For this reason, when the Lord invites the Jewish people to repentance, he enjoins no second circumcision upon those who . . . were circumcised. . . . He urges only conversion of heart."[130] Likewise, God's promises in infant baptism remain steady, sturdy, and true, even when encountered by unbelief.[131] Calvin does not impose rebaptism on account of our unfaithfulness, but encourages change of heart.[132]

Infant baptism is justified because of its close linkage with circumcision. In the Old Testament, circumcision was a prototype of a sacrament given to Israel. It is a sign that a male child has been born into the covenantal family of God and is possessed of spiritual promises sealed to them in circumcision. Circumcision has no bearing on what the child thinks, does, or believes. It simply says that here is a child born within the family of God. Likewise, in the New Testament, it is inconceivable that God should have neglected to give the people some corresponding signs. Like Zwingli before him, Calvin argues that we should baptize infants, not because they believe, but simply because it is an external sign that the child has been born within a believing community, and a celebration of that child's birth. Calvin argues for the covenantal justification of infant baptism. As the children of the old covenant were sealed with God's promises, so the children of the new have the same promises. The children of the Jews were called "a holy seed" (Ezra 9:2); the children of Christians are considered "holy" (1 Cor 7:14). In the time of the Old Testament, circumcision confirmed the covenant; in the New Testament, baptism confirmed it. "The covenant is common, and the reason for confirming it is common. Only the manner of confirmation is different—what was circumcision for them was replaced for us by baptism. Otherwise, if the testimony by which the Jews were assured of the salvation of their posterity is taken away from us, Christ's coming would have the effect of making God's grace more obscure and less attested for us than it had previously been for the Jews."[133] Calvin warns against neglecting the baptizing of infants, arguing that once the testimony of God's goodness is removed from us, it leads to a disastrous consequence, that the promise of God

130. *Inst.* 4.15.17.
131. *Inst.* 4.15.17.
132. *Inst.* 4.15.17.
133. *Inst.* 4.16.6.

set forth before our sight may eventually vanish.[134] Hence "if Christian infants cannot be baptized," McGrath notes, "they are placed at a disadvantage to Jewish infants, who are publicly and outwardly sealed into the covenant community through circumcision."[135] Unlike his Anabaptist opponents, Calvin expressly avows that elect children who, after receiving the sign of regeneration, die in infancy will be saved by "the power, incomprehensible to us, of the Spirit, in whatever way he alone foresees will be expedient."[136]

Both the parents and the infants benefit from infant baptism. First, it gives their parents a firmer assurance that God manifests his grace to their posterity, that he acknowledges them as his children as soon as they are born, and that he includes them as members of the church.[137] "For God's sign, communicated to a child as by an impressed seal, confirms the promise given to the pious parent, and declares it to be ratified that the Lord will be God not only to him and to his seed; and that he wills to manifest his goodness and grace not only to him but to his descendants even to the thousandth generation [Exod 20:6]."[138] This not only fills their hearts with gratitude for God's care for their children, but also gives parents stimulus to teach the faith to their beloved children,[139] with the hope that one day they reach the age when they can understand the virtue of baptism, and be stirred to obey God.[140] The fervent desire for renewal springs "from learning that they were given the token of it in their first infancy in order that they might meditate upon it throughout life."[141] In this regard, Godfrey writes, "Baptism constantly remains a visible word, calling them to faith."[142]

Second, infant baptism possesses value for the children. Being grafted into the body of the church, they are somewhat in closer proximity to the care of all church members. Calvin's defense of infant baptism is an implication of his conception of the church as the mother in whose bosom Christians nestle. Baptism animates in children a powerful

134. *Inst.* 4.16.32.
135. McGrath, *Reformation Thought*, 224.
136. *Inst.* 4.16.21.
137. *Inst.* 4.16.32.
138. *Inst.* 4.16.9.
139. *Inst.* 4.16.32.
140. *Inst.* 4.16.32.
141. *Inst.* 4.16.21.
142. Godfrey, *Pilgrim and Pastor*, 106.

impetus to worship God, by whom they were received into divine favor via "a solemn symbol of adoption," long before they could perceive him as Father.[143]

Calvin sees value in confirmation, not as a sacrament, but as a public expression of faith made at a relatively early age. This was practiced by the ancient Christians, who delivered an account of their faith in the presence of the church. A boy of ten years old, for example, may be examined on the articles of faith. If he was found ignorant of any or failed to understand them, he would be taught.[144] This reinforces the parental role in the instruction of their children.

While the sacrament of baptism is given to infants, the sacrament of the Lord's Supper is denied to them. Calvin sees the Supper as "solid food,"[145] given to the mature, those who have passed tender infancy. In keeping with the apostolic instruction in 1 Corinthians 11:26–29, he deduces that those who come to the table are capable of discerning the body of Christ, of practicing self-examination, of proclaiming the cross of Christ, and of remembering the force and benefit of Christ's work.[146] None of these applies to the infants, as they fail to understand them. Just as the signs of circumcision and the Passover differ in application, so too do the corresponding signs of baptism and the Supper. Circumcision, which corresponds to our baptism, was applied to infants (Gen 17:12). The Supper's antecedent, the Passover, was not open to all indiscriminately—only to those who were mature enough to grasp its meaning (Exod 12:26).[147] Likewise, the Supper is appointed for adults.

## EUCHARISTIC RELOCATION: ASCENSION AND THE HOLY SPIRIT

The Lord's Supper is a constant means by which Christ sustains and strengthens us in the life he has regenerated by his word. The pious find "greater assurance and delight" in this sacrament; "in it they have a witness of our growth into one body with Christ such that whatever is his may be called ours. As a consequence, we may dare assure ourselves that

143. *Inst.* 4.16.9.
144. *Inst.* 4.19.13.
145. *Inst.* 4.16.30.
146. *Inst.* 4.16.30.
147. *Inst.* 4.16.30.

eternal life, of which he is the heir, is ours; . . . This is the wonderful exchange which, out of his measureless benevolence, he has made with us; that, becoming the Son of man with us, he has made us sons of God with him."[148] The power of the sacrament is applied to believers but withheld from the wicked. Brian Gerrish notes, "The eucharistic gift therefore benefits those only who respond with the faith that the proclamation itself generates."[149] The Supper is poison to Judas, not because it is an evil thing, but a good thing that "an evil man evilly received."[150]

Calvin opposes the Roman Catholic view that a worthy reception of the Supper requires the communicants to be pure. For Calvin, the Supper was instituted to purify us and help us against sin and ought to attract us with joy and yearning. Those who wait until they have already perfected themselves to receive it no longer have need of any sacramental help. The Supper does not benefit the healthy, righteous, and rich; rather, it is medicine for the sick, alms for the poor, and forgiveness for sinners.[151] Calvin detests the papists' practice of sacrificing Christ anew. The belief that the Mass as a sacrifice procures the forgiveness of sins commits "a most pestilential error."[152] The Mass detracts from the finished and completed sacrifice of Christ on the cross. It is a blasphemy against Christ; it insults Christ, undermines the efficacy of his cross, deprives us of the benefit which comes from it, and invalidates the sacrament as God's action.[153] It changes the sacrament from a gift God gives to the church into an offering she gives to God. Such action is sacrilegious, as it converts the Mass into the occasion for the appeasement of God's wrath. For Calvin, the Supper is a liturgical enactment of God's provisions that the communicants receive with gratitude.

The fundamental eucharistic question concerns the location of Christ's body. Is Christ's body attached to the elements or separated from them? Rome taught the doctrine of transubstantiation, that the bread and wine are miraculously transformed into Christ's body and blood, though the elements only appear as bread and wine. Calvin considers such teaching superstitious and idolatrous, as if the body of Christ was localized.[154]

148. *Inst.* 4.17.2.

149. Gerrish, *Grace and Gratitude*, 139.

150. *Inst.* 4.14.15, citing Augustine, *John's Gospel* 26:11–12.

151. *Inst.* 4.17.42.

152. *Inst.* 4.18.1.

153. *Inst.* 4.18.1.

154. *Inst.* 4.17.12; 4.17.36.

Lutherans upheld the doctrine of ubiquity, that Christ's body is in the sacrament, while denying any change in substances. Christ's bodily presence is to be explained according to their usage of the *communicatio idiomatum*: The divine attribute of ubiquity is predicated of the humanity of Christ.[155] Both, Calvin argues, fail to consider any other way to partake of Christ than his descent into the bread; and thus they know nothing of the descent of the Spirit by which we ascend to God to sit with Christ at God's right hand in the heavenly places. Following Chrysostom, Calvin relates the whole force of our participation in Christ to the Holy Spirit.

> And there is no need of this for us to enjoy a participation in it, since the Lord bestows this benefit upon us through the Spirit, so that we may be made one in body, spirit, and soul with him. The bond of this connection is therefore the Spirit of Christ, with whom we are joined in unity, and is like a channel through which all that Christ himself is and has is conveyed to us. For if we see that the sun, shedding its beams upon the earth, casts its substance in some measure upon it in order to beget, nourish, and give growth to its offspring—why should the radiance of Christ's Spirit be less in order to impart to us the communion of his flesh and blood?[156]

Just as the sun shines its rays upon the earth to nourish it, so the radiance of Christ's Spirit imparts to us Christ's flesh to nourish us. As the Spirit vivifies the word and creates faith as an outcome, so he effects the connection of the sign and the reality signified on account of the sacramental promise "This is my body."

McGrath holds that, for Luther, Christ is not merely "*behind*" the sacraments; he is "*in*" them as well.[157] Christopher Elwood argues that, for Calvin, Christ is available not *in* the signs but "*through*"[158] them. By the Spirit, Christ is truly present through the symbols, the means of our participation in his benefits. The material elements are not empty signs, pointing to an absent Christ, but effective signs pointing to an ever-present Christ. Horton writes, "The bread and wine neither become the gift, as in Rome's view, nor simply remind us of the gift, as Zwingli implied; rather, the Spirit gives us Christ when we receive the bread and the wine

155. Helm, *Ideas*, 75.

156. *Inst.* 4.17.12. Note 35 cites *Sermon on the Holy Spirit* in Chrysostom's *Opera* (Basel, 1530), 5.379.

157. McGrath, *Reformation Thought*, 209, italics original.

158. Elwood, *Brief Introduction*, 55–56, italics original.

as his saving pledge."[159] As instruments, the elements actually deliver to the believing participants Christ and the fruits of his death. Christ "testifies and seals in the Supper—not by presenting a vain and empty sign, but by manifesting there the effectiveness of his Spirit to fulfill what he promises. And truly he offers and shows the reality there signified to all who sit at that spiritual banquet, although it is received with benefit by believers alone, who accept such great generosity with true faith and gratefulness of heart."[160] Through faith, the Spirit unites communicants on earth with their glorified Redeemer in heaven, enabling them to feed on Christ's life-giving body there. Regarding how this occurs, Calvin confesses, "I rather experience than understand it."[161] But he is convinced of the Spirit-actuated basis for that experience:

> Even though it seems unbelievable that Christ's flesh, separated from us by such great distance, penetrates to us, so that it becomes our food, let us remember how far the secret power of the Holy Spirit towers above all our senses, and how foolish it is to wish to measure his immeasurableness by our measure. What, then, our mind does not comprehend, let faith conceive: that the Spirit truly unites things separated in space.[162]

The Spirit connects the sign to the reality signified, making possible a real communion of believers with the flesh and blood of Christ in the ascended throne, without requiring the descent of Christ into the bread. He accomplishes this, not by dragging Christ down from heaven to us, but rather by raising us to him, to the ascended position where Christ is now seated. As criticism of the Roman and Lutheran views of the real presence, Calvin writes,

> But greatly mistaken are those who conceive no presence of the flesh in the Supper, unless it lies in the bread. For thus they leave nothing to the secret work of the Spirit, which unites us to Christ. To them, Christ does not seem present unless he comes down to us. As though, if he should lift us to himself, we should not as much enjoy his presence.[163]

159. Horton, *Christian Life*, 135.
160. *Inst.* 4.17.10.
161. *Inst.* 4.17.32.
162. *Inst.* 4.17.10.
163. *Inst.* 4.17.31.

Calvin's critique stems not only from a christological perspective, with its emphasis on Christ's ascension, but also from a pneumatological ground, with its emphasis on the secret work of the Holy Spirit, who draws us up into the heavenly sanctuary. It is precisely in the antithesis between the descent of the Spirit and the ascent of Christ that sacred partaking of Christ's flesh and blood receives its true meaning.[164] Calvin speaks of "the manner of descent by which [the Spirit] lifts us up to himself,"[165] to become sharers in Christ's exalted position with his Father. The mediation of the Spirit does not undermine Christ's true humanity but underscores it. Butin writes,

> Not only does Christ [in the Spirit] condescend to manifest himself to believers by means of visible, tangible, created elements; at the same time by the Spirit, the worshipping church is drawn into the heavenly worship of the Father through the mediation of the ascended Christ, who is seated with the Father in the heavenlies. For Calvin, this accentuates, rather than diminishes, the true humanity of Christ.[166]

The Spirit ushers us into "God's reality," says Julie Canlis, "not him into us."[167] The Spirit lifts us upward and places us in Christ, to benefit from him true participation in his life through the Supper, the vehicle of participation. Hence, Calvin writes,

> it was established of old that before consecration the people should be told in a loud voice to lift up their hearts. Scripture itself also not only carefully recounts to us the ascension of Christ, by which he withdrew the presence of his body from our sight and company, to shake from us all carnal thinking of him, but also, whenever it recalls him, bids our minds be raised up, and seek him in heaven, seated at the right hand of the Father [Col. 3:1–2]. According to this rule, we ought rather to have adored him spiritually in heavenly glory than to have devised some dangerous kind of adoration, replete with a carnal and crass conception.[168]

Just as God descends in human flesh to lift us heavenward, so God descends in word and sacrament to lift us heavenward. Calvin uses the

164. *Inst.* 4.17.26.

165. *Inst.* 4.17.16.

166. Butin, *Revelation*, 118.

167. Canlis, *Calvin's Ladder*, 163.

168. *Inst.* 4.17.36.

idea of the believer's "*spiritual ascent*"[169] into heaven in his understanding of the Lord's Supper.

> Now that the Mosaic ceremonies are abolished we worship at the footstool of God, when we yield a reverential submission to his word, and rise from the sacraments to a true spiritual service of him. Knowing that God has not descended from heaven directly or in his absolute character, but that his feet are withdrawn from us, being placed on a footstool, we should be careful to rise to him by the intermediate steps. Christ is he not only on whom the feet of God rests, but in whom the whole fulness of God's essence and glory resides, and in him, therefore, we should seek the Father. With this view he descended, that we might rise heavenward.[170]

God helps our ascent to God by his Spirit, who descends to empower word and sacrament. "It is thus that the Holy Spirit condescends for our profit, and in accommodation to our infirmity, raising our thoughts to heavenly and divine things by these worldly elements."[171] The upward movement of eucharistic worship has as its basis the Spirit, by whom believers rise up "to seek Christ there [heaven] in the glory of his Kingdom, as the symbols invite us to him in his wholeness," to feed on him, and "enjoy him at last in his wholeness."[172] Douglas Farrow says, "It is *we* who require eucharistic relocation."[173] At every eucharistic celebration, it is not that Christ is relocated to earth, to feed us from below, but that believers are relocated to heaven, where Christ nourishes us with his body from above. The union with Christ we experience in the Supper transforms the recipients, not the elements themselves. What is communicated to us from his ascended throne is not so much Christ's body but rather life-giving power from his body. In Calvin's words, "from the substance of his flesh [the ascended] Christ breathes life into our souls—indeed, pours forth his very life into us—even though Christ's flesh itself does not enter us."[174] Christ's body is life-giving, so the faithful communicants enjoy the fruits of Christ's life-giving death that are imparted to them by the Spirit.

169. Godfrey, *Pilgrim and Pastor*, 82, italics original.

170. *Comm. Ps.* 132:7, *CP* 5:150.

171. *Comm. Ps.* 132:7, *CP* 5:150.

172. *Inst.* 4.17.18.

173. Farrow, *Ascension and Ecclesia*, 177, italics original; also cited in Canlis, *Calvin's Ladder*, 163.

174. *Inst.* 4.17.32.

In partaking of Christ's substance, we feel the power of his life transmitting into us, just as we eat bread and feel its nutrients invigorating our bodies. "We are therefore bidden to take and eat the body which was once for all offered for our salvation, in order that when we see ourselves made partakers in it, we may assuredly conclude that the power of his life-giving death will be efficacious in us."[175]

With Augustine, Calvin denies "bodily presence" but affirms "spiritual presence."[176] Quoting Augustine:

> [Though Christ has] ascended into heaven . . . he is here, for the presence of majesty has not withdrawn [cf. Heb. 1:3]. Therefore, we always have Christ according to the presence of majesty; but of his physical presence it was rightly said to his disciples, "You will not always have me with you" [Matt. 26:11]. For the church had him in his bodily presence for a few days; now it holds him by faith, but does not see him with the eyes.[177]

The ascended Christ "is excepted from the category of creatures,"[178] and his presence is not withdrawn according to his majesty. Christ is really present in the Supper, or else faith becomes "a mere imagining" of his presence.[179] Such a perspective steers Calvin away from Eutyches, who, by "removing the distinction between [Christ's two] natures and urging the unity of the person, . . . made man out of God and God out of man."[180] Such mingling of the two natures deviates from what became Chalcedonian Christology, which Calvin affirms. Calvin charges, "What sort of madness, then, is it to mingle heaven with earth rather than give up trying to drag Christ's body from the heavenly sanctuary?"[181] We partake of Christ's presence in his ascension and session at the Father's right hand. We share in the kingdom he acquires, which is

> neither bounded by location in space nor circumscribed by any limits. Thus Christ is not prevented from exerting his power wherever he pleases, in heaven and on earth. He shows his

175. *Inst.* 4.17.1.

176. *Inst.* 2.16.14, citing Augustine, *John's Gospel* 78.1 (MPL 35.1835; tr. NPNF 7.340f.).

177. *Inst.* 2.16.14, citing Augustine, *John's Gospel* 50.13 (MPL 35.1763; tr. NPNF 7.282).

178. *Inst.* 1.13.14.

179. *Inst.* 4.17.6.

180. *Inst.* 4.17.30.

181. *Inst.* 4.17.30.

> presence in power and strength, is always among his own people, and breathes his life upon them, and lives in them, sustaining them, strengthening, quickening, keeping them unharmed, as if he were present in the body. In short, he feeds his people with his own body, the communion of which he bestows upon them by the power of his Spirit. In this manner, the body and blood of Christ are shown to us in the Sacrament.[182]

Paul teaches that "Christ dwells in us only through his Spirit" (cf. Rom 8:9). By the Spirit, believers "possess Christ completely and have him dwelling in us."[183] Though Christ's body is not enclosed underneath the earthly elements, the "whole Christ" is not removed from the Supper. With Lombard, Calvin does not hesitate to say that the "whole Christ" is everywhere, yet not "the whole of that which is in him."[184] In the Supper, Christ reveals himself in "a special way": "the whole Christ is present," yet not in "his wholeness," for his body, though glorified, is circumscribed in heaven.[185] Partee writes, "Calvin affirms the local, heavenly presence [of Christ's body] by insisting that Christ while present to faith is not present in, with, or under the elements. Christ is absent from us in the body which is in heaven, but Christ dwells in us by the Spirit."[186] Believers by the Spirit commune not with a disembodied Christ, but "the whole Christ."[187]

Though Scripture does not prescribe how often the Lord's Supper is to be administered, Calvin encourages a frequent use of it—"at least once a week"[188]—so that we might grow in "eucharistic piety"[189] before God, fostering reverent worship, and before people, fostering "the bond of love."[190] Calvin affirms that the Lord's Supper

> was ordained to be frequently used among all Christians in order that they might frequently return in memory to Christ's Passion, by such remembrance to sustain and strengthen their

182. *Inst.* 4.17.18.

183. *Inst.* 4.17.12.

184. *Inst.* 4.17.30, citing Lombard, *Sentences* 3.22.3 (MPL 192.804).

185. *Inst.* 4.17.30.

186. Partee, *Theology*, 285.

187. See Helm, *Calvin*, 119–20.

188. *Inst.* 4.17.43.

189. Gerrish, "Calvin's Eucharistic Piety," 52–65. The phrase "eucharistic piety" is Gerrish's.

190. *Inst.* 4.17.38.

> faith, and urge themselves to sing thanksgiving to God and to proclaim his goodness; finally, by it to nourish mutual love, and among themselves give witness to this love, and discern its bond in the unity of Christ's body.[191]

## CONCLUSION

Christian piety is not a private, subjective phenomenon, devoid of its social reality. In this regard, Calvin's piety can be labeled an ecclesial piety. Spiritual flourishing does not take place in a vacuum; it does not overlook the ecclesial dimension of faith, the context in which piety is nurtured and increased. God's fatherly love admits us to the church, "her school" (the church as my mother) from which we will not graduate until we enter heaven. To remove ourselves from her bosom is to be removed of forgiveness or salvation. The offices of doctors and ministers, elders and deacons, the preached and celebrated word—these are all instituted means of growth in piety. For Calvin, the optimism of grace is the dynamism of our continuation with the communion of the church that has the creative power of the word of God as her foundation. Believers will not diminish in power, knowing that, for the perfecting of their faith, God dispenses his riches to them through various means of his choice: through preaching, baptism, the Lord's Supper, and absolution. Such a vision of God as a multimedia communicator ought to strengthen our communion with the church rather than separate us from it; it should inspire in us a piety of gratitude. God "inwardly fulfills what he outwardly designates,"[192] delivering the benefits of Christ's mediatorial activity to his people through these diverse forms of the gospel; this is completed by the Holy Spirit who creates faith in that word of promise. God gives himself in his word and the sacraments, without giving up his majesty. In his self-giving, God remains transcendently majestic, yet not in such a way that he cannot be reached. Calvin's vision of the majesty of God mediated through the maternal care of the church serves to draw us nearer to God, even as God has drawn near to us via word and sacrament. The intimacy of God's presence is no less vivid or valid in our times than it was in the times of old. Through the word we hear and celebrate, God abides with us, just as he did with the prophets and apostles, through

191. *Inst.* 4.17.44.

192. *Inst.* 4.17.5.

whom God's presence was mediated. The increase of piety is prefaced upon the instrumental causality of the forms of his word by which Christ and his benefits are made effective in us by the Spirit. The word in the power of the Spirit can transform lives and create new situations through the varied and distinct graces of God it delivers. Assurance of faith is based upon the presupposition that God is true to his promise and cannot negate himself. He cannot abandon his people to death but appoints them to life via the word of life we proclaim, celebrate, and hold fast. The church is not a fruit of the human attempt to grasp God; rather it is a gift of God which we grasp by faith. The abundant fruits of Christ's life-giving death continue to benefit those who remain within the body of Christ. As a consequence, Calvin exults, "We should so revere such a father with grateful piety and burning love, as to devote ourselves wholly to his obedience and honor him in everything."[193] Calvin's vision of the church ought to instill in us patience and perseverance until the last day, when the church triumphant, without spots or blemishes, to which we look forward, will appear.

193. Calvin, OS 1:76, as cited in Beeke, "Calvin on Piety," 136.

# Bibliography

## PRIMARY SOURCES


Bretschneider, Karl Gottlieb, et al., eds. *Corpus Reformatorum.* 101 vols. Halle and Braunschweig: Schwetschke, 1834–1909.

Calvin, Jean. *Ioannis Calvini opera quae supersunt omnia.* Edited by Wilhelm Baum et al. 59 vols. *Corpus Reformatorum*, vols. 29–87. Braunschweig: Schwetschke, 1863–1900.

Calvin, John. *Against the Fantastic and Furious Sect of the Libertines Who Are Called "Spirituals."* In *Treatises Against the Anabaptists and Against the Libertines*, translated and edited by Benjamin Wirt Farley, 187–326. Grand Rapids: Baker, 1982.

———. *Calvin's Commentaries.* 46 vols. 1844–55. Reprint, 22 vols. Grand Rapids: Baker, 1979.

———. *Calvin's New Testament Commentaries.* 12 vols. Edited by David W. Torrance and Thomas F. Torrance. Grand Rapids: Eerdmans, 1959–72.

———. *Commentaries on the Book of the Prophet Jeremiah and the Lamentations.* Translated and edited by John Owen. 5 vols. Reprint, Grand Rapids: Baker, 1979.

———. *Commentaries on the Four Last Books of Moses.* Translated by Charles William Bingham. 4 vols. Reprint, Grand Rapids: Eerdmans, 1950.

———. *Commentaries on the Twelve Minor Prophets.* Translated by John Owen. 5 vols. 1847. Reprint, Grand Rapids: Eerdmans, 1950.

———. *Commentary on the Book of the Prophet Isaiah.* Translated by William Pringle. 4 vols. Reprint, Grand Rapids: Baker, 1979.

———. *Commentary on the Book of Psalms.* Translated by James Anderson. 5 vols. Reprint, Grand Rapids: Eerdmans, 1949.

———. *Institutes of the Christian Religion.* Edited by John T. McNeill. Translated by Ford Lewis Battles. 2 vols. Library of Christian Classics, vols. 20–21. Philadelphia: Westminster, 1960.

———. *Institutes of the Christian Religion.* Translated by Henry Beveridge. 3 vols. Edinburgh: Calvin Translation Society, 1845.

———. *Instruction in Faith.* Edited and translated by Paul T. Fuhrmann. Philadelphia: Westminster, 1949.

———. *John Calvin's Sermons on the Ten Commandments.* Edited and translated by Benjamin W. Farley. Foreword by Ford Lewis Battles. Grand Rapids: Baker, 2002.

———. *The Mystery of Godliness and Other Sermons*. Grand Rapids: Eerdmans, 1950.

———. *On God and Political Duty*. Edited by John T. McNeill. 2nd ed. New York: Liberal Arts, 1956.

———. *Selected Works of John Calvin: Tracts and Letters*. Edited by Henry Beveridge and Jules Bonnet. 7 vols. Grand Rapids: Baker, 1983.

———. *Sermons on the Epistle to the Ephesians*. Translated by Leslie Rawlinson and S. M. Houghton. Carlisle, PA: Banner of Truth Trust, 1998.

———. *Sermons on Galatians*. Translated by Kathy Childress. Edinburgh: Banner of Truth Trust, 1997.

———. *Theological Treatises*. Translated by J. K. S. Reid. Philadelphia: Westminster, 1954.

———. *Tracts Relating to the Reformation*. Vol. 1. Edited by Henry Beveridge. Edinburgh: Calvin Translation Society, 1844.

## SECONDARY SOURCES

Ames, William. *The Marrow of Theology*. Translated from the third Latin edition, 1629, and edited by John D. Eusden. Boston: Pilgrim, 1968.

Augustine of Hippo. *The City of God*. In *The Nicene and Post-Nicene Fathers*, Series 1, Vol. 2, *St. Augustin's City of God and Christian Doctrine*, edited by Philip Schaff, translated by Marcus Dods, 1–511. Buffalo, NY: Christian Literature, 1887.

———. *The Trinity* (*De Trinitate*). Edited and translated by Edmund Hill. Series 1, vol. 5 of *The Works of St. Augustine: A Translation for the 21st Century*. 2nd ed. Edited by John E. Rotelle. New York: New City, 2016.

Austin, J. L. "Performative-Constative." In *The Philosophy of Language*, edited by J. R. Searle, 13–22. London: Oxford University Press, 1971.

Avis, Paul D. L. *Church in the Theology of the Reformers*. Louisville: Westminster John Knox, 1981.

Barth, Karl. *Church Dogmatics*. Translated by G. T. Thomson et al. 14 vols. Edinburgh: T&T Clark, 1936–67.

Beach, J. Mark. "The Real Presence of Christ in the Preaching of the Gospel: Luther and Calvin on the Nature of Preaching." *Mid-American Journal of Theology* 10 (1999) 77–134.

Beeke, Joel R. "Calvin on Piety." In *The Cambridge Companion to John Calvin*, edited by Donald K. McKim, 125–52. Cambridge: Cambridge University Press, 2004.

———. "John Calvin on Prayer as Communion with God." In *Taking Hold of God: Reformed and Puritan Perspectives on Prayer*, edited by Joel R. Beeke and Brian G. Najapfour, 27–42. Grand Rapids: Reformation Heritage, 2011.

Beeke, Joel R., and Brian G. Najapfour, eds. *Taking Hold of God: Reformed and Puritan Perspectives on Prayer*. Grand Rapids: Reformation Heritage, 2011.

Billings, J. Todd. *Calvin, Participation, and the Gift: The Activity of Believers in Union with Christ*. Oxford: Oxford University Press, 2007.

———. "John Calvin's Soteriology: On the Multifaceted 'Sum' of the Gospel." *International Journal of Systematic Theology* 11 (2009) 428–47.

———. *Union with Christ: Reframing Theology and Ministry for the Church*. Grand Rapids: Baker Academic, 2011.

———. "Union with Christ and the Double Grace: Calvin's Theology and Its Early Reception." In *Calvin's Theology and Its Reception: Disputes, Developments, and New Possibilities*, edited by J. Todd Billings and I. John Hesselink, 49–71. Louisville: Westminster John Knox, 2012.

———. "United to God Through Christ: Assessing Calvin on the Question of Deification." *Harvard Theological Review* 98 (2005) 315–34.

Billings, J. Todd, and I. John Hesselink, eds. *Calvin's Theology and Its Reception: Disputes, Developments, and New Possibilities.* Louisville: Westminster John Knox, 2012.

Bouwsma, William J. *John Calvin: A Sixteenth-Century Portrait.* Oxford: Oxford University Press, 1988.

Bray, Gerald L., ed. *Galatians, Ephesians.* Reformation Commentary on Scripture. New Testament 10. Downers Grove, IL: IVP Academic, 2011.

Butin, Philip W. *Revelation, Redemption, and Response: Calvin's Trinitarian Understanding of the Divine–Human Relationship.* New York: Oxford University Press, 1995.

Calhoun, David B. "Prayer: 'The Chief Exercise of Faith' (3.20)." In *A Theological Guide to Calvin's Institutes: Essays and Analysis*, edited by David W. Hall and Peter A. Lillback, 347–67. Phillipsburg, NJ: P&R, 2008.

Canlis, Julie. "Calvin, Osiander, and Participation in God." *International Journal of Systematic Theology* 6 (2004) 169–84.

———. *Calvin's Ladder: A Spiritual Theology of Ascent and Ascension.* Grand Rapids: Eerdmans, 2010.

———. "To Thine Own Self Be True? John Calvin and the Mystery of Human Identity." *Crux* 52 (2016) 13–21.

Chester, Stephen J. *Reading Paul with the Reformers: Reconciling Old and New Perspectives.* Grand Rapids: Eerdmans, 2017.

Clark, John C. "'The Principal Point on Which Our Whole Salvation Turns': Calvin on the Vicarious Humanity of Jesus Christ." Pages 128–48 in *Dogmatics and Devotion*, edited by Myk Habets and Bobby Grow. Vol. 2 of *Evangelical Calvinism.* Eugene, OR: Pickwick, 2017.

Clark, John C., and Marcus Peter Johnson. *The Incarnation of God: The Mystery of the Gospel as the Foundation of Evangelical Theology.* Wheaton, IL: Crossway, 2015.

Crisp, Oliver D. *Retrieving Doctrine: Essays in Reformed Theology.* Downers Grove, IL: InterVarsity, 2010.

———. *The Word Enfleshed: Exploring the Person and Work of Christ.* Grand Rapids: Baker Academic, 2016.

Davis, Thomas J. *This Is My Body: The Presence of Christ in Reformation Thought.* Grand Rapids: Baker, 2008.

De Klerk, Peter, ed. *Calvin and the Holy Spirit.* Calvin Studies 6. Grand Rapids: Calvin Studies Society, 1989.

DeVries, Dawn. "Calvin's Preaching." In *The Cambridge Companion to John Calvin*, edited by Donald K. McKim, 106–24. Cambridge: Cambridge University Press, 2004.

Dowey, Edward A., Jr. *The Knowledge of God in Calvin's Theology.* Grand Rapids: Eerdmans, 1994.

———. "Law in Luther and Calvin." *Theology Today* 41 (1984) 146–53.

Dyrness, William A. "Calvin: Creation, Drama, and Time." In *The Origins of Protestant Aesthetics in Early Modern Europe: Calvin's Reformation Poetics*, 53–83. Cambridge: Cambridge University Press, 2019.

Earnshaw, Rebekah. "The Usefulness of Divine Majesty According to Calvin in Genesis." *Calvin Theological Journal* 51 (2016) 181–203.

Edmondson, Stephen. *Calvin's Christology*. Cambridge: Cambridge University Press, 2004.

Elwood, Christopher. *A Brief Introduction to John Calvin*. Louisville: Westminster John Knox, 2017.

Faber, Jelle. "The Saving Work of the Holy Spirit in Calvin." In *Calvin and the Holy Spirit*, edited by Peter De Klerk, 1–11. Calvin Studies 6. Grand Rapids: Calvin Studies Society, 1989.

Farrow, Douglas. *Ascension and Ecclesia*. Grand Rapids: Eerdmans, 1999.

Gaffin, Richard B., Jr. "Justification and Union with Christ (3.11–18)." In *A Theological Guide to Calvin's Institutes: Essays and Analysis*, edited by David W. Hall and Peter A. Lillback, 248–69. Phillipsburg, NJ: P&R, 2008.

Ganoczy, Alexandre. *The Young Calvin*. Translated by David L. Foxgrover and Wade Provo. Philadelphia: Westminster, 1987.

Garcia, Mark A. "Imputation as Attribution: Union with Christ, Reification and Justification as Declarative Word." *International Journal of Systematic Theology* 11 (2009) 415–27.

———. "Imputation and the Christology of Union with Christ: Calvin, Osiander and the Contemporary Quest for a Reformed Model." *Westminster Theological Journal* 68 (2006) 219–51.

Garlington, Don B. "Calvin's Doctrine of Prayer: An Examination of Book 3, Chapter 20 of *Institutes of the Christian Religion*." *Baptist Review of Theology* 1 (1991) 21–36.

———. "Imputation or Union with Christ? A Response to John Piper." *Reformation & Revival* 12 (2003) 45–113.

George, Timothy. *Theology of the Reformers*. Rev. ed. Nashville: Broadman, 2013.

Gerrish, Brian A. "Calvin's Eucharistic Piety." In *Calvin Studies Society Papers, 1995–1997*, edited by David Foxgrover, 52–65. Grand Rapids: Calvin Studies Society, 1998.

———. *Grace and Gratitude: The Eucharistic Theology of John Calvin*. Minneapolis: Augsburg Fortress, 1993.

———. "Theology Within the Limits of Piety Alone: Schleiermacher and Calvin's Doctrine of God." In *Reformatio Perennis: Essays on Calvin and the Reformation in Honor of Ford Lewis Battles*, edited by B. A. Gerrish and Robert Benedetto, 67–87. Eugene, OR: Pickwick, 1981.

———. "'The Unknown God': Luther and Calvin on the Hiddenness of God." In *The Old Protestantism and the New: Essays on the Reformation Heritage*, 131–59. Chicago: University of Chicago Press, 1982.

Girgensohn, Herbert. *Teaching Luther's Catechism*. 2 vols. Translated by John Doberstein. Philadelphia: Muhlenberg, 1959–60.

Godfrey, W. Robert. "Calvin, Worship, and the Sacraments (4.13–19)." In *A Theological Guide to Calvin's Institutes: Essays and Analysis*, edited by David W. Hall and Peter A. Lillback, 368–89. Phillipsburg, NJ: P&R, 2008.

———. *John Calvin: Pilgrim and Pastor*. Wheaton, IL: Crossway: 2009.

Haas, Guenther H. "Calvin's Ethics." In *The Cambridge Companion to John Calvin*, edited by Donald K. McKim, 93–105. Cambridge: Cambridge University Press, 2004.

Hall, David W., and Peter A. Lillback, eds. *A Theological Guide to Calvin's Institutes: Essays and Analysis*. Phillipsburg, NJ: P&R, 2008.

Harkness, George. *John Calvin: The Man and His Ethics*. New York: Holt, 1931.

Helm, Paul. *Calvin: A Guide for the Perplexed*. London: T&T Clark, 2008.

———. *John Calvin's Ideas*. Oxford: Oxford University Press, 2004.

Hesselink, I. John. *Calvin's Concept of the Law*. Allison Park, PA: Pickwick, 1992.

———. *Calvin's First Catechism: A Commentary*. Columba Series in Reformed Theology. Louisville: Westminster John Knox, 1997.

———. "The Development and Purpose of Calvin's Institutes." Pages 209–16 in *Articles on Calvin and Calvinism*, edited by Richard C. Gamble. Vol. 4 of *Influences upon Calvin and Discussion of the 1559 Institutes*. New York: Garland, 1992.

———. "Law." In *Encyclopedia of the Reformed Faith*, edited by Donald K. McKim, 215–16. Louisville: Westminster John Knox, 1992.

———. "The Role of the Holy Spirit in Calvin's Doctrine of the Sacraments." *Acta Theologica*, Supplementum 3 (2002) 66–88.

Holder, R. Ward, ed. *Calvin and Luther: The Continuing Relationship*. Göttingen: Vandenhoeck & Ruprecht, 2013.

Horton, Michael. *Calvin on the Christian Life: Glorifying and Enjoying God Forever*. Wheaton, IL: Crossway, 2014.

Huijgen, Arnold. *Divine Accommodation in John Calvin's Theology: Analysis and Assessment*. Göttingen: Vandenhoeck & Ruprecht, 2013.

Jansen, John F. *Calvin's Doctrine of the Work of Christ*. London: James Clarke, 1956.

Johnson, Marcus Peter. "Luther and Calvin on Union with Christ." *Fides et Historia* 39 (2007) 59–77.

———. *One with Christ: An Evangelical Theology of Salvation*. Wheaton, IL: Crossway, 2013.

Jones, David Clyde. "The Law and the Spirit of Christ (2.6–9)." In *A Theological Guide to Calvin's Institutes: Essays and Analysis*, edited by David W. Hall and Peter A. Lillback, 301–19. Phillipsburg, NJ: P&R, 2008.

Jones, Serene. *Calvin and the Rhetoric of Piety*. Louisville: Westminster John Knox, 1995.

Kolb, Robert, and Carl R. Trueman. *Between Wittenberg and Geneva: Lutheran and Reformed Theology in Conversation*. Grand Rapids: Baker Academic, 2017.

Lane, Anthony N. S. *John Calvin: Student of Church Fathers*. Edinburgh: T&T Clark, 1991.

———. "John Calvin: The Witness of the Holy Spirit." In *Faith and Ferment*, 1–17. Westminster Conference Papers. London: Westminster Conference, 1982.

———. *A Reader's Guide to Calvin's Institutes*. Grand Rapids: Baker Academic, 2009.

Lane, Belden C. *Ravished by Beauty: The Surprising Legacy of Reformed Spirituality*. Oxford: Oxford University Press, 2011.

———. "Spirituality as the Performance of Desire: Calvin on the World as a Theatre of God's Glory." *Spiritus: A Journal of Christian Spirituality* 1 (2001) 1–24.

Leith, John H. "Calvin's Doctrine of the Proclamation of the Word and Its Significance for Today." In *John Calvin and the Church: A Prism of Reform*, edited by Timothy George, 206–29. Louisville: Westminster John Knox, 1990.

———. *John Calvin's Doctrine of the Christian Life*. Louisville: Westminster John Knox, 1989.

———, ed. *Calvin Studies 6*. Colloquium on Calvin Studies. Davidson, NC: Davidson College, 1992.

Loggie, Robert Douglas. "Chief Exercise of Faith: An Exposition of Calvin's Doctrine of Prayer." *The Hartford Quarterly* 5 (1965) 65–81.

Lopes, Nicodemus Augustus, and José Manoel da Conceicao. "Calvin, Theologian of the Holy Spirit: The Holy Spirit and the Word of God." *Scottish Bulletin of Evangelical Theology*, 15 (1997) 38–49.

Luther, Martin. *D. Martin Luthers Werke: Kritische Gesamtausgabe*. 65 vols. Weimar: Hermann Böhlau, 1883–1929. Abteilung 1: Schriften vols. 1–56.

———. *Luther's Works: American Edition*. Edited by Helmut T. Lehman. Vols. 31–55. Philadelphia: Fortress, 1957–86.

———. *Luther's Works: American Edition*. Edited by Jaroslav Pelikan. Vols. 1–30. St. Louis: Concordia, 1955–73.

———. *Luther's Works: American Edition*. New series. Edited by Christopher Boyd Brown et al. Vols. 56–82. St. Louis: Concordia, 2009–.

McGrath, Alister E. "Evangelical Theological Method. A State of the Art." In *Evangelical Futures: A Conversation on Theological Method*, edited by John G. Stackhouse, 15–38. Grand Rapids: Baker, 2000.

———. *Iustitia Dei: A History of the Christian Doctrine of Justification*. 4th ed. Cambridge: Cambridge University Press, 2020.

———. *A Life of John Calvin: A Study in the Shaping of Western Culture*. Oxford: Blackwell, 1990.

———. *Reformation Thought: An Introduction*. 5th ed. Oxford: Blackwell, 2021.

McKee, Elsie Anne. "John Calvin's Teaching on the Lord's Prayer." In *The Lord's Prayer: Perspectives for Reclaiming Christian Prayer*, edited by Daniel L. Migliore, 88–106. Grand Rapids: Eerdmans, 1993.

McKim, Donald K., ed. *The Cambridge Companion to John Calvin*. Cambridge: Cambridge University Press, 2004.

———, ed. *Readings in Calvin's Theology*. Grand Rapids: Baker, 1984.

McNeill, John T. *A History of the Cure of Souls*. New York: Harper & Row, 1951.

———. "Introduction." In *Institutes of the Christian Religion*, edited by John T. McNeill, translated by Ford Lewis Battles, 1:xxix–lxxi. 2 vols. Library of Christian Classics, vols 20–21. Philadelphia: Westminster, 1960.

———. "Introduction." In *On God and Political Duty*, edited by John T. McNeill, vii–xxvi. 2nd ed. New York: Liberal Arts, 1956.

Melanchthon, Philip. *Loci Communes* (1535). In *Corpus Reformatorum*. Vol. 21. Edited by Karl Gottlieb Bretschneider and Heinrich Ernst Bindseil. Braunschweig: Schwetschke, 1854.

Mesa, Ivan. "John Calvin's Trinitarian Theology of Prayer." *Puritan Reformed Journal* 7 (2015) 179–92.

Miller, Ross C. "Calvin's Understanding of Psalm-Singing as a Means of Grace." In *Calvin Studies 6*, edited by John H. Leith, 35–48. Colloquium on Calvin Studies. Davidson, NC: Davidson Colleges, 1992.

———. "Music and the Spirit: Psalm-Singing in Calvin's Liturgy." In *Calvin Studies 6*, edited by John H. Leith, 49–58. Colloquium on Calvin Studies. Davidson, NC: Davidson College, 1992.

Milner, Benjamin Charles, Jr. *Calvin's Doctrine of the Church*. Studies in the History of Christian Traditions 5. Leiden: Brill, 1970.

Muller, Richard A. *Calvin and the Reformed Tradition: On the Work of Christ and the Order of Salvation*. Grand Rapids: Baker Academic, 2012.

———. *Christ and the Decree: Christology and Predestination in Reformed Theology from Calvin to Perkins*. Grand Rapids: Baker Academic, 2008.

———. *The Unaccommodated Calvin: Studies in the Foundation of a Theological Tradition*. Oxford: Oxford University Press, 2002.

Neuser, W., ed. *Calvinus ecclesiae doctor*. Kampen: Kok, 1978.

Ng, Lok Ping. "Nature in the Thought of John Calvin." *Churchman Journal* 132 (2018) 301–10.

Ngien, Dennis. *Grace and Law in Galatians: Justification in Luther and Calvin*. Eugene, OR: Cascade, 2013.

———, ed. *The Interface of Science, Theology, and Religion: Essays in Honor of Alister E. McGrath*. Eugene, OR: Pickwick, 2019.

———. *The Suffering of God According to Martin Luther's Theologia Crucis*. Bern: Lang, 1995.

Niesel, Wilhelm. *The Theology of Calvin*. Translated by Harold Knight. Philadelphia: Westminster, 1956.

Oberman, Heiko A. "Preaching and the Word in the Reformation." *Theology Today* 18 (1961) 16–29.

Olson, Jeannine E. "Church and Society: Calvin's Theology and Its Early Development." In *Calvin's Theology and Its Reception: Disputes, Developments, and New Possibilities*, edited by J. Todd Billings and I. John Hesselink, 193–215. Louisville: Westminster John Knox, 2012.

Packer, J. I. "Calvin the Theologian." In *John Calvin: A Collection of Distinguished Essays*, edited by G. E. Duffield, 149–76. Grand Rapids: Eerdmans, 1966.

Parker, T. H. L. *Calvin: A Biography*. Philadelphia: Westminster, 1975.

———. *Calvin: An Introduction to His Thought*. Louisville: Westminster John Knox, 1995.

———. *Calvin's Doctrine of the Knowledge of God*. Grand Rapids: Eerdmans, 1959.

Partee, Charles. "Calvin's Central Dogma Again." *The Sixteenth Century Journal* 18 (1987) 191–99.

———. *The Theology of John Calvin*. Louisville: Westminster John Knox, 2008.

Piper, John. *John Calvin and His Passion for the Majesty of God*. Wheaton, IL: Crossway, 2009.

Plantinga, Alvin. *Warranted Christian Belief*. Oxford: Oxford University Press, 2000.

Potter, Mary Lane. "The 'Whole Office of the Law' in the Theology of John Calvin." *Journal of Law and Religion* 3 (1985) 117–39.

Price, Timothy Shaun. "A Comparative Analysis of John Calvin and Martin Luther Concerning the First and Second Commandments." *Ashland Theological Journal* 40 (2008) 61–73.

Quistorp, Heinrich. *Calvin's Doctrine of the Last Things*. Translated by Harold Knight. Richmond, VA: John Knox, 1955.

Richard, Lucien Joseph. *The Spirituality of John Calvin*. Atlanta, GA: John Knox, 1974.

Schreiner, Susan E. *The Theater of His Glory: Nature and the Natural Order in the Thought of John Calvin*. Durham, NC: Labyrinth, 1991.

Schreiner, Thomas. *Faith Alone: The Doctrine of Justification*. Grand Rapids: Zondervan Academic, 2015.

Sharp, Larry. "The Doctrine of Graces in Calvin and Augustine." *Evangelical Quarterly* 52 (1980) 84–96.

Shepherd, Victor. *The Nature and Function of Faith in the Theology of John Calvin*. Macon, GA: Mercer University Press, 1988.

Stackhouse, John G., ed. *Evangelical Futures: A Conversation on Theological Method*. Grand Rapids: Baker, 2000.

Steinmetz, David. *Calvin in Context*. Oxford: Oxford University Press, 1995.

Tamburello, Dennis E. *Union with Christ: John Calvin and the Mysticism of St. Bernard*. Louisville: Westminster John Knox, 1994.

Tan, Jimmy Boon-Chai. *How Then Shall We Guide? A Comparative Study of Ignatius Loyola and John Calvin as Spiritual Guides*. Eugene, OR: Pickwick, 2023.

Taylor, W. David O. *The Theater of God's Glory: Calvin, Creation, and the Liturgical Arts*. Grand Rapids: Eerdmans, 2017.

Thomas, Derek W. H. "The Mediator of the Covenant (2.12–15)." In *A Theological Guide to Calvin's Institutes: Essays and Analysis*, edited by David W. Hall and Peter A. Lillback, 205–25. Phillipsburg, NJ: P&R, 2008.

Thompson, John. *Modern Trinitarian Perspectives*. Oxford: Oxford University Press, 1994.

Torrance, James B. "The Vicarious Humanity and Priesthood of Christ in the Theology of John Calvin." In *Calvinus Ecclesiae Doctor*, edited by W. H. Neuser, 69–84. Kampen: Kok, 1978.

Torrance, T. F. *Calvin's Doctrine of Man*. Westport, CT: Greenwood, 1957.

———. "Truth and Authority: Theses on Truth." *Irish Theological Quarterly* 39 (1972) 215–42.

Troeltsch, Ernst. *The Social Teaching of the Christian Churches*. Vol. 2. Translated by Olive Wyon. New York: Harper & Brothers, 1960.

Tylenda, Joseph N. "Calvin's Understanding of the Communication of Properties." *Westminster Theological Journal* 38 (1975) 54–65.

———. "Christ the Mediator: Calvin versus Stancaro." Pages 161–72 in *Calvin's Opponents*, edited by Richard C. Gamble. Vol. 5 of *Articles on Calvin and Calvinism*. New York: Garland, 1992.

Van 't Spijker, Willem. *Calvin: A Brief Guide to His Life and Thought*. Grand Rapids: Westminster John Knox, 2009.

Van Vlastuin, Willem. "Kuyper's Spirituality in Its Calvin-Context." *Church History and Religious Culture* 101 (2021) 526–45.

Venema, Cornelis P. "Calvin's Doctrine of the Last Things: The Resurrection of the Body and the Life Everlasting (3.25 et al.)." In *A Theological Guide to Calvin's Institutes: Essays and Analysis*, edited by David W. Hall and Peter A. Lillback, 441–67. Phillipsburg, NJ: P&R, 2008.

Wallace, Ronald S. *Calvin's Doctrine of the Christian Life*. Edinburgh: Oxford & Boyd, 1959.

———. *Calvin's Doctrine of the Word and Sacrament*. Grand Rapids: Eerdmans, 1957.

———. *Calvin, Geneva and the Reformation: A Study of Calvin as Social Reformer, Churchman, Pastor and Theologian*. Grand Rapids: Baker, 1988.

Ware, Bruce A. "The Role of Prayer and the Word in the Christian Life According to John Calvin." *Studia Biblica et Theologica* 12 (1982) 73–91.

Warfield, Benjamin B. *Calvin and Augustine*. Phillipsburg, NJ: P&R, 1980.

Webb, Stephen H. *The Divine Voice: Christian Proclamation and the Theology of Sound*. Grand Rapids: Baker Academic, 2004.

Wendel, François. *Calvin: Origins and Development of His Religious Thought*. Translated by Philip Mairet. Grand Rapids: Baker, 1982.

Wengert, Timothy J. "Philip Melanchthon and John Calvin Against Andreas Osiander: Coming to Terms with Forensic Justification." In *Calvin and Luther: The Continuing Relationship*, edited by R. Ward Holder, 63–88. Göttingen: Vandenhoeck & Ruprecht, 2013.

Wolterstorff, Nicholas. *Until Justice and Peace Embrace: The Kuyper Lectures for 1981 Delivered at the Free University of Amsterdam*. Grand Rapids: Eerdmans, 1983.

Wright, David F., et al. *Calvinus Evangelii Propugnator: Calvin, Champion of the Gospel*. Grand Rapids: Calvin Studies Society, 2006.

Wright, Terry J. *Providence Made Flesh: Divine Presence as a Framework for a Theology of Providence*. Eugene, OR: Wipf & Stock, 2009.

Wyatt, Peter. *Jesus Christ and Creation in the Theology of John Calvin*. Eugene, OR: Pickwick, 1996.

Zachman, Randall C. *The Assurance of Faith: Conscience in the Theology of Martin Luther and John Calvin*. Minneapolis: Fortress, 1993.

———. "Did the Death of Christ Appease the Wrath of God? Luther and Calvin on the Purpose of the Death of Christ." In *The Interface of Science, Theology, and Religion: Essays in Honor of Alister E. McGrath*, edited by Dennis Ngien, 66–85. Eugene, OR: Pickwick, 2019.

———. *Image and Word in the Theology of John Calvin*. Notre Dame: University of Notre Dame Press, 2007.

———. *Reconsidering John Calvin*. Cambridge: Cambridge University Press, 2012.

———. "The Universe as a Living Image of God: Calvin's Doctrine of Creation Reconsidered." *Concordia Theological Quarterly* 61 (1997) 299–312.

———. "Why Should Free Scientific Inquiry Matter to Faith? The Case of John Calvin." In *Knowing Creation: Perspectives from Theology, Philosophy, and Science*, edited by Andrew B. Torrance and Thomas H. McCall, 69–86. Grand Rapids: Zondervan, 2018.

Zahl, Simeon. *The Holy Spirit and Christian Experience*. New York: Oxford University Press, 2020.

———. "Tradition and Its 'Use': The Ethics of Theological Retrieval." *Scottish Journal of Theology* 71 (2018) 308–23.

www.ingramcontent.com/pod-product-compliance
Lightning Source LLC
LaVergne TN
LVHW100527110826
845146LV00002B/802

* 9 7 9 8 3 8 5 2 5 3 3 7 1 *